BEYOND DELICIOUS COOKBOOK

RECIPES & STORIES FROM THE ORIGINAL GHOST WHISPERER

MARY ANN WINKOWSKI & DAVID POWERS

BEYOND DELICIOUS COOKBOOK

RECIPES & STORIES FROM THE ORIGINAL GHOST WHISPERER

YES

MORE THAN 100 RECIPES FROM THE DEARLY DEPARTED

CLERISY PRESS

Editor: Emily Beaumont
Proofreader: Jenna Barron
Cover and interior design: Hilary Harkness
Typesetter: Karla Linder

10 9 8 7 6 5 4 3 2 1

Beyond Delicious: The Ghost Whisperer's Cookbook
First Edition 2011
Second Edition 2025
© 2011 and 2025 by Mary Ann Winkowski and David Powers

CLERISY PRESS
an imprint of AdventureKeen
2204 First Ave. S., Ste. 102
Birmingham, AL 35233
800-678-7006; fax 877-374-9016

Visit **clerisypress.com** for a complete listing of our books and for ordering information.

Distributed by Publishers Group West
Printed in China

Cataloging-in-Publication Data is on file with the Library of Congress.
ISBN 978-1-57860-429-6 (pbk.); 978-1-57860-403-6 (ebook)

CONTENTS

DESSERTS

MISCELLANEOUS

FINAL THOUGHTS

To my husband, Ted; my daughters, Amber and Tara;
and all the "foodie spirits" with the great recipes.
—*M. A. W.*

For Abby, who managed to do as I asked, despite everything.
—*D. P.*

ACKNOWLEDGMENTS

My thanks to the following people:

- Richard Hunt and his wife, Linder Hunt, for her expertise with the recipes.

- Jack Heffron, for the short time that I worked with you.

- Scott Schwimmer, my attorney, who loves me even when I do not listen.

- Jen Gates, my literary agent, whose great advice is only a phone call away.

- Jill Parsons Stern for having great friends in the right places.

- David Powers—I could not have done it without you. Amazing you could make sense of my rambling; your talent makes a great story. Thanks also to your wife, Elizabeth, and your children for letting me have your extra time for our project.

- My family and friends, always in my thoughts.

- Most important, my clients who encountered chatty earthbound spirits with fond memories of food—we can all enjoy the fruits of those reminiscences!

—*Mary Ann Winkowski*

One of the first things I remember is how proud I was when I wrote a "story" about a truck when I was about 6 years old, and how excited my parents were to read all 10 words of it. My parents, Kay and Ken, were supportive of my efforts then and have never stopped being supportive of me—even when I switched my major from journalism to creative writing, and later when I took a job as a coffee-shop barista after leaving college, so I'd have enough spare time to write. Thanks for everything, Mom and Dad.

My wife, Elizabeth, has always been just as supportive, never batting an eye when we made the "five-year plan" after getting married, where she would work full-time and I would write, before we both settled down and got real jobs. Without her and without those five years, I know I would never have been able to keep writing at the forefront of my life, and without her now, all these years later, I know I would never find the time and peace of mind to keep writing. Thanks, Elizabeth—you always make it mean something, even when it doesn't.

I must also thank my children, Gabe, Evie, and Phina, who somehow managed to play quietly while I sat at the computer in a corner of the living room and wrote up the stories for this book.

I know it was hard for them to understand why they had to be so quiet, especially in the dead of winter when they couldn't go outside to play, but they managed to pull it off with only a few disasters. Thanks for reminding me what it's like to be a kid, my little turkeys.

Of course, it goes without saying that I owe Mary Ann more thanks than I'll ever be able to muster. Her level-headed, no-nonsense, and honest approach to everything—including her own amazing ability—is a trait that sets her far apart from the crowd. Without it, I don't think I could have gotten through this book. And without her confidence in me, even when I lacked confidence in myself, I wouldn't have had a book to get through in the first place. Thank you, Mary Ann—I will never be able to repay you for everything you've done for me and everything you've taught me over the decades.

I'd also like to thank my college roommate and ever-present friend since then, Erich Burnett. He not only gave me my first paid writing assignment, but he also helped me hone my journalistic skills to the point that I was later able to join him on the editorial staff at *Scene* in Cleveland. He was also the person who introduced me to Mary Ann when she told him she needed to find a ghostwriter—for that, Erich, I can never thank you enough.

Finally, I'd like to thank my brother, who never did anything more with his stories than entertain me. Don't think I've forgotten those nights, Andrew, when we'd sit up after we were supposed to be in bed and you'd make up stories on the fly, right as you told them to me. Without your tales of "The Veil of Black A" and "Starship One," I don't think storytelling would ever have occurred to me as a career choice.

—David Powers

INTRODUCTION

When I first began to help people communicate with earthbound spirits and to help those spirits cross over, I had very little to go on. At first, my grandmother was always with me because I was just a child. But because Grandma didn't have the same ability, she wasn't really able to give me much insight into how I should go about things. Along the way, I picked some ideas up myself, was told some things directly by the spirits, and had my abilities extended by whatever Power gave me this gift in the first place.

One of the hints I picked up from my own experiences was to always take a notepad and pen with me into every job. It seems so obvious now, but back when I first started doing this in earnest, it didn't occur to me. Usually the spirits were family members and I could just pass their messages on directly, or they were completely unrelated, and, to be frank, no one really cared what they said as long as they said goodbye.

Bess was the spirit who taught me to keep a notebook and pen with me at all times, and she was also the first ghost to ever give me a recipe. I'd never thought about lost recipes until Bess either. In hindsight, I should have expected both things: the need for paper and pen, and the need to pass along recipes.

Food is everywhere. We have to eat to survive, if nothing else, but, for most of us, food defines our days. Morning is the time between breakfast and lunch; afternoon comes before dinner. Yet eating is much more than survival or a way to break up the day. It is social. We conduct business lunches, raise money with pancake breakfasts, and share the day's events with loved ones over dinner—and it wasn't too long ago that eating was only half the experience. The other half was preparation. Average kitchens had stovetops crammed with pots of simmering soup stock, drying racks holding freshly baked bread, and chopping boards festooned with diced vegetables.

Times have changed. In this age of toaster-pastry breakfasts, power lunches, and fast-food dinners, eating has become a chore and cooking is considered a hassle. Even so, most of us still define good times and good memories with food: the cookies baked by a favorite aunt or the chicken soup you always had at Grandma's. I'm sure, somewhere out there, some people even fondly remember the aroma of a nut roll made by a woman named Bess.

Eleanor, the woman who called me about Bess, lived alone. Eleanor's husband had been dead for years, and since then she had become more involved with her church. That's where Eleanor must have first encountered Bess—when she was alive, I assume. Eleanor loved to bake, and her specialty was nut rolls. There was only one problem, as Bess explained when I got to Eleanor's house: "She can't bake worth a tinker's cuss."

Bess must have been 80 when she died, and she was now actively trying to get Eleanor to stop baking her nut rolls: She'd blow out the pilot light on the stove, she'd steal key ingredients, she'd put the butter that Eleanor had left out to soften back into the fridge—anything she could think of. Eleanor was actually baking the day I went out there, and the house smelled delicious.

"She goes around giving those nut rolls of hers away, and everyone just throws them out. I mean, look at them!" Bess offered, motioning to the cooling rack where Eleanor's signature nut rolls were. I turned and gave them a harder look, and Bess was right. They *smelled* good, but they sure didn't *look* good. They weren't roll-shaped, for one thing, and they looked more pasty than golden-brown.

"What?" Eleanor wondered, seeing me turn to look at her baking. "What's the ghost saying?"

Fortunately, I do not have to talk with earth-bound spirits out loud. For me, the whole conversation takes place in my head. That has saved me a lot of heartache over the years because it allows me to filter what the spirits are saying. Not that I ever make up things or put words in their mouths, but I can soften the blows when need be. Some ghosts—just like the people they were in life—have very little tact. The things they say can be mean and hurtful, even if they don't mean them that way. So talking to them in my head gives me the chance to rephrase

things and be more polite, sometimes even more diplomatic.

"Oh, we're just talking about baking," I replied carefully. I didn't quite know how to tell this sweet old woman that her special nut rolls were so bad that most people threw them away the second she'd gone. One glance told me that Eleanor derived a lot of pleasure from baking.

"Do you only notice things happening when you're going to bake?" I asked, turning to Eleanor.

"Yes."

"Well, Bess was a baker too," I said. "So that explains that."

"Oh, does she like my baking?" Eleanor asked hopefully.

"Tell her I like her *cooking,*" Bess said. "She makes good meatloaf and decent chili, and her stew doesn't look bad. She just can't *bake.* Can you stop her from baking?"

"No," I told the ghost. "It makes her happy. I'm not going to tell her that, and once I'm done here, you won't be able to bother her anymore. So you might as well go into the White Light once I've made it for you."

We cook because of that connection to food that is always there. We want to cook for sustenance and joy. What I've learned over the years in talking with spirits is that this connection with food is not broken after death. In fact, some spirits become earthbound *because* of food. Perhaps there's a recipe they didn't intend to take to the grave, or that was passed on incorrectly, and they need to make sure it survives. Maybe they don't like a relative's cooking and are literally haunting them in the hopes of correcting the error. Sometimes they even understand that food can heal in little ways, but only if it's prepared correctly, with the love and attention that should be poured into every dish.

Eleanor certainly had the love and attention to put in her nut rolls; she just didn't have a good recipe.

"Her nut roll recipe really is just awful," Bess almost pleaded. "How about I give you *my* nut-roll recipe for her to use?"

"So?" Eleanor cut in. "What's she saying about my baking?"

"Oh, nothing much," I replied. "Do you have a pen and paper? She's so thankful that you called and got me out here to help that she wants to give you a recipe—*her* recipe for nut rolls."

"A secret recipe?" Eleanor breathed, her eyes widening and sparkling. She got up breathlessly and fetched me something to write on and with.

"I don't know if it's secret," I answered truthfully. "But this is the first time a ghost has ever given me a recipe."

Eleanor smiled broadly, and I could see it in her eyes that this one "secret" recipe summed up for her everything she remembered from her childhood about her family's cooks—and all the "secret" recipes she wished she had now.

I also have fond memories of the wonderful smells that always came from Grandma's house. On my mother's side—the Italian side—it was Grandma's spaghetti sauce and Grandpa's pizza. There was homemade wine, with the fragrant aroma of grapes always drifting up from the basement. On my father's Bohemian side, the food was heavier but just as memorable and delicious: nut rolls and doughnuts and the weighty scent of yeast and hops for Granddad's beer. Visits were little more than one long excuse to eat and drink. The food never ran out, and the beer and wine flowed in an endless stream.

That was the era, though. Saturday was for cooking and baking for the next week, so when we visited, there was always something fresh and delicious to be had. Cooking, baking, preparing food—that's just the way it was.

Now we try to pack all those food-related memories into holidays, and we spend a week off work trying to cook from scratch without really knowing what to do. We follow recipes designed not for taste and nutrition, but for efficiency and show. We try to cram everything into one or two special meals, or one big meal a week, and invariably something goes wrong, or the food doesn't come out right, or it just doesn't taste like you remember it tasting when Grandma made it.

This book sets out to right the wrongs that so many earthbound spirits have perceived. These are recipes so beloved that the living asked me to get them before a loved one crossed over, or so meaningful that a loved one wanted to make sure they were kept by those left behind. These are simple dishes from typical homes with basic kitchens from all over the country. The best part: The recipes in this book can't help but also inspire the kind of love and attention that fills homes with mouthwatering aromas and creates long-lasting memories.

These recipes make some of the best home-cooked meals you can find because they actually come from homes, straight from the kitchens of the mothers, grandmothers, uncles, and grandfathers who prepared—and perfected—them over a lifetime. We say it's difficult in our modern society to find the time to make a fresh soup, but we still feel like we should try, and for good reason. Nothing will ever beat a home-cooked meal for nutrition, value, and satisfaction—that's one thing every spirit who has passed on a recipe from beyond agrees on.

Eleanor called a few weeks after my visit and after Bess had crossed over. She was overjoyed but also circumspect. No one had ever asked for her nut-roll recipe before, but since she started using Bess's recipe, suddenly people were, and she didn't know if she should give it out. She figured it should remain a secret recipe—but I found out much, much later, when she died herself, that Eleanor had shared her secret recipe with almost everyone in the parish!

And now I'm passing on all these "secret" recipes to you. I think you'll agree with me that everything in this book is *Beyond Delicious*.

BESS'S NUT ROLL

½ cup plus 1 tablespoon water, divided

1 cup granulated sugar, divided

1 cup walnuts

Dash of vanilla extract or grated lemon peel

1 cake (packet) yeast

¾ cup warm potato water (water that potatoes have been boiled in)

3 eggs, beaten

½ cup lard or butter

Dash of salt

4 cups all-purpose flour

1 egg white

▸ Preheat oven to 350°. Boil ½ cup water and ½ cup sugar in a saucepan; cool. Stir in walnuts and pound into a paste. Stir in vanilla until smooth.

Dissolve yeast into ¾ cup potato water with a pinch of sugar. Stir in remaining ½ cup sugar, 3 eggs, lard, salt, and flour. Cover and let dough rise in a warm place (85°), free from drafts, for about 1 hour. Roll dough out into a rectangle. Spread evenly with nut mixture, and roll up into a log. Let dough rise again until doubled in size. Place roll, seam side down, on a baking sheet lightly greased with butter.

Whisk together egg white and remaining 1 tablespoon water; brush onto roll. Bake for 30–35 minutes.

Sometimes when her back was turned, she'd
hear a scrape or a whoosh, and when she'd
turn back, a chair would be pulled out from
the table or a pot or pan would be taken
down from the pot rack. Not to mention the
baby, whose eyes seemed to follow the air
as if watching someone walk by.

—Swedish Pea Soup

SOUPS

CAULIFLOWER SOUP

The long New England winters had given Ann much more than a passing interest in "hand piece" work—linens, scarves, doilies, anything crocheted. If it involved handiwork, she loved it, not only to make herself but also to buy and collect. (To be honest, it was more the latter.) She spent her winters poring over her collection and marveling at the ingenuity and craftsmanship that had gone into every piece, running her fingertips over the fine stitchery with reverence. The only thing she wished for was to know more about the seamstresses and embroiderers who had made each one.

Some of the linens she'd been given by friends and relatives, and she knew their stories, of course, but more often than not she spent her time rummaging through thrift stores and boxes at church sales, amassing new finds she could go over in more detail once she was snowed in. It was these she always wondered about, and it was a unique find that would finally afford her some insight into the artisan.

A lot of the pieces she found were close to ruin with stains and rips. These she'd carefully nurse back to their former glory with gentle hand-washings and by applying her own talents for repairs. Even so, sometimes she found pieces that practically disintegrated the moment they touched the soapy water, and sometimes the fabric was so worn that there was nothing left to hold the rips together.

That was the case with the box of flour-sack dish towels she'd found at a farmhouse estate sale. It was a set of eight, and she took them all but wasn't sure any of them would survive. The fabric hadn't been designed for longevity, and the towels had been stuffed in a box for who knew how long. But they were beautifully embroidered with colorful vegetables—bell peppers, carrots, onions—and a relevant message or thought regarding each one, such as "Don't cry" for the onions. Only four of them were in good enough shape to be salvaged. Fortunately, one of the four she saved was also the most distinctive. The picture was of cauliflower, but instead of a short message, this one contained a recipe for cauliflower soup.

The cauliflower-soup towel was also the reason the woman who had made them had not crossed over after she died. Apparently, she had stitched the recipe incorrectly, and she was more concerned about the soup coming out right than she was about crossing over!

"It's two to three egg *yolks*, not two to three whole eggs," she explained to me after sharing her handiwork secrets and inspirations with Ann.

"Eggs in soup?" I checked. I had imagined the mistake had been the eggs in the first place.

"Oh yes," she replied. "You'd not believe the difference they make."

The cauliflower-soup towel was also the reason the woman who had made them had not crossed over after she died. Apparently, she had stitched the recipe incorrectly, and she was more concerned about the soup coming out right than she was about crossing over!

CAULIFLOWER SOUP

1 medium-size head cauliflower
6 cups chicken stock, heated
1 tablespoon all-purpose flour
1 tablespoon butter
2–3 egg yolks
½ cup whipping cream
Salt and black pepper to taste
6 fresh mushrooms (optional),
    cut into strips and sautéed in butter

▶ Cook cauliflower in salted boiling water in a large pot for 20 minutes or until tender; drain off water. Remove 6–8 florets, and mash remaining cauliflower in pot. Stir in hot stock, and whisk in flour. Stir in butter until mixture becomes a smooth paste. Let simmer for a few minutes. Meanwhile, beat egg yolks with cream in a small bowl. Add egg mixture to cauliflower paste, a little at a time, stirring constantly to avoid curdling. Add salt and pepper. Top with reserved florets and, if desired, mushrooms.

GRANDMA'S PICKLED-BEET SOUP

Eve didn't look at it as anything but a labor of love, but ever since her mother had died she'd been left to care for her father. He was suffering from dementia, and his thoughts skipped wildly from topic to topic, never resting on any single one for very long. He certainly couldn't manage alone, and Eve was only too willing to help.

It was his anger that made her wonder if she was really up to the task. One of the topics his thoughts seemed to flit to more often than the others was—of all things—pickled-beet soup, and when he started rambling about that, Eve knew it wouldn't be long before the anger came. He never did anything violent, which is why she'd not seriously looked into a home for him, but he did yell during these outbursts. The strangest thing was, when he was yelling, he also seemed to be at his most lucid. His thoughts seemed connected and logical and, in fact, very much as if she were only hearing one side of an argument.

He was voicing an ongoing argument about pickled-beet soup.

He would even look into the room as if there was someone there. He'd follow this invisible someone with his eyes, shouting and interjecting—and being cut off mid-sentence. That scared Eve, too, but for other reasons beyond her father's mental health. It made her think about ghost stories and the uneasy theories that said some crazy people might not be crazy

at all, but they only seem that way because we can only hear half the conversation.

It was at that point that she called me. She'd had enough and she had to know who was crazy: her or her father. Or both.

As it turned out, her father certainly had dementia and Eve wasn't crazy to wonder about ghosts. Eve's grandmother was also living with her, watching over her son. Eve had been convinced it was her mother—her father's wife—but it wasn't. It was her grandmother, who'd had three girls and one boy and doted on her boy above all the others.

Grandma wasn't helping her boy's mental health—or physical health—by being there, though. At first she was affronted when I told her this, but then she calmed down.

"I'm just upset because he's not getting his pickled-beet soup," Grandma explained.

"Pickled-beet soup?" I wondered, glancing over at Eve. Eve nodded her head slowly.

"That makes sense—he's often yelling about beet soup."

When I looked over at him, his eyes weren't looking at us; they were following his mother. He could see and hear her just as well as I could. Grandma smiled sweetly at her boy, then turned back to me.

"I keep telling him that soup will make him feel better, and that's when he gets upset. No one can make his soup like I can. Not even his wife could, and Eve certainly can't."

He would even look into the room as if there was someone there. He'd follow this invisible someone with his eyes, shouting and interjecting—and being cut off mid-sentence. That scared Eve, too, but for other reasons.

I told Eve what her grandmother said, and Eve agreed that she wasn't much of a cook.

"But will she try, if I give her the recipe?" Grandma asked me. "Please? For my boy? Will she try and make his soup?"

Eve agreed to try, and Grandma agreed to cross over once she'd given us the recipe. Two weeks later, Eve called me to tell me how the soup had turned out.

"The house doesn't smell so good," she admitted. "I had to move the pot to the detached garage while it was stewing, but you wouldn't believe it, Mary Ann." I could hear her getting a bit emotional, but she gathered herself and explained, "When he ate that soup, my father actually cried with joy."

She paused, then added, "It must be an acquired taste."

GRANDMA'S PICKLED-BEET SOUP

6 large or (10 small) beets
4 cups lukewarm water
1 slice sour rye bread
Salt and black pepper to taste
Dash of granulated sugar (optional)
Sour cream (optional)

▶ Scrape and dice beets; place in a large pot. Cover with 4 cups water and place bread on top. Cover loosely and let stand for 4 days in the warmest part of the kitchen. The liquid should be sour and tasty by that time (depending on the weather). Should mold appear, carefully skim it off. Discard bread; add salt, pepper, and, if desired, sugar. Soup may be served hot or cold with sour cream, if desired. Tightly covered, it may be stored in the refrigerator for later use.

BAT WINGS

MRS. WHITE'S CLEAR CONSOMMÉ

Ruth Johnson was nothing if not frugal. She counted pennies and clipped coupons, and when she saw a good deal at the secondhand shop, she didn't think twice about taking it. So it was with the cooking pot she came across one day: It was the right size, and the lid, of all things, was spectacular. She'd been looking for something bigger to make her applesauce in, and she couldn't help but grin with glee at finally finding it.

Then the problems began.

First, it was the lightbulbs in the kitchen constantly burning out. Then it was the radio going on the fritz. Around the same time, Ruth started feeling run-down, which she attributed to her suddenly restless nights. But it wasn't until she saw the shadow that she thought she'd better call someone.

Just outside her bedroom door, she had a night-light in the hallway, and she would see it go out, then come back on again—only she knew it wasn't turning on and off. No, she could just tell that someone was walking in front of it and blocking it from her view momentarily. As reasonable as she was frugal, Ruth knew when she was up against something she needed help with. She hadn't lived 60 years and not learned when it was time to ask for help.

When I arrived at Ruth's small bungalow, where she'd lived for 25 years, I confirmed immediately that there was a ghost because she was standing there glaring at us before I even got in the door. Her name was Mrs. White, and she clearly didn't appreciate sass from anyone. The ghost's hair was gray and tied up in a severe bun, and she refused to give me her first name.

"Mrs. White," she said curtly. "Everyone calls me Mrs. White."

Realizing that small talk was not going to work, I got right to the point: "Why are you here? Do you know Ruth?"

She stood up straight and glared. "No, I don't know her. She's just using my pot wrong. Ask her—isn't her applesauce always burning?"

Ruth agreed that it was. Her new pot, as perfect as it was, always seemed to burn her applesauce.

"That's because the pot was made for consommé, not for fruit," Mrs. White said in a haughty tone.

"Consommé?" I checked. "Do you mean broth—soup stock?"

"I mean *consommé!*" she retorted. "I used to cook for the wealthiest family in four counties. I know what broth is, and I know what my pot is for!"

That's when it all became clear. Ruth had brought home more than just a good pot from the secondhand store. She had also brought home Mrs. White, whose pot it had been, and the old cook was angry about how Ruth was using it. When I explained this, Ruth was actually overjoyed.

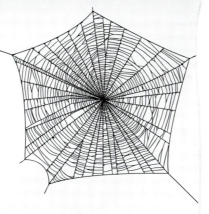

MRS. WHITE'S CLEAR CONSOMMÉ

¼ pound chicken giblets or chicken meat, cut into small pieces

¼ pound veal

2 pounds beef brisket

10 cups cold water

Salt to taste

Dash of freshly ground black pepper

2 medium-size onions, preferably baked

1 large leek

2 or 3 carrots

1 celery root

1 parsley root

Few sprigs parsley

½ head Savoy cabbage (optional)

1 bay leaf

1 bouillon cube

Crackers or noodles (optional)

▶ Place chicken, veal, and brisket in a large pot. Cover meat with 10 cups cold water (5 cups water to 1 pound meat); bring to a boil. Skim carefully. When no more fat comes to the surface, lower flame and add salt; pepper; onions; leek; carrots; celery root; parsley root and sprigs; cabbage, if desired; bay leaf; and bouillon cube. Cover and let simmer for 3 hours. Skim fat, strain, and discard bay leaf. Serve with crackers or noodles, if desired.

Around the same time, Ruth started feeling run-down, which she attributed to her suddenly restless nights. But it wasn't until she saw the shadow that she thought she'd better call someone.

"I've always wanted to make my own soup stock!" she cried. "Will she give me her recipe if I promise not to use that pot for anything else?"

"If she promises to call it consommé! And only if she cleans the pot well first," Mrs. White decided, but I could tell by the twinkle in her eye that she'd gotten what she really wanted. Her consommé was clearly a great source of pride for her, and she didn't want the recipe to join her in the grave.

NEW ENGLAND CLAM CHOWDER

Mothers like to believe their children will mature as they get older. In many ways they do, but they can also stay the same bickering siblings they've been since they were little. I don't know if that's any more true for twins, but Tammy and Terry from Rhode Island were still petty and argumentative when I met them when they were in their 40s.

Don't get me wrong—they were still close. They lived in the same development, and their families often got together for dinners and cookouts. Tammy was a nurse and Terry was a teacher, so neither of them had a career to lord over the other, but one thing seemed to bring out the inner bickering girls: Mom's cooking. Or, more specifically, Mom's recipes.

Their mother, Martha, had been a private caterer, what Terry called her "cottage industry." She hadn't been rich, but she'd been a great cook and she'd turned it into a business to put her girls through college. That's what Mom had wanted more than anything, and she had apparently gone out of her way to not share her recipes when she was alive because she didn't want the girls to follow her into her business. She wanted them to get good jobs with good pay, which they'd done.

Now Martha had known when she was dying, so they'd had time to plan for their last goodbyes. Often, they would sit with her and talk about growing up and the antics they'd all gotten up to. One day, Martha asked what they wanted of her. She wanted to make sure that each one got something of hers they really wanted, and she wanted them to have it before she died.

But they both wanted her recipes.

Finally, Martha decided they would divide them and that they would have to share them if one ever wanted a recipe the other one had. They agreed, and the recipes found new homes. One of the recipes that Tammy got was for New England clam chowder, which Terry had always loved, so she asked for a copy of it. Tammy was only too happy to give it to her, but when Terry made it, it just didn't taste the way she'd remembered—and Terry had an idea of why because she had not faithfully copied a recipe from her stack that her sister had wanted. She left out an important ingredient to keep the recipe special—something of Mom's that was hers and hers alone. She had the feeling Tammy had done the same thing with the clam chowder.

This was something they found to argue about, each accusing the other of transcribing recipes wrong on purpose. As it turned out, neither of them was wrong about the other.

"I had a feeling something like this would happen," Martha told me when I arrived. Terry had called me out because of odd things that had been going on around the house, but Martha was upset with both of them. "Tell them I'm very disappointed they couldn't share. And tell them I'm not leaving until they *do* share."

This was something they found to argue about, each accusing the other of transcribing recipes wrong on purpose. As it turned out, neither of them was wrong about the other. "I had a feeling something like this would happen."

Fortunately, maturity did finally kick in, and the sisters agreed again to share.

"Prove it," Martha demanded. "Tell Tammy to tell her sister what she did with that clam chowder recipe."

Tammy 'fessed up immediately and told her sister about the missing ingredient, then Terry admitted her own guilt in copying down some recipes incorrectly.

"Well now, just to be sure," I said. "Why doesn't Mom give *me* the recipe so we can check it?"

Martha thought that was a great idea, so she did and the recipe was a match for the corrected recipe Tammy had just given Terry.

NEW ENGLAND CLAM CHOWDER

2 slices salt pork, diced
1 large onion, minced
2½ cups water
3 large potatoes, diced
1 quart milk
1 quart clams, picked over and chopped fine, with juice
3 tablespoons butter
Freshly ground black pepper to taste
Crackers

▶ Fry salt pork in a large saucepan; add onion and sauté until it begins to brown. Add 2½ cups water and potatoes; bring to a boil, reduce heat, and simmer for about 15 minutes or until potatoes are tender. Add milk and return to a boil. Scald clams with their juice, and stir into potato mixture. Add butter and pepper, and serve immediately with crackers.

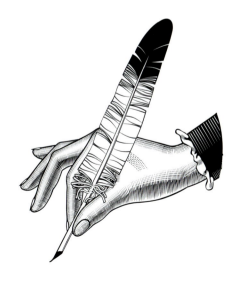

OXTAIL SOUP

The sound was coming from Sam's room. A soft whirring, like an electric train that had been left on and now was looping endlessly on its track. Sam certainly had a hard time remembering to put his toys away, but Mary gave her 7-year-old boy a pass. He had leukemia, and though it was in remission, he was still sickly, and she didn't figure a nagging mother would do much to help when all was said and done. But this was different. It was 3 o'clock in the morning and it seemed like a bit of nagging wouldn't hurt compared to Sam staying up all hours playing with his trains.

Mary cracked the door to her son's room and looked in. Sure enough, his train was looping on its track, but there were no lights on, except for the night-light, and Sam was huddled in his bed.

"Sam?" she whispered. "Sam, honey, are you up playing with your trains?"

"No," he replied feebly. "It's Adam. He's keeping me awake again."

A chill always worked its way up Mary's spine at the mention of Adam, but she was long past being scared. "Go away, Adam," she said firmly to the room. "Leave him alone. He needs sleep."

The train stopped. She waited for the follow-up—maybe a stuffed animal would come flying through the air at her, or maybe Adam would kick a ball across the room—but nothing happened.

"I mean it, Adam," Mary added, then she moved over and tucked Sam back in, kissing him lightly on the forehead. "I'll call Mary Ann tomorrow."

"The ghostbuster?" he asked with wide eyes. Mary nodded and smiled at her son.

In the morning, though, it never seemed as bad, and Mary forgot about calling until that afternoon when she set about making a cake. First the electric mixer died, then the electric stove just wouldn't turn on. But when the radio came on by itself and the mixing bowl moved a fraction of an inch, she remembered and she called.

When I got there, I saw the boy first. He looked mischievous but not mean. Then I saw the old lady in the kitchen. She looked bossy, to put it nicely, and she was too. Neither ghost was related to anyone in the family. Adam, the boy, had followed Sam home the last time he'd left the hospital, and the woman—Miss Ellie, Adam called her—had followed Adam.

"He was up to no good," she explained regarding why she'd followed Adam, but she would not say why she was earthbound—she wasn't much for small talk. Adam didn't really know what had happened to him, either. All he could remember was that his dad had had a car wreck, then suddenly everyone was gone. I wanted to find out more, but Miss Ellie kept interrupting.

"That boy would be feeling better if she'd cook right!" she was squawking.

First the electric mixer died, then the electric stove just wouldn't turn on. But when the radio came on by itself and the mixing bowl moved a fraction of an inch, she remembered and she called.

"Who? Adam?" I checked.

"No! The sick one. He'd feel better if his mother would cook from scratch! She uses canned soups for everything!"

"Sam loves soup," Mary explained when I relayed the message. "Sometimes we get take-out soup—he just loves the oxtail soup we get from the soup shop down the road—but we do also go through a lot of cans of soup. We can't eat takeout every day."

"Well, she doesn't like that," I said. "She says she's been trying to stop you from cooking from cans." Mary nodded with understanding. "She also says she has a recipe for oxtail soup that's better than medicine."

"*Really*?" Mary gasped. "Sam loves oxtail soup! Will she give me the recipe?"

Miss Ellie was only too happy to oblige. And whether it was the ghosts finally being away from him or the soup, Sam did start to get his energy back, and Miss Ellie's oxtail soup quickly became his favorite meal.

OXTAIL SOUP

2 oxtails, cut into pieces
1 tablespoon all-purpose flour
3 tablespoons bacon fat or lard
1 carrot, diced
1 large onion, diced
2 quarts cold water
2 stalks celery
2 sprigs parsley
1 bay leaf
2 tablespoons barley
Salt, black pepper, and
 cayenne pepper to taste
1 teaspoon Worcestershire sauce
¼ cup sherry (optional)

▶ Roll oxtails in flour to coat. Melt bacon fat in a large pot; sauté carrot, onion, and oxtails in drippings. When meat is browned, add 2 quarts cold water. Stir in celery, parsley, and bay leaf (tied together). Bring to a boil, shake in barley, and simmer for about 1½ hours. Stir in salt, black pepper, and cayenne pepper. Simmer, skimming occasionally, for 1½ more hours. Remove large bones and bundle of celery, parsley, and bay leaf, returning meat from bones to soup. Stir in Worcestershire sauce and, if desired, sherry; serve soup very hot.

SWEDISH PEA SOUP

Whether they put it on themselves or not, young brides always feel pressure to please their in-laws, and Nancy was no different. She was also quite sure she wasn't being overly sensitive. She'd was a New York City girl, born and raised, and her husband was Swedish. Needless to say, there was some culture clash, but the one thing she hadn't expected was that some people in Sweden still "promised" their children to wed the children of other families. Not arranged marriages, exactly, more like an anticipation or an expectation. Jon, her husband, had been so promised, a small thing he had failed to mention when they met at a youth hostel.

"It's ridiculous anyway," he said dismissively when it came up later. "Nobody really follows that stuff anymore."

Still, it was rough visiting his family. To say she was shunned might be a bit of an exaggeration, but it was certainly how Nancy felt. No one in the family even tried to speak English to include her in conversations, and something in the way they laughed and glanced at her told her they were making fun of her in a language she didn't understand. All except Helga, Jon's aunt. She was the exact opposite. She went out of her way to make Nancy feel welcome, to teach her useful phrases and words, and to show her around when they were there.

Then the baby came along. The baby not only forced the Swedish family to come to terms with it—that the marriage was real and was for good—but it also meant they were going to visit them in New York. Nancy was petrified. Not only was she a new mother, but Aunt Helga had recently died and so she would not be there to comfort Nancy. And to top it all off, their house was suddenly haunted.

Nancy and Jon had lived in the same place for years, and Nancy had lived there before that "forever," and there had never been anything amiss before. Now, however, she could hear footsteps in the house when she knew she was quite alone, and things would move. Sometimes when her back was turned, she'd hear a scrape or a whoosh, and when she'd turn back, a chair would be pulled out from the table or a pot or pan would be taken down from the pot rack. Not to mention the baby, whose eyes seemed to follow the air as if watching someone walk by.

This was too much for Nancy, so she called me and I went out to visit her. Nancy expected the worst, like a demon or something—too much TV, I suppose—but what she got was the best: Aunt Helga had been hanging around and she still wanted to help.

"They're coming to visit," Aunt Helga explained. "My sister and her husband are convinced Nancy doesn't keep a good house, and they are quite certain she isn't a good cook. They will pick and pick and pick at her when they're here."

This was too much for Nancy, so she called me and I went out to visit her. Nancy expected the worst, like a demon or something.

"So what can she do? How can you help?" I wondered.

"Pea soup," Aunt Helga replied with a proud smile.

"Pea soup?"

She nodded dramatically. "They *love* my pea soup. If Nancy makes them my pea soup, she will win them over for good." I opened my mouth to reply, but Aunt Helga held up a hand to stop me so she could finish. "Maybe not at first. Maybe not right away. But trust me, that soup will win their hearts."

"Okay," I agreed. "Give me the recipe."

Aunt Helga made sure I took it down with exacting detail—she was very sure this soup would help. I called Nancy back a few weeks after I knew the in-laws would be gone, to see how it went.

"You wouldn't believe it!" she said. "Aunt Helga was right! They loved the soup, and they were so surprised that I'd gone out of my way to learn to make it that they melted almost after the first bite. Jon's mother even hugged me when they left!"

SWEDISH PEA SOUP

1 medium-size onion, finely diced
2 celery ribs, finely diced
2 carrots, finely diced
2 leeks, diced
¾ pound (3 sticks) butter
¾ pound green split peas
3 quarts chicken stock
1 ham hock (fresh, not smoked)
2 bay leaves
2 teaspoons thyme
Salt and black pepper to taste
1 medium-size potato, finely diced

▶ In a large pot, simmer onion, celery, carrots, and leeks with butter over low heat. Add peas, chicken stock, ham hock, bay leaves, thyme, salt, and pepper. Bring to a boil. Add potato and simmer slowly for 2 hours. If soup is too thick, add more stock.

At first, he just sort of gave me the chills. He had this odd stare and way of looking through you that made you uneasy. In fact, that's why Joann had called me in the first place. Nothing specific had happened, but she felt watched.

—Secret Harvard Beets

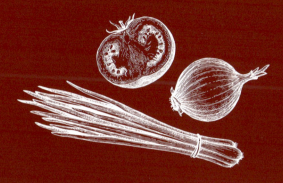

VEGETABLES AND SIDES

CREOLE TOMATOES

Angelo had a tiny plot in a community garden in one of the close-in suburbs of Cleveland. He was a big Italian man, about 75, and he'd lived in the neighborhood his whole life, watching it slowly deteriorate over the years as people moved out to the newer suburbs.

Angelo's wife had died long ago, but one of the traditions he'd kept up that he'd shared with her was cooking. They had both enjoyed cooking and also canned their own vegetables, but lately he had stopped experimenting and stuck primarily to tomatoes.

"He has no imagination," the ghost in his home told me. The ghost was an older African American man, and he tutted with pity and shook his head. "He grows peppers sometimes—he could do so much with all those tomatoes he grows! Annie would give him some of her onions too."

I looked at Angelo and decided that criticizing his cooking might not be the best way to broach the ghost's concern. "Do you know an Annie?" I finally asked. He sort of paled, then caught himself and sat up straight.

"Sure," he said. "She's a woman who lives on my street. She tends the garden plot next to mine. Why do you ask?"

"This ghost thinks she might be willing to trade some of her vegetables with you, for some tomatoes."

"Yeah?" Angelo checked. "And who's this guy, then?"

"My name's Arthur," the ghost told me. "I'm Annie's father."

"It's Annie's dad."

"Well, tell him to get out!" Angelo said. I could tell he was secretly scared, and it only took a look to get him to continue. "Annie told me once she sees her dad in her house from time to time. He's been dead for a while. I figured she was, you know, crazy."

"She's not," I assured him.

"She's been asking me a lot about my tomatoes lately," he added thoughtfully. "Like, what I plan to do with all of them and if I ever make fried green tomatoes—stuff like that."

"And?" I asked, bringing up the reason for Arthur's visits. "What are you going to do?"

Angelo shrugged. "Make spaghetti sauce. You know, some folks don't know what to do with tomatoes."

I glanced at Arthur apologetically, then said to Angelo, "I think they might. Arthur says he has a good recipe for tomatoes."

"I know what to do with tomatoes!" Angelo replied defensively.

"Sure he does," Arthur disagreed. "He knows how to cut them up and put them on things. He cuts them up and puts them on eggs. He slices them and puts them on a sandwich. He has no imagination! Look, ask him to give a message to my Annie. Tell him to let her know that I love her and Della and Peg, and I'm very proud of all of them."

Angelo balked at the idea. "She'd think I was nuts!" he exclaimed.

"Did she ever tell you her father's name?" I wondered.

"No."

"Did she ever tell you that her mother was also dead, and that her name was Margaret?"

"No."

"Well, that's the other part of the message—he wants me to help him cross over now so he can see Margaret again. Now, how else would you know that stuff?"

I turned back to Arthur. "Did you ever see Angelo's wife around, Arthur?"

"Carmella? Sure I did."

I turned back to Angelo. "Do you think Carmella would want you to do this?"

Angelo practically fell out of his chair. "How'd you know my wife's name?"

"How do you think?"

At that moment, I realized that, despite him calling me, until that second he hadn't fully believed any of it. "Now if you don't mind," I said. "I'm going to get Arthur's tomato recipe before he crosses over. Are you going to give Annie his message?"

"Yeah," Angelo agreed. "I'll give it to her."

A couple of weeks later, I called Angelo, to make sure he'd delivered Arthur's message. Annie had been appreciative. She gave him some peppers and onions, so he gave her some tomatoes. Angelo told her about the recipe too.

CREOLE TOMATOES

4 large tomatoes

2 green bell peppers, finely chopped

1 small onion, finely chopped

Salt and cayenne pepper to taste

4 tablespoons butter or meat drippings, divided

½ cup water

2 tablespoons all-purpose flour

1 cup milk

4 slices toast

▶ Preheat oven to 400º. Cut tomatoes in half crosswise; place, cut sides up, in a baking dish. Sprinkle with green bell peppers, onion, salt, and cayenne pepper. Dot with 2 tablespoons butter. Pour ½ cup water into dish; bake for 20 minutes or until tomatoes are tender.

Melt remaining 2 tablespoons butter in a saucepan; brown flour in butter. Add milk and liquid from baking pan, stirring over high heat until boiling. Reduce heat, add additional seasonings to taste, and cook for 3 minutes. Serve tomatoes on toast, pouring sauce over top. Makes 4 servings.

HAZEL'S GREEN BEAN CASSEROLE

Dorothy called me at a complete loss. I don't know why people take so long to realize they have something going on that won't go away and won't be explained away. But they do, and when they get to me, they're usually frazzled.

Dorothy lived with her daughter, Tina, and Tina's twin boys, Pete and Paul. The twins were 5 years old, and they hadn't slept in their own room for months. What especially troubled Dorothy was that it wasn't just some nameless fear that drove them away—nothing to do with typical fears of closets or the dust bunnies under the bed. No, the twins were pretty specific: They were afraid of Hazel, the old lady with funny hair and no teeth. Not only that, the twins had been pretty sickly for the past several months, and Dorothy thought that was only making things worse.

"But they just won't stop talking about this Hazel woman," Dorothy told me.

When I got to the house, Tina gave me some more insight. She was the head nurse at a nursing home, and a woman named Hazel had died right around the time the boys started seeing this lady with funny hair and no teeth. I was about to ask if that was an accurate description of the Hazel at the nursing home when the ghost walked into the kitchen where we were talking.

I have to be honest—this was one of the few times a ghost actually gave me the willies. I absolutely and completely understood why those poor twin boys were afraid to be in the same room with her. She looked old—*really old*—and she was thin, like a skeleton. She didn't appear to have any teeth, which gave her jawline a caved-in look, and her hair—what was left of it—stuck up in oddly twisted wisps on the top of her head.

"Tina, what was going on with Hazel before she died?" I asked politely.

"Mostly it was dementia," Tina replied. "Hazel must have been 90. She wouldn't eat. She couldn't hold a conversation. She quite literally wasted away."

"I can see that," I said softly, but it didn't help me get over the shock of her appearance. I asked Hazel why she was there, and she replied in that strange sucking way that toothless people do.

"Tina was always so nice to me," she said. "I had twins, too, and I loved when her boys came and visited her at work."

By this time the boys had come up from where they were playing in the basement, with an assortment of what looked liked canned food and frozen bagged vegetables. When they saw Hazel, they both stopped and scooted away from her, toward their mother. There's no doubt that they could see her, just as well as I could.

"What do you have?" Tina asked her boys. Pete handed her a bag of green beans and Paul handed over a can of soup.

What especially troubled Dorothy was that it wasn't just some nameless fear that drove them away—nothing to do with typical fears of closets or the dust bunnies under the bed. No, the twins were pretty specific.

"Oh, I know what they want," Dorothy said. "They want me to make them a green bean casserole for dinner."

"That's a terrible recipe!" yelled Hazel.

"Excuse me?" I questioned. It was time for this woman to cross over, I can tell you that.

"She came into the nursing home and made that all the time. I *hated* it! We all hated it! I used to make a green bean casserole that is *much* better than that—healthier too. Those boys should try mine!"

"All right," I said. "Give me the recipe and I'll let her know, but then you have to leave."

She didn't really agree, but she gave me the recipe and she did leave. I told the boys it was okay now, that Hazel was going away. I was hoping they'd be able to see the White Light and see her go into it, but if they did, they didn't tell.

HAZEL'S GREEN BEAN CASSEROLE

2 (9-ounce) packages frozen French-style green beans

1 cup water

3 tablespoons butter

½ cup minced onion

3 ounces slivered almonds

2 tablespoons all-purpose flour

2 teaspoons salt

½ teaspoon black pepper

½ teaspoon dry mustard

2 teaspoons Worcestershire sauce

1 cup sour cream

1 cup milk

1 cup grated sharp cheddar cheese

1 (4-ounce) package French-fried onion rings

▶ Cook green beans for about 5 minutes in 1 cup boiling salted water; drain. Melt butter in a saucepan. Add onion and almonds, and cook over medium heat, stirring constantly, until onion is transparent. Stir in flour, salt, pepper, mustard, and Worcestershire sauce until mixture bubbles. Remove from heat and gradually add sour cream and milk, stirring constantly for 2 or 3 minutes. Do not boil. Add green beans. Toss gently until well coated.

Preheat oven to 350º. Pour green bean mixture into a casserole dish. Sprinkle with grated cheese and spread onion rings on top. Bake for 10–15 minutes. Serve immediately, piping hot.

MUSHROOM PATTIES

Carl was a mushroom hunter. He picked mushrooms as a hobby—not to examine them, but to eat them. My parents used to do that, too, but it's not a hobby you can take lightly. When it comes to mushrooms, you really have to know what you're doing and you have to be really careful. If you pick the wrong mushrooms—and they may even look like the "right" mushrooms to pick—you can end up violently sick, or worse, dead.

Carl was an avid mushroom-picker, and the best time to go out was in autumn, when it was cold and rainy. Carl would go out with his wife and a group of fellow pickers, and they'd come back with baskets full of mushrooms, which they'd clean, can, and freeze. One fall, there was a new guy in the group, someone Carl had never seen before. In fact, no one seemed to know him, which wasn't that strange since they publicized their outings at the library.

The new guy settled right in with them and seemed to know quite a bit about mushrooms. At one point, he stopped to pick a type of mushroom none of the others recognized. He assured everyone they were delicious and perfect for canning because they had a good, strong flavor. Carl picked some, as did another guy, but most of the group, not knowing the variety themselves, passed.

That had been October. When Carl called me in May, he said things hadn't been right in his house since then.

"Did you eat the mushrooms?" I wondered.

"Well, just a taste," Carl replied. "We fried a couple and tried them, and they did have a good flavor, so we canned the rest. Neither of us got sick or felt the least bit bad, so we didn't think any more of it. But come December, there was this absolutely horrible smell wafting up from the basement. Turns out, those mushrooms had popped the cans and were completely rotten, so we threw them out."

Carl did have a ghost in the house—a rugged, outdoorsy-looking man with a full beard and a knowing twinkle in his eyes. He nodded slowly at me and said, "I did that."

"You ruined the mushrooms?" I checked.

"I popped the cans. Those mushrooms were poisonous," he said evenly. "I also ruined that other fella's cans. But I can't find the last guy to ruin his."

"Carl, did anyone else say those mushrooms went off?" I asked him.

"Yes!" Carl answered. "The same exact thing happened to the other guy who picked them!"

"The guy who told you about them?"

"No, no—he never came back to the group. The other guy who picked them that day, from our regular group."

"Oh," I looked back over at the ghost. "And how do you know they were poisonous?"

"I picked mushrooms too," he said. "That's my land they were on. I don't mind them out there foraging. But they don't know how to cook mushrooms right."

But come December, there was this absolutely horrible smell wafting up from the basement.

"Okay," I said evenly before I relayed the critique to Carl.

"That's ridiculous!" Carl protested. "I know every recipe there is!"

"No, you don't," the ghost said with a grin, then proceeded to give me a recipe for mushroom patties!

"So you came home with Carl because of the mushrooms?" I wondered, once he was done giving me the recipe.

"That's right. Those mushrooms were bad. I just wish I could find that other guy . . . ."

Carl and his wife had been lucky not to get sick. He had no idea how to get in touch with the other man, though, so I asked the ghost if he was ready to move on. I was shocked when he said no, more so because his tone was not at all argumentative, just very matter-of-fact.

"I wasn't a religious man," he explained. "And I enjoy walking the Earth."

"Well, you won't be able to come back here once I leave," I warned him. He just smiled and winked.

"That's okay—I'll see him when he's out picking mushrooms!"

MUSHROOM PATTIES

1 pound mushrooms

1 medium-size onion, grated

Butter

Salt and black pepper to taste

2 white rolls, moistened in milk and mashed

2 whole eggs, lightly beaten

1 tablespoon chopped fresh parsley

Breadcrumbs

Pan-fried potatoes (optional)

▶ Wash, clean, and chop mushroom caps and stems. Cook grated onion in a little butter in a skillet; when onion begins to brown, add mushrooms. Add salt and pepper, and simmer, covered, for about 5 minutes. In a bowl, mix mushroom mixture thoroughly with mashed rolls, eggs, and parsley; shape into patties. Roll in breadcrumbs and fry in hot butter until golden brown. Serve patties with pan-fried potatoes, if desired. Makes 4 servings.

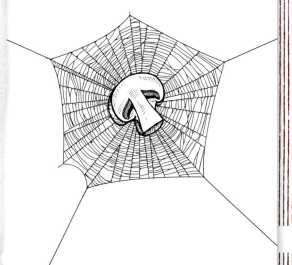

SECRET HARVARD BEETS

Joann's husband, Mike, was a social worker at a group home, and to be honest, I'm amazed there was only one ghost that had come home with him. Those who work around troubled people—like the police and firemen and paramedics—tend to bring home ghosts more often than other people. When someone dies in a high-stress situation, maybe they just tag along with whoever was trying to help them.

The ghost's name was Jerry. At first, he just sort of gave me the chills. He had this odd stare and way of looking through you that made you uneasy. In fact, that's why Joann had called me in the first place. Nothing specific had happened, but she felt *watched*. She could sense Jerry's eyes on her, watching her in the odd way he had. It was an intense stare, and I'm sure even the least in-tune person would have been able to feel his eyes on them. He just gave you the willies. He made you think of someone in a Stephen King book.

"It feels like someone's playing with my hair at night," Joann whispered. "I even feel like he's watching me in . . . the bathroom."

"I'm sure he is," I agreed slowly. Then I said to the ghost, "So why are you here?"

"I don't know," he said in an odd cadence. "I came home with Mike. I like Mike. Mike is my friend. He's my friend, so I came home with him. He likes me. He's my best friend."

"Oh," I breathed with dawning realization. "Joann, I think this ghost is mentally challenged. Did Mike ever mention any mentally challenged guests at the group home?"

"Yes!" she gasped. "Oh my God! Is it Jerry? Jerry was handicapped—he died right around when I started feeling weird."

The ghost nodded, then his brow furrowed. "They tied me to a bed. They tied me up to give me medicine. Is that why I'm here?"

Before I could get more out of him, Joann's cousin came waltzing through the front door. She stopped when she saw our faces. I'm sure my own expression echoed her surprise, as there, walking in right behind her, was another ghost.

"And who are you?" I said to the ghost, but of course Joann's cousin thought I was talking to her.

"I'm Jeanne, Joann's cousin."

I apologized for the mistake and explained about the ghost who had followed her in, which of course got them both trying to outdo each other as far as who was freaked out more.

"So who are you?" I asked her again.

"Jeanne's mother, Mable," she said politely. "You can see . . ." she glanced at Jerry. "Us?"

"Yup," I admitted. I knew that telling Jeanne her mom was with her would all but end anyone caring about Jerry, though, so I went back to him before telling her. I was a little confused because I don't normally run into mentally handicapped ghosts. As best I can tell, they have a spirit guide who helps them cross over. I wasn't sure how Jerry had missed his.

When I asked him, he said he did remember the White Light and that he'd seen his grandpa in it, beckoning him to join him. The problem was his spirit guide, who had come to help him.

"But I didn't want to go," Jerry said. "I was scared. I always have to go with people, but I didn't want to go with him."

I could see how he would have been afraid, but it made me wonder what kind of spirit guide he had if they just left him to roam the Earth. Jerry said he wanted to see his grandpa again, so I was sure he'd cross over. Which brought me back to Mable.

When I told the girls, there were the usual hysterics and tears and wails. Aunt Mable had died of cancer, so they'd got most of the good-byes out of the way when she was alive. She'd stayed behind because her daughter was pregnant at the time and she'd wanted to see the baby. When everyone had calmed down again, I asked if there was anything else they wanted to say or ask before I made the White Light and let the two ghosts cross over.

"Jeanne? Can I ask Aunt Mable something?"

"Sure! Of course!" Jeanne gushed.

"Well, she used to make this really delicious beet recipe, and I was wondering if she'd give it to me? It's just so good!"

Mable was glad to be asked, you could tell, but she pretended to play hard. "That was my secret recipe," she said slowly before she broke into a smile. "But of course I'll give it to Joann!"

SECRET HARVARD BEETS

1½ tablespoons butter

½ cup brown sugar

1½ teaspoons cornstarch

⅔ cup fresh orange juice

2 tablespoons grated orange rind, divided

3 cups diced cooked or canned beets, drained

4 shakes each salt and black pepper

▶ Melt butter in a large saucepan. Mix together sugar and cornstarch; stir into butter. Stir in orange juice gradually and cook, stirring constantly, until mixture is thickened. Blend in 1 tablespoon orange rind and beets. Add salt, pepper, and remaining 1 tablespoon orange rind. Makes 8 servings.

SPANISH CORN AND SPANISH ZUCCHINI

The home in the Los Angeles hills was beautiful. It was one of the movie mansions from the 1940s and sort of off the beaten path.

The owners were Betty, a corporate lawyer, and her husband, Bob, an accountant. They were no-nonsense people who had quickly reached a point in their lives where they felt entitled to what they had and looked down on those who had not. They were cold but polite, even to each other, and their two children—5-year-old Gracie and 7-year-old Eric—seemed to look to their live-in nanny, Rita, for the affection and attention most children get from their parents.

To be honest, I was amazed they'd called me in the first place. It did take them a while to call, Betty admitted, but it had finally gotten to the point where their logical explanations were failing. The kids were always sickly, but they wrote that off as kids being kids, but the workers who came to restore or refurbish parts of the mansion were another story. They'd work for a few days, then leave and never come back. The footsteps, the glimpses of moving shadows, the missing tools that turned up later in other parts of the house—it was too much, and Betty and Bob were sick of trying to find replacements.

Not to mention the kids. Gracie hadn't slept in her own bedroom for months, afraid of the woman who stood and watched her in the night. Gracie said the woman had a long braid on one side of her head, tied off with a blue ribbon. Eric stayed in his own bed, but only because he was afraid to move. His closet door liked to open and close by itself, and his toys would move across the floor of their own volition. Sometimes he could feel the ghost tugging on his covers.

Still, when I got there, the buttoned-down, business-minded husband and wife were still dismissive. Betty didn't like me telling them about their unwanted guests.

There was a male ghost there who did not like Betty. He's what I'd call "residue" from a case she'd won, so he already had a chip on his shoulder. Besides that, he thought she was arrogant and controlling, and he wanted to make life hard for her because of it. There was also a female ghost, a Mexican woman who looked exactly as Gracie had described. She may have been genuinely concerned for the health of the children and the food they ate, as she said, or she may have been slightly embarrassed that Rita, who was also Mexican, was not preparing any of her country's more traditional dishes.

"I've been trying to tell her," the female ghost said, nodding toward Rita, "but she won't listen!"

I asked Rita if this meant anything to her, and she seemed ashamed to speak. Finally, she admitted that the food Betty and Bob wanted her to make was very simple, just meat and potatoes.

"There are no colors in the food!" the ghost cried. "No colors!"

"Colors?" I asked. "Do you mean colors, like vegetables?"

"Yes! Of course!" she agreed. "Those kids would be much healthier if they ate better! I gave her the recipes!"

That was when Rita remembered the dreams. She had actually dreamed of two recipes, one for Spanish corn and one for Spanish zucchini. She'd also found some of the ingredients pulled out on the counter, like a tomato one day and a zucchini the next—items she hadn't even purchased!

Well, I could tell this conversation was not pleasing Betty, who clearly believed she could do no wrong, especially when it came to picking the right foods for her family. She must have suspected it was some plot cooked up between me and the nanny to make her look dumb—at least that's what the expression on her face said. So I made it seem like a big joke.

"Why don't we get these recipes?" I suggested to Betty with a wink. "Then she can cross over and leave you alone."

Betty seemed unsure, so I winked again. The ghost was standing behind me, so she didn't see it.

"Okay," Betty finally agreed.

I don't know if Rita was ever allowed to make the dishes, but Betty and Bob did refer me to several other people after I'd helped the two spirits cross over.

SPANISH CORN

2 cups canned corn

¼ teaspoon granulated sugar

2 tablespoons chopped green bell peppers

1 egg, beaten well

2 tablespoons chopped pimientos

½ cup cracker crumbs

1 tablespoon finely chopped onion

½ cup milk

1 tablespoon salt

2 tablespoons melted butter

▶ Preheat oven to 350º. Combine all ingredients and pour into a buttered baking dish. Bake for 25 minutes.

SPANISH ZUCCHINI

1 medium-size onion, finely chopped

1 clove garlic, finely chopped

2 tablespoons olive oil

1 pound small unpeeled zucchini, sliced

1 can tomato paste

½ cup boiling water

1 (4-ounce) container pimiento cheese

Salt and black pepper to taste

▶ Simmer onion and garlic in oil in a saucepan until tender. Add zucchini slices; cover and cook until tender. Add tomato paste, ½ cup boiling water, and pimiento cheese. Add salt and pepper. Cook mixture slowly for 5 minutes. Makes 6–8 servings.

STIR-FRIED SUGAR SNAP PEAS

Every once in a while a story comes along that reminds me what I'm dealing with. I know it sounds odd, but when you can see and talk to ghosts every day, like I can, you sort of forget sometimes what that really means: It means these people lived and died. It means they left loved ones behind. I know they say police detectives get calloused to the crimes they witness day in and day out, so it shouldn't be surprising that I've developed a certain amount of detachment. Just like with the police, it's a coping mechanism. But every now and again there is a story that still hits me, even when I retell it decades later. This is one of those stories.

When I was about 22, I was referred to a man, Tim, who was married to a Japanese woman, Kim. This would have been during the late 1960s, and back then I wasn't on TV or the radio, and no one wrote about me in newspapers or magazines. If you'd heard of me, it was because someone you knew had met me. And if you called me, it was because you were honestly at your wit's end.

Tim called me because he was worried about the children of the house. He heard them late at night, when they should have been sleeping, talking to their deceased mother. They'd laugh and giggle, pause as if listening, then reply. It was his wife who told him who it was they were talking to—because they were speaking to their mother in Japanese. Their mother, Mia, was Kim's sister, and she was dead.

Tim and Kim were in the process of adopting the children. They'd come to the US with their parents and their baby sibling to visit their Aunt Kim, but on the way from the airport, they were in a terrible car accident. Their parents and the baby were killed, leaving them in the care of an aunt and uncle they'd never met in a country they'd never seen before.

When I got to the house, I knew there was a ghost there, but she wasn't with us. Tim told me what had happened and that Kim was convinced it was her sister.

"The kids aren't adjusting. They'd never met us before, and now they just wait to see their mother at night," he explained. "I know it sounds horrible, but if they're going to stay with us, they have to get used to us. They won't even eat our food—they want their mother to cook for them."

The kids were upstairs sleeping, so I went up to see their room, and sure enough, there was Mia. One of the things I can't explain about my ability, but that I am certainly thankful for, is that I can understand ghosts when they speak to me, no matter what language they speak in, and they can understand me.

"Mia?" I checked. She nodded and sort of half-smiled. "Can you come downstairs with me?" She nodded again and followed me.

When we got downstairs, I asked her why she was there.

"My husband took the baby into the White Light after the crash," she said. "We agreed that I'd stay behind and watch over the other two." It was all I could do not to start crying at that point, but I kept my composure.

"Do you want Tim and Kim to have the children?" I asked.

"Oh, yes," she agreed. "They can't go back to Japan. We wanted to move to America anyway."

"Mia, you aren't helping them, though. They need to get used to how things are now. They can't do that with you here. And you just sap their energy when you're around—that makes them sick."

"I know," she agreed sadly. "But I just can't leave my babies."

"I know," I replied—it was getting tougher to stay calm. "You know, once you cross over you can come back and check on them anytime you want, and it won't bother them."

"Really?"

"Yes." I paused. "Now is there anything I can tell Tim and Kim before you cross over? Anything to help them help the kids?"

"Of course," she said kindly, then listed all their favorite things, all their likes and dislikes. She also said that she had been a chef with her husband in Japan, and she wanted Kim to make some of her recipes for them.

"Their favorite is sugar snap peas," she said.

"Well, let's start with that one, then," I suggested, and she gave me the recipe.

STIR-FRIED SUGAR SNAP PEAS

¼ cup chicken broth
2 tablespoons dry sherry
2 teaspoons oyster sauce
3 tablespoons peanut oil
⅔ cup thinly sliced scallions
1 pound sugar snap peas
   (snow peas)

▶ Combine broth, sherry, and oyster sauce in a small bowl. Heat a wok over high heat and add peanut oil. Add scallions, then peas. Stir-fry for 2 minutes. Add broth mixture and toss until snow peas are well coated. Cook for no more than 2 minutes. Peas should be crisp-tender. Serve hot in a heated dish.

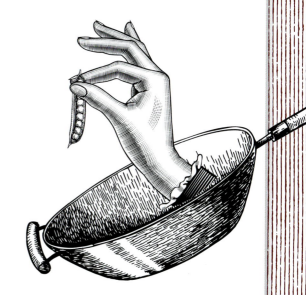

STUFFED KOHLRABI

My Bohemian grandfather used to grow kohlrabi, also known as German turnip. I remember going out into his garden and picking it fresh; then we'd clean it, salt it, and eat it raw. I thought it was delicious, and because that was how my grandfather always served it, I never thought of cooking it. Furthermore, I never thought of stuffing it with meat and cooking it—but that changed when I met Hannah.

Hannah was Emma's mother, and she'd been dead for about six years. Emma lived in rural Ohio in a place known as the Dumpling Valley. She was Amish, and her friend Sharon, who was not Amish, had called me for her.

"It's terrible for them," Sharon told me on the phone. "You have to come out."

"Does Emma know you've called me?" I asked before we got too far into the conversation. I'd done some work with the Amish before, and as in many devoutly religious communities, someone who could see and talk to ghosts wasn't always welcome.

Sharon assured me that Emma knew about the call, but she agreed that I should time my trip so that her husband and older sons wouldn't be around. Sharon explained how she would watch the chickens in the yard sometimes and it looked just like they were being chased—the birds hopping and flapping about as if being kicked at. The animals in the barn would become similarly spooked; inside, the lanterns they used would just go out.

"And these aren't like our lanterns," Sharon assured me. "This is their only light after dark because they don't have electricity. These lanterns are designed to never go out unless you put them out." She went on to tell me that things would go missing and whole rows of sewing would be unraveled, almost as they watched. Not to mention that the kids—all eight of them—were constantly getting sick.

"And they also say they've seen their grandmother," she concluded.

"Grandma's dead?" I assumed.

"Yes," Sharon confirmed. "And she was . . . well, she was the queen of the family, for lack of a better word. She was harsh and rigid and very traditional. She always said Emma married the wrong man."

When I got to the house, Hannah was there, and she was everything I'd been told. I could tell that she didn't like me. I almost got the sense that she didn't believe I could see and talk to her—just as she probably would have felt when she was alive. But, of course, I could see and talk to her, and I did.

"Are you upset about something?" I asked pleasantly.

"She married the wrong man," Hannah spat back. "If she'd married who I'd wanted her to marry, she'd be living on a farm twice this size!" Aaron, Emma's husband, was Amish, but he did a lot of woodworking for the non-Amish, and that upset Hannah. That wasn't all that had Hannah upset, though. She spent several minutes cutting down Emma's garden, her cooking, her sewing, and just about everything else the poor woman did. She was especially annoyed that Emma was not growing kohlrabi.

"She wants to know why you're not growing kohlrabi," I summed up diplomatically.

"Why would I?" Emma retorted. "I always hated kohlrabi, so why would I grow it?"

"That's because she won't stuff it!" her mother replied in a clipped tone, and I suddenly got what this was about. This was about a recipe that Hannah was particularly proud of that Emma refused to make.

"Did your mother make stuffed kohlrabi?" I asked Emma.

She made a gagging sound and nodded.

I looked at Hannah. "If she says she'll make that recipe for the kids, will you cross over?"

She didn't answer. "You're not doing any good here, you know. You're making the kids sick, scaring the animals—"

"I know that!"

"And I don't think you're going to break up their marriage—"

"I don't *want* to break up their marriage. I just want her to know she did it wrong."

"I think Emma knows how you feel. So why don't you give me the recipe and then cross over?"

She opened her mouth to snap at me again, then shut it, sighed, and finally said, "All right."

STUFFED KOHLRABI

6–8 kohlrabi

½ pound beef or pork, ground with a meat grinder

½ white roll, moistened in milk and mashed

1 small onion, minced and lightly browned in butter

1 whole egg, lightly beaten

Salt and black pepper to taste

Granulated sugar to taste

1 tablespoon butter

1 tablespoon all-purpose flour

▶ Preheat oven to 350°. Peel kohlrabi carefully and cut into halves lengthwise; scoop out centers with a potato scoop (do not discard). Combine ground beef, mashed roll, onion, egg, salt, pepper, and sugar. Stuff kohlrabi with meat mixture, and arrange in a baking dish; add a shallow amount of water. Add salt and a little sugar to water, and place scooped-out kohlrabi pieces in dish. Bake, tightly covered so kohlrabi will steam, for 30 minutes or until tender. Melt butter in a saucepan; stir in flour, adding a little cooking liquid, until thoroughly blended. Spoon over kohlrabi before serving.

SURPRISE POTATO DUMPLINGS

Sometimes people just want to be remembered. We can't all have buildings or streets named after us, but we do all touch others in ways that will help us be remembered after we're gone. Veronica had been forgotten.

Shelly had called me because her son, Donny, was always talking to a "lady with a ponytail on top of her head, but with no tail." Donny was 4-going-on-40, as his mother said—very well-spoken for a 4-year-old. I'm not sure he was quite 40, but he did certainly seem to speak and comprehend above his age group.

When I got to the house, Donny was thrilled.

"Grandma is mad!" he explained of his excitement. "She's mad because Mommy and Daddy can't talk to her and she wants to talk to a grown-up."

"Grandma?" I repeated, glancing at Shelly.

"That's just what he calls her," she said. "But it can't be his grandmother—they're both still alive."

At that moment the ghost walked into the room, and I saw exactly what Donny meant about a ponytail with no tail on top of her head—only I called it a bun. She looked like your pretty typical old lady, and I couldn't imagine her having a mean bone in her body, but she also looked sad—and relieved.

"Here," Donny said, interrupting my train of thought. He thrust some pictures he'd drawn into my hands.

"What are these?"

"Grandma told me to draw these," he said. I flipped through and saw lots of crayon pictures of food. "Look," Donny said, pulling out one in particular. "That's green beans, and that's corn, and that's meat, and *that* is the surprise!"

He pointed at a blob in one corner of the plate. "Are they potatoes?" I asked.

"No," he said thoughtfully. "Well, maybe . . . but *surprise* potatoes."

"He's been going on about that surprise for months," Shelly said. "We don't have any idea what he's talking about, but this Grandma he talks to is very adamant about it."

"Why is it a surprise?" I asked Donny.

"Because there's something inside it!"

At that moment I remembered that this lady was standing in the room with us, so I looked at her and asked, "What is this?"

"It's a potato dumpling surprise!" she said cheerfully. "Oh, it's so good to talk to you! I'm a relative of theirs. Donny is named after my husband."

I told Shelly this, but she shook her head. "We just liked the name Donald."

"My great-grandfather was Donald," Shelly's husband called in from the other room—where he was pretending not to be interested. "But that's not who he's named after."

"That was my husband," this ghost said. She said her name was Veronica.

"Nope," Shelly's husband reported from the other room. "His wife was named Elizabeth."

"That was his first wife," Veronica explained. "I was his second wife. He died about six months after we got married."

I wasn't sure how that exactly qualified her to be a relative, per se—certainly not by blood—but since she went on to tell me that she'd been wandering from family member to family member for the last 60 years "trying to get some respect," I thought it best to let things slide. In the meantime, Shelly's husband had gotten on the phone and called his mother. After some back and forth with her, he returned with the news.

"It's true," he stated simply. "He did have a second wife named Veronica." Then he vanished into the basement and came back up with a huge box stuffed with old photographs. While he dug through them, I explained to Veronica that she wasn't doing anyone any good by hanging around, and she agreed. She said she didn't stay too long in any one place.

"But Donny—he just has to try my surprise dumplings," she said. "My husband loved them so much, and he *is* named after him."

"That's her!" Donny suddenly shrieked, pointing at an old photograph in his dad's hand. "That's Grandma!"

His dad flipped it over and read the back: "Donald's second wife, Veronica."

Shelly was quite happy to take down the recipe after that, and she promised to make it for her Donald.

SURPRISE POTATO DUMPLINGS

1 cup bread cubes
Bacon fat
2 cups mashed potatoes
2 tablespoons butter, divided
1 egg
1 tablespoon finely chopped onion
¾ cup all-purpose flour
1¼ teaspoons salt
Dash of black pepper
3 cups water
1 cup milk
½ cup fine, dry breadcrumbs

▶ Brown bread cubes in bacon fat in a skillet. Heat mashed potatoes in a separate pan; stir in 1 tablespoon butter, and allow to cool. Whisk in egg, onion, flour, salt, and pepper; blend well. Form potato mixture into 12 egg-size balls. Wrap each ball around 4–5 cubes of fried bread.

Bring 3 cups water and 1 cup milk to a gentle boil (milk keeps the dumplings white). Add dumplings and cook, covered, for 7 minutes.

Meanwhile, melt remaining 1 tablespoon butter; stir in breadcrumbs to coat. Remove dumplings with a strainer; place on a large platter. Sprinkle with buttered breadcrumbs before serving.

SWEET CABBAGE WITH CARAWAY SEEDS

One of the things people don't realize is that I see ghosts all the time. Some people think I only see them when I visit a house I've been called to, but the truth is, I see and hear them almost every day, just as you see and hear people when you go to the mall. Not that there's a constant parade of ghosts bothering me every hour of every day, but they're there. I've just learned to tune them out over the years.

Every once in a while, though, they just can't be ignored—like the Polish twins I came across one year at a church down the road from my house. My husband, Ted, and I had gone down to the church to buy some pierogis. It was during Lent, and most of the churches in our neighborhood sell pierogies as a fundraiser during that time, so it had become a tradition for us. Ted loves the sauerkraut filling, but I prefer the cheese. I remember thinking as we drove to the church that day that I really needed a good recipe for pierogies. Most of them were homemade by the parishioners, and I'd seen ghosts at the neighborhood churches plenty of times before—I wondered if maybe some of those ghosts were former parishioners who might have a good recipe to share.

Unfortunately, I came to learn that pierogi recipes are closely guarded secrets. I should have guessed as much—the church we bought from made you go around the back and knock on a locked door to get in. You practically needed a password just to buy pierogies!

Once we were inside, a woman politely took our orders, then went in the back to put them together. As she went through the door to the kitchen, I saw a woman—a ghost—come out.

I'd seen this spirit around before from time to time, but I'd never made contact of any kind with her. I was mulling over my pierogi-recipe plan and thinking of asking her when another ghost came into the room behind her—a ghost that looked exactly like the first one.

Twins, I breathed to myself. In all my years, I couldn't remember seeing twins, at least not twins who had both failed to cross over, haunting the same place. They even had the same clothes; the same hairstyle; and the same sour, disgusted look on their faces. They were also the same age, I realized, which meant they must have died at nearly the same time.

Recovering from the mild shock of seeing twin ghosts, I was about to catch their eyes and let them know I could see them when the one who had entered second looked at her sister and said harshly, "Listen, Helga—I told you that's not the way you make it!"

The first ghost I'd seen rolled her eyes and replied, "That may be, Olga. And it may be that you're the better cook, but I'm a better baker! And I *know* you can make it that way!"

I couldn't believe it. Having just gotten over the fact that they were twins, now I was standing there listening to them argue— loudly. Ted couldn't see or hear a thing, of course, which honestly amazed me—they were going at each other at top volume, presumably bickering over some recipe or other. I know I was staring because Helga cut herself off mid-sentence and looked right at me. I just couldn't look away.

"Olga?" she said in a loud whisper. "Olga! That lady over there? I think she can see us!"

"Yes, I can," I said. "And I can hear you too."

"Well, what do you want?" Olga snapped.

"How about a recipe for pierogies?" I asked.

"We'll never give that away," Helga said. "That's a family recipe, and it died with us."

"How did you die?" I wondered, trying to smooth things over. Olga explained that they had died in a house fire. From what I could gather, they must both have been overcome by smoke. They also explained that this had been their church and that they just liked hanging around, seeing what the ladies were cooking.

"There might be an even better kitchen if you cross over," I offered. In truth, I have absolutely no idea what's on the other side, but they didn't know that!

At that moment, the woman came back with our orders. While Ted was paying, I asked the ladies again for their pierogi recipe, but they declined. So I offered them a trade: I'd make the White Light so they could cross over if they gave me a good recipe before they left—it didn't have to be pierogies, but something worth sharing nonetheless. Here is that recipe.

SWEET CABBAGE WITH CARAWAY SEEDS

2 small heads white cabbage, cored and cut into small sections

2–3 ounces salt pork or bacon, minced

1 medium-size onion, minced

2–3 teaspoons caraway seeds

3 tablespoons bouillon

Salt and black pepper to taste

2 teaspoons all-purpose flour

½ teaspoon Kitchen Bouquet

▶ Parboil cabbage in salted water to cover in a large pot for 10 minutes; drain, removing cabbage to a bowl. Heat salt pork in pot until transparent; add onion, cooking until lightly brown. Add cabbage, caraway seeds, bouillon, salt, and pepper. Add water to cover and bring to a boil; simmer, tightly covered, stirring occasionally, until cabbage is soft (about 1 hour). Dust with flour and add Kitchen Bouquet; stir and let simmer for another 5 minutes. Makes 6–7 servings.

SWEET RAISIN STUFFING

The male ghost in Vye's house was the one who was causing all the problems. He'd broken the furnace twice, as well as the hot-water heater, costing Vye and her husband money in repairs. The extra bills were causing them to be more stressed than usual, and then the ghost was feeding on that extra energy. For most earthbound spirits, that's all they're after: a bit more energy. It's how they sustain themselves and also why they act as a draining force, often making the living sickly and anxious. This ghost was doing it partly for that reason—to heighten the energy for him to use—but also because he was just an ornery cuss.

He was even ornery to me when I got out to Vye's house. He refused to give me his name or any information about why he was there or how he'd died. Based on his description and behavior, Vye's husband later pieced together that it had been a guy he knew from work who had died recently—a guy he had never gotten along with who obviously held a grudge even after death. Fortunately, he was also easy to get rid of. When I made the White Light, he went into it almost without me asking him to leave.

The smaller problems Vye had noticed—like flickering lights, the TV turning off for no reason, and a general sense of unease—could just as easily have been caused by the man, but the woman who was also there undoubtedly caused some of it too. She was an older woman, and she looked prim and proper, much like a stereotypical old maid, with a high-collared blouse. She was even wearing a cameo pin.

"Grandma Pet!" Vye said with certainty, when I described her.

The woman smiled and nodded, but I was a bit confused by the name. "Pet?" I asked. "Is that a nickname?"

"Sort of," Vye said. "All the girls in the family are named after flowers. I'm Violet, but they call me Vye. My sister is Daisy. And grandma was Petunia, so we called her Grandma Pet."

Grandma Pet had died three years before, and she turned out to be a bit difficult to deal with. Not in getting her to cross over, but in getting her to tell Vye the answer to her question: "What did Grandma Pet do to her stuffing that made it so good?"

Grandma Pet just smirked at me when Vye asked, so I prodded her for the answer, but she just shook her head. "No, she has the recipe. She knows how to make it."

"We all have the recipe!" Vye cried when I told her what Grandma Pet had said. "But it *never* tastes as good as hers did! Every Thanksgiving and Christmas, it's always the same: We spend all of dinner talking about how much we miss Grandma Pet's stuffing!"

"Could you get the recipe you have and read it back to her?" I asked Vye. "Maybe something was left out when you copied it down."

Vye did as I asked, and Grandma Pet just smirked the whole time she was reading it.

When she was done, Grandma Pet said, "She copied it right. There's nothing missing."

"And the proportions are right?" I checked.

"It's the right recipe," she said again, but I could just tell by the way she was smirking that there was something she was leaving out, so I started letting my annoyance show.

"I can tell you're leaving something out—is it really that important that your recipe stays so secret?" I asked.

She replied with a slight arrogance. "At least they haven't forgotten me."

"Forgotten you?" I asked in disbelief. "Is that how you want to be remembered? As the grandma who deliberately gave them the wrong recipe for her stuffing? As the grandma who refused to give up the secret even in her very last moment to tell it? Wouldn't you rather be remembered for giving them a *good* recipe instead of giving them the *wrong* recipe?"

Her smirk faltered. She scuffed her feet a bit, thinking on what I'd said. Finally, she raised her head, stood straight, and said, "It's the eggs."

"The eggs?" I said, then added to Vye, "Get ready to write this down." I got out my pad and pen, too, to write it down with her.

"You have to separate the eggs. The yolks have to be creamed with the butter and then mixed with the other ingredients, but the egg whites have to be beaten separately until they're stiff, then folded into the stuffing after everything else is mixed together."

SWEET RAISIN STUFFING

1 tablespoon butter

3 eggs, separated

Turkey or chicken liver (use whatever comes with your bird), chopped

6 heaping tablespoons breadcrumbs

Salt and black pepper to taste

Dash of nutmeg

2 whole cloves

1 teaspoon granulated sugar

1 heaping tablespoon fresh chopped parsley

¾ cup raisins

▶ Preheat oven to 350º. Cream butter and egg yolks in a large bowl. Stir in chopped liver. Add breadcrumbs, salt, pepper, nutmeg, cloves, sugar, parsley, and raisins; mix thoroughly. Beat egg whites until stiff, and fold into raisin mixture. Transfer to a buttered baking dish and bake for 30 minutes.

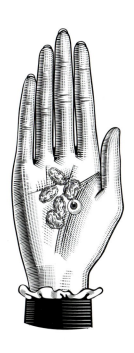

TENNESSEE CORN FRITTERS

The thing I love about visiting with all these ghosts is that I get to go to all these neat locations to meet them. I've been all over the country helping people and helping earthbound spirits cross over—sometimes I think I should forget the ghost stories and just write a travel book! And even though the bulk of my work has been local to me, in Ohio, I've still visited some pretty neat places right here in my own state.

Take Barbara, for example. She lived on a real dude ranch that was practically in my backyard, complete with cowboy hats and horse wranglers. She raised show horses for kids to show at competitions, and she employed about five or six ranch hands to help her. She'd not been having a lot of problems, but she had actually been seeing a ghost with her own eyes, and her ranch hands had been complaining that they kept bumping into someone in the kitchen, except there was no one there to bump into.

"She doesn't look dangerous," Barbara said of the ghost. "She's sort of, you know, roly-poly. She has scraggly hair and she's missing some teeth, but she's always laughing. Looks like she's having the time of her life!"

"Are the ranch hands seeing her too?" I asked her when I got out there. I was looking around, but I couldn't see this roly-poly woman anywhere.

"I don't think they've seen her," Barbara replied. "But they are pretty wound up about

it. They said I had to do something, so I called you."

"I don't see a ghost anywhere, Barbara," I admitted.

"Oh, she'll be down in the kitchen. My husband, Bruce, is there now, cooking dinner for everyone—that's usually when she shows up."

So we went down to the mess hall and, sure enough, there she was. She did look quite disheveled but, just as Barbara said, not dangerous. In fact, I'd have said she was jovial, if anything. As soon as she realized I could see her as well as hear her, I got her full attention.

"What's you name?" I asked her.

"Tilly."

"Tilly, do you know anyone here?"

"No, no," she laughed. "I came up with my horses."

"You did what?"

"From Tennessee." She nodded at Barbara and added, "She bought some horses from my ranch, and I came up with them."

I checked this fact with Barbara and she confirmed that it was absolutely true. She had bought some horses from a ranch in Tennessee the year before, and she had started seeing Tilly shortly thereafter.

"I was the cook," Tilly went on to explain. "And that boy there, he misses his home-cooked Tennessee meals."

The "boy" she was referring to was a ranch hand named Bobby who had moved up from

She'd not been having a lot of problems, but she had actually been seeing a ghost with her own eyes, and her ranch hands had been complaining that they kept bumping into someone in the kitchen, except there was no one there to bump into.

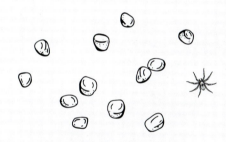

Tennessee for the job. Tilly said he was especially missing real Tennessee corn fritters.

"If I give the recipe to Barbara so her husband can make it for Bobby, will you go into the White Light?" I offered, making a deal I've struck many times over the course of my life.

"Those horses are in good hands," she decided. "So yes, I suppose my work here is done now."

TENNESSEE CORN FRITTERS

¾ cup sifted all-purpose flour
½ teaspoon salt
Dash of black pepper
¾ teaspoon baking powder
2 eggs, beaten
1½ cups corn cut from cob
Milk (optional)
Vegetable cooking spray or oil
Maple syrup

▶ Stir together flour, salt, pepper, and baking powder. Add beaten eggs; corn; and, if desired, a little milk. Drop by rounded tablespoonfuls onto a hot, well-greased griddle or frying pan, and cook until golden brown on both sides. (If using creamy canned corn instead of fresh, add an additional 2 tablespoons flour to absorb extra moisture.) Serve fritters with warm maple syrup. Makes 6 servings.

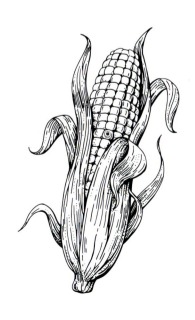

Jenna was incensed. She just knew her
husband was playing a prank on her, even
though he swore up and down that he was
not. This time, he put the box in his truck
and said he'd dump it at work. The next
day, Jenna came home and found the same
box back in the same spot as it had been
every week.

—Clara's Creamed Veal with Biscuits

MAIN DISHES

AUNT POLLY'S APPLE MEATLOAF WITH BROWN GRAVY

If a minor calls me, I usually don't call back. Nine times out of ten they've called without their parents' knowledge or permission, and just as often they've seen too many movies. Zach's call piqued my interest, however. Not only did he leave his mother's number for me to call back, but he also claimed that odd messages had been appearing on a digital memo pad he and his mother used to leave notes to each other. I hadn't heard of earthbound spirits communicating so directly with people who couldn't otherwise hear or see them.

"Really, I just want to clear my name," Zach said on the message he left me. "Mom thinks I'm doing it to be funny, but I'm not."

I called Laura, his mother, right back. She explained that this digital memo pad was a feature on their new microwave that allowed you to leave short messages, like "At my friend's house" or "Went to the store." Recently other messages had appeared too. Usually these were just one or two words that didn't make a whole lot of sense, like "meatloaf" or "Polly."

Then Laura confessed to why she hadn't called. "I'm pretty sure there is something going on," she admitted. "And I'm afraid it's my ex-husband." She explained that her ex-husband had died while they were going through their divorce—not in a sinister way or anything they could attribute to the split. He'd had an aneurysm and was just . . . gone.

I went out to the house and quickly put Laura's mind at ease. The spirit was not her ex-husband but an older woman, and her name was Polly. Polly had been the aunt of her ex-husband.

"His *aunt*?" Laura wondered. "What on Earth would *she* want?"

Polly had been dead for 15 years and had actually been around for a while. Zach reminded her of her nephew, and she liked to watch over him, plus they had taken one of her bedroom sets after she died (earthbound spirits seem to get attached to things!). Then, since Ian—the ex-husband—had died, the energy in the house had increased from the stress. When they got the new microwave, she discovered she could use the memo pad to leave messages.

"But only right after they argue or if Zach has friends over," Aunt Polly said.

"And right around the full moon?" I guessed. Polly nodded and grinned. These were all "energy boosts" for spirits that would allow for bursts of physical interaction.

Polly then said she wanted me to give Laura her old recipe for apple meatloaf.

"Ian loved it," she explained. "I think Zach will love it too."

Laura was quite thrilled to have the recipe, as long as Polly gave her the recipe for the brown gravy that went with it too. Aunt Polly, of course, agreed to share it.

Recently, other messages had appeared too. Usually these were just one or two words that didn't make a whole lot of sense.

AUNT POLLY'S APPLE MEATLOAF WITH BROWN GRAVY

1 large onion, finely chopped
2 tablespoons butter
2½ pounds ground beef
1½ cups fresh breadcrumbs
2 cups finely chopped apples, peeled and cored
3 eggs, beaten
1 tablespoon chopped parsley
½ teaspoon black pepper
2 teaspoons salt
¼ teaspoon allspice
1 tablespoon prepared mustard or ¼ teaspoon dry mustard
¼ cup ketchup
Brown Gravy (recipe below)

▶ Preheat oven to 350º. Sauté onion in butter until soft. Combine onion, meat, bread-crumbs, apples, eggs, parsley, pepper, salt, allspice, mustard, and ketchup in a large bowl, mixing thoroughly. Form mixture into a loaf and place in a 10x14-inch baking pan. Bake for 1 hour. Remove from oven; let stand for 15 minutes before serving with Brown Gravy.

BROWN GRAVY

1½ tablespoons all-purpose flour
2 tablespoons bacon fat or drippings
1½ cups water or beef stock
Salt and pepper to taste

▶ Brown flour in fat. Stir in 1½ cups water; bring to a boil. Add salt and pepper; simmer for 5 minutes. Serve over meatloaf or on the side. (If using drippings from roasted meat, drain all but 2 tablespoons from roasting pan.)

BEN'S ROAST BEEF ON A SPIT

Animals often sense—or see—earthbound spirits where humans don't. The trick for the humans is to pay attention to the behavior of their animals. That was the case with Crystal and her brother, TJ, who owned a dairy farm in central Ohio. Yes, Crystal said she always felt eyes on her when she was in the barn milking and feeding the cows, but she assumed it was just the cows looking at her. Then she and TJ noticed that milk production had gone down and the cows seemed more skittish than usual.

The farm had originally belonged to their grandfather. Their parents' generation hadn't wanted anything to do with it, but it had stayed in the family, and Crystal and TJ eventually took it over. TJ had earned a degree in animal husbandry, and his sister had studied to be a veterinary technician. They both loved animals and the allure of farming, and despite how hard the work was, they really enjoyed it. The farm they had wasn't big—maybe 50 cows—but it was just like a postcard, with the nice well-kept farmhouse and the big red barn. It also had a ghost named Ben.

Ben had been a farmer in the same area and had actually known the siblings' grandparents when they had been alive. He was a leathery-looking old farmer: clean-shaven with a full head of white hair, but obviously a man who had worked his whole life out in the sun and weather. He was quick to make clear that he

was a *gentleman*. He did watch Crystal while she worked out in the barn, but he never went into the house and he never watched the "kids" doing anything private.

"I just like to watch them work," he said. He went on to reminisce about his own farming glory days, mentioning that all the farmers in the area used to get together once a year and have a huge cookout, where they'd spit-roast half a cow. TJ and Crystal smiled when I told them that.

"I remember those," TJ said, his eyes sparkling. "We'd come all day and visit with Grandma and Grandpa. They'd roast a cow and a pig. We'd just play games and eat all day. And I have never had beef as good as that beef again."

"Ask him why they don't do it anymore, if he liked it so much," Ben said.

TJ explained that the sense of community was gone. A lot of the farms had changed hands or been bought out, and it was just too expensive now to even bother getting together with the neighbors. Everyone just basically kept to themselves. They were civil and they helped each other out in a pinch, but they just didn't visit like they used to.

"Well then, he could just make it for himself!" Ben suggested, but TJ shook his head dismally.

"I don't have the faintest idea how to cook a cow like that," he admitted.

Crystal said she always felt eyes on her when she was in the barn milking and feeding the cows, but she assumed it was just the cows looking at her. Then she and TJ noticed that milk production had gone down and the cows seemed more skittish.

Ben had a fix for that too: "Then he can use my recipe. I'll give it to him."

He did, and Crystal called me back several weeks later to say they'd tried it and it came out perfectly. "Of course, we had to cut down the proportions to match a 3- or 4-pound roast, but TJ swears it tastes just like he remembered."

"And how's the milk production now?" I checked.

"Oh, that's back up again, ever since you helped Ben cross over."

BEN'S ROAST BEEF ON A SPIT

3–4 pounds sirloin roast
2–3 tablespoons olive oil
Juice of ½ lemon
3–4 onions, sliced
Salt and black pepper to taste
Melted butter for basting
1 tablespoon all-purpose flour

▶ Place meat in a large baking dish; rub with olive oil and sprinkle with lemon juice. Cover top and bottom with onion slices. Let stand for 3 hours.

An hour before cooking, season meat with salt and pepper. Preheat rotisserie and cook on spit at a very high temperature, brushing frequently with melted butter. (Be sure to catch all the drippings in a gravy pan.) When meat is well browned, dust with flour. Allow to dry out, and brush again with butter. The roast should be ready in 35–50 minutes, depending on size and desired degree of doneness.

BING'S BLACK-AND-BLEU RIB STEAKS

Jack called me, and he was now a true believer. Before when his wife, Darlene, suggested they had a ghost in the house, he shooed her off and told her to stop reading so many books about ghosts.

"But after what I've seen recently . . . ," he admitted, "We need you."

Jack liked to grill. He had one of those huge stainless-steel grills with all the burners and side tables and the hooks for hanging grilling tools, and he thought himself quite the master grill chef. But just lately, whenever he grilled, strange things would happen. Sometimes it was relatively benign, like the fuel tanks for the grill would both be empty because the valves had been left open. That he could write off as his own sloppiness, even though he started being extra-careful about it the first time it happened. Sometimes the grill would suddenly go out, just like someone had blown out a candle, or it just wouldn't light in the first place, even with full fuel tanks. But what made him finally admit something was going on was the day the end of the grill raised off the ground and then dropped.

"Just like someone had grabbed the towel rod, picked up the end an inch or two, and let it go," he said. "Spilled my basting sauce all over the patio. I'm telling you, something doesn't want me using that grill."

There was a male ghost in the house, and when I got there, he was standing looking at us with a silly grin on his face. His name was Bing, like Bing Crosby, and he had lived close by. His dad had been a butcher, so he'd been hanging out at the old butcher shop down the street, where Jack bought his steaks for the grill.

"He always comes in and asks for steaks that are leaner than the last time," Bing said. "Once he leaves, the butchers make fun of him—they always give him the leanest ones they have. His steaks are tough because he doesn't know how to cook them!"

Eventually, Bing had followed Jack home to see just what he was doing to ruin these steaks, and that's when he'd decided to stay and try to stop him from doing it the wrong way.

"He flips them all the time," Bing said. "You're supposed to cook one side, then the other, with one flip. But he stands there flipping them back and forth, back and forth, and he ruins them!" Bing went on to say that he shouldn't be grilling steaks on an open flame like that in the first place. Bing thought the best way to cook steak was to make pan steaks.

"And even then, it's all in the spices," he said. "It doesn't matter how you cook a steak—if you don't spice it right, it won't be good."

"You know," I said to him. "I don't really think it's your place to be here correcting Jack's grilling. He enjoys it, the steaks are good enough, and, to be honest, before I leave this house, you will have left first."

But just lately, whenever he grilled, strange things would happen. Sometimes it was relatively benign, like the fuel tanks for the grill would both be empty because the valves had been left open. That he could write off as his own sloppiness.

That stumped Bing. He mumbled that it wasn't just Jack, that he'd actually been going around the whole neighborhood seeing how other people cooked their steaks, and he was quite convinced they all were doing it wrong.

"See?" I said. "So there's nothing you can do about it. That's how people cook their steaks now."

"Give him my recipe, then," he replied as if he was cutting me a deal. "Give him my recipe for black-and-bleu steak and I'll go."

"Black and *blue?*" I checked.

"Not the color," he laughed. "*Bleu,* as in the cheese. Although the cheese is optional because not everyone likes it."

"All right," I agreed with a sigh. "Give me the recipe, and then you'll have to go."

BING'S BLACK-AND-BLEU RIB STEAKS

SPICE RUB
1 tablespoon paprika
1 tablespoon black pepper
2 tablespoons coarse sea salt
1½ teaspoons garlic powder
1 teaspoon cayenne pepper
1 teaspoon oregano
1 teaspoon thyme

STEAKS
½ tablespoon olive oil
4 (8-ounce) rib steaks
8 ounces bleu cheese, crumbled

▶ To make spice rub, combine paprika, black pepper, salt, garlic powder, cayenne pepper, oregano, and thyme in a small bowl.

To make steaks, add oil to a skillet (or cast-iron skillet) over medium-high heat. Coat steaks with spice rub. Place steaks in pan, and sear. After a few minutes, turn steaks over to finish cooking to desired degree of doneness. Sprinkle steaks evenly with bleu cheese, and allow to melt on top. Remove steaks from pan and serve immediately.

BLANCHE'S BRAISED BEEF SHORT RIBS

I was invited to a private party by Nancy. It was a potluck luncheon put on by a group of nurses who all worked together, and I was asked to do one of my "ghost chats." I give these private talks to allow for a more personal interaction with the guests, but I don't do any kind of collective "ghostbusting" for them. I'd be there all day if I spoke with everyone individually and helped them with their issues! This party was no different—I saw five spirits attached to guests the moment I walked in, and this being the party room of a condo complex, other ghosts came and went over the course of the afternoon.

There's always an exception, of course. Being nurses, Nancy and her friends had a lot of ghost stories to share, and they were a really nice and fun bunch, so I decided it wouldn't hurt to help with just one ghost, especially because this ghost had caught my eye and I just had to know what her story was. She'd been poring over the potluck dishes all afternoon, tutting at some of them and shaking her head at others. She was about 50 and had come in with one of the guests.

"There are a few ghosts here now," I admitted to the group. "But there's one in particular I'd like to know more about." I caught the ghost's eye and asked her—privately—if she minded being "outed" and she rushed right over to me, all smiles.

"Not at all!" she said.

"Well, what's your name?"

"Blanche," she said. "They all know me. I died of breast cancer. I was one of the dumb nurses who was always giving everybody else advice, then ignoring it myself. By the time I got myself checked, it was far too late."

"And what's with the food?" I wondered. "Why are you turning your nose up at all of it?"

"Oh, it's just all the same old food these girls always made for our parties," she said. "Now, ask them why, with all of them who got the recipe from me, no one made braised beef short ribs?"

So I turned my attention back to the group of nurses and explained who it was. They all gasped, then were overjoyed and started sharing stories about Blanche, even though I had just gotten done telling them she was standing right there and could hear every word they were saying! Then I got to the question of the braised short ribs, and everyone got quiet and guilty.

Finally, Nancy spoke up and said that it was true, someone always wanted the recipe when Blanche made it for their potlucks, but she admitted that, speaking for herself, she ended up losing the recipe later. A lot of other heads nodded in agreement.

"Will she give it to us again?" Nancy asked. "And this time I promise I won't lose it!"

Blanche agreed to give them the recipe, but she said that the real reason she'd been

This party was no different—
I saw five spirits attached to
guests the moment I walked
in, and this being the party room
of a condo complex, other ghosts
came and went over the course
of the afternoon.

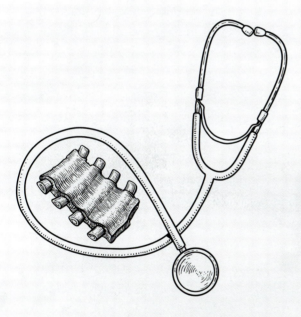

hanging around "the girls" was to make sure they didn't make the same mistake as her, and that they followed their own advice to their patients and got regular checkups and all that. It was an easy deal for them to make, and I think Blanche crossed over happy at having passed on a very important message.

BLANCHE'S BRAISED BEEF SHORT RIBS

1 cup canola or vegetable oil
4 pounds beef short ribs
Salt and black pepper to taste
All-purpose flour
2 medium-size onions, chopped
3 celery ribs, chopped
2 carrots, chopped
3 garlic cloves, minced
2 whole cloves
½ teaspoon thyme
1 cup canned tomatoes
1 cup red wine
Beef broth (optional)
Prepared horseradish sauce

▶ Heat oil in an oven-safe skillet. Season ribs with salt and pepper, and roll in flour. Place in hot oil and brown on all sides. Remove ribs and keep warm.

To the same skillet, add onions, celery, carrots, garlic, cloves, and thyme. Sauté until vegetables are soft. Stir in tomatoes and simmer, stirring occasionally, for about 10 minutes.

Preheat oven to 350º. Return ribs to pan; add wine, cover, and bake for 1¼ hours or until tender. If sauce becomes too dry, add beef broth, if desired. Place ribs on a serving platter. Season sauce with additional salt and pepper; strain over ribs. Serve with horseradish sauce.

BREAKFAST BAKE CASSEROLE

Linda and Gale were the kind of sisters whose bond went beyond the mere familial relationship. They'd always been close. After their parents died when the sisters were 19 and 22, that closeness helped them both and only grew exponentially. It was also how Gale knew—*knew*—her sister was in the house with her.

Linda had been dead more than a year when Gale called me. She'd died of cancer, leaving her 8- and 10-year-old boys behind. I knew there was a spirit in the house, but I wasn't convinced yet that it was Linda. Most cancer patients cross over immediately—they have had a long, hard battle to the end; they've said their goodbyes a hundred times; and they're just ready to move on.

But Linda was in the house all right. She'd stayed for Gale, to help her care for her kids! The sisters had lived right next door to each other, and since Gale didn't work and Linda did, Gale often watched her nephews after school. Gale had her own children, too, and the cousins got along famously—it was hardly a strain, but Linda said she felt bad. Linda's husband traveled a lot for work, and now that Linda was gone, Gale often had to watch the kids overnight.

"Gale's always been there to watch my kids," she said. "It's not fair. I couldn't just leave her with all that extra work."

"Believe it or not, you probably aren't helping too much, though," I said gently. Gale had

already told me her daughter had seen Aunt Linda in the house, and it had scared her. I guess we're just conditioned to think ghosts are scary, aren't we? But besides that, there were the colds and headaches and all the other things that come when a ghost is draining the energy from the living.

"I know," Linda admitted dismally. "But I also just feel *horrible* about something."

"What?" I wondered. "Is there something you forgot to mention before you died?" That was not at all uncommon—seems like even the spirits who tell me they had everything sewn up when they died can still think of just one last thing to say. One last regret to own up to, or one last apology to make.

"No, no, this was after I died," Linda said. "My boy, Jack, really hurt Gale's feelings at Christmas, and that's just not right. Not with all she does for them."

Apparently Gale had tried to make one of her nephew's favorite recipes just after Christmas, something his mom always used to make. It had been their first Christmas without Linda, and she was trying to do something, however small, to let her boys know that Linda would never be forgotten. Only she hadn't made it right, and Jack had told her so in no uncertain terms. Gale had felt bad and Jack only made it worse.

"It's just not right," Linda said again. "Look, can you give her the recipe for me, so she can

They'd always been close. After their parents died when the sisters were 19 and 22, that closeness helped them both and only grew exponentially. It was also how Gale knew—knew—her sister was in the house with her.

make it right? She put potatoes in it, and that's what Jack hated so much."

"Sure," I said. "Of course I can."

"And one other thing," Linda added with an amused smirk. "Ask Gale why she didn't just go next door and get my recipe box."

Gale chuckled at that. "Well, I guess I never thought of it!"

BREAKFAST BAKE CASSEROLE

3 cups ham, diced
1 tablespoon dry mustard
3 cups cheddar cheese, shredded
1 tablespoon all-purpose flour
3 cups French bread cubes
3 tablespoons melted butter
4 eggs
3 cups milk

▶ Combine all ingredients in a bowl, and pour mixture into a large baking dish. Refrigerate overnight.

In the morning, preheat oven to 350º. Bake for 1 hour.

CHICKEN LEFTOVER PUFF

A number of earthbound spirits in houses are relatives of the people who currently live there, or the house was once theirs. Usually there is some connection to the home for them, but not always. There are also "nosy neighbor" ghosts, who have stuck around for some reason and now just wander from place to place, seeing what people are up to. To be honest, those are the kind of spirits that irk me. If they're going to hang around, they should at least stay somewhere meaningful or be with their loved ones, not just flit from home to home, bothering random people. It's not polite, and impolite people annoy me, whether living or dead!

Sheila had one of these nosy-neighbor ghosts in her house, named Ruth. Ruth was older, cranky, and irritable—I imagine in life she was one of those old ladies who stood on the front porch and waggled a rolled-up newspaper at the neighborhood kids for being too loud. Now she was still making people uncomfortable.

Sheila's husband was a long-haul truck driver, so he was gone quite often for long stretches of time. Sheila was terrified of being in the house without him. She didn't live in a bad neighborhood, and the neighbors on the other side of the duplex were always there to help her out. She had two children, a boy of 7 and a girl of 5, and they always slept in the bed with her when her husband wasn't there. It just felt safer that way.

Sheila was afraid because she heard things in the house: steps on the stairs, bumps in the attic, scraping sounds like furniture being moved. She'd also see things from time to time—never directly, but out of the corner of her eye. A shape that moved, then was gone. She could have written it off to the house "settling" and her nerves when her husband was on the road, but their dog was obviously seeing things too. For no reason, the old German shepherd would growl at the air and its hackles would go up.

All of this was because of Ruth. She annoyed the dog because she hated dogs—she'd even locked it in the closet once!—and she annoyed Sheila because . . . well, because she was a nosy neighbor. When I got there, Ruth lit into me like I was the one upsetting her, yelling at me about Sheila's husband always being gone and the dog being too big and the kids being too loud. But what really got her was that Sheila wasted food. Apparently, Sheila didn't save any food for leftovers, she just threw it away. Ruth was appalled.

"My kids don't eat leftovers," Sheila said with a shrug. "Even if I saved them, they wouldn't eat them, so they'd still get thrown away. You tell her that if she knows a recipe for leftovers that doesn't seem like leftovers to a couple of kids, I'll make it."

"Oh, I have the perfect recipe," Ruth said haughtily, as if Sheila had offended her with

She'd also see things from time to time—never directly, but out of the corner of her eye. A shape that moved, then was gone. She could have written it off to the house "settling" and her nerves when her husband was on the road.

the challenge. Old-lady ghosts are just like living old ladies—they always think they're right!

So I took down the recipe and told Ruth that she had to go. She wasn't doing anyone any good by staying, and she clearly wasn't enjoying herself, so why not cross over? For once, she didn't argue, and since Sheila agreed that the recipe looked pretty good and she'd start making it for the kids, there was really nothing left for Ruth to do but leave.

CHICKEN LEFTOVER PUFF

1½ cups sifted all-purpose flour
2 teaspoons baking powder
½ teaspoon salt
2 eggs, separated
1 cup milk
1 cup leftover chicken, cut fine
2 teaspoons grated onion
¼ cup grated raw carrot
2 tablespoons melted butter
2 cups White Sauce (recipe below)
   or leftover chicken gravy

▶ Preheat oven to 425°. Stir together flour, baking powder, and salt in a large bowl. Add well-beaten egg yolks and milk. Add chicken, onion, carrot, and melted butter. Mix well. Fold in stiffly beaten egg whites. Transfer chicken mixture to a greased (with butter) baking dish; bake for about 30 minutes. Serve with White Sauce.

WHITE SAUCE

6 tablespoons butter
4 tablespoons all-purpose flour
2 cups milk
½ teaspoon salt

▶ Melt butter in a saucepan; add flour and mix well. Add milk slowly, stirring constantly. Stir until thick; add salt.

CHICKEN-NOODLE CASSEROLE

Men rarely call for my help, mostly because most men don't believe in what I can do. It doesn't bother me—it's just one of those facts I've learned along the way. I swear, a ghost could hit some of the husbands I've met over the head with a broomstick and they still wouldn't believe. Ralph believed, though.

Ralph's dogs had been acting strange, as he put it, for about the last six months. He lived alone—never married, no kids—with his dogs, and they'd got used to each other's rhythms pretty well. He was usually home from the factory where he worked by 2 o'clock in the afternoon, and he'd take the dogs for a walk or just run them around in the backyard. He had three dogs. Two were mother and son, and the other was a stray female he inherited. Life was pretty routine for Ralph, so he tended to notice even the slightest thing that was peculiar.

The first thing that clued him in to something being amiss was that his male dog took to rolling over and exposing his belly when they were in the backyard. He'd done that as a pup for his mother, of course, but he didn't do it very often anymore. Now he did it all the time. He'd be running across the yard after a ball, and he'd suddenly just drop and roll over, a sheepish, ears-back look on his face.

There were other things too. All three of the dogs would growl in the house when they'd never growled before. Usually it was the male, and Ralph's first thought had been that the

dog was going funny, but then he noticed the females doing it too. They'd just stand and stare at the air in an empty room and growl.

"Yup, there's a ghost here," I agreed, looking at the man standing before me, a giant Rottweiler at his feet. "And he's got a dog with him."

"Are you kidding?" Ralph checked. "I didn't think dogs had, you know, ghosts."

"Oh sure," I said. "I've seen all kinds of animal ghosts. And it's that dog that's making your dogs act strange."

"Rocky don't mean no harm," the ghost said. "He's just no good with other dogs, especially ones that took his house. I'm Ernie, by the way." He actually extended his hand to me to shake before he caught himself and withdrew it, chuckling nervously.

"Ralph, how long have you lived here?"

"Twenty years, at least."

"Do you remember who you bought the house from?"

"No, not this house," Ernie cut in. "Rocky's protecting *his* house, out in the yard."

"Did you buy a doghouse recently?" I asked Ralph. He narrowed his eyes and thought for a second.

"You know, I did. I built the other two, but I saw a great price on a used one and figured I couldn't make a third for less, so I bought it."

"How long ago was that?' I checked. "About six months?"

"Yeah," Ralph agreed.

There were other things too. All three of the dogs would growl in the house when they'd never growled before. Usually it was the male, and Ralph's first thought had been that the dog was going funny, but then he noticed the females doing it too.

"Well, you got more than a bargain, Ralph. You also got a ghost named Ernie and his dog, Rocky."

Once the mystery was solved, Ralph was ready to see that Ernie and his dog crossed over, and Ernie had no problem with that. What he did have a problem with was Ralph's cooking.

"If you can call it cooking," he elaborated. "He just eats sandwiches and hot dogs. You know, I lived alone too—well, except for Rocky—and I used to cook. I used to make this great chicken-noodle casserole. He could even make it the night before and warm it up when he got home."

I gave the recipe to Ralph. He took one look at it and smiled widely. "This looks *great*! No veggies! I *hate* veggies!"

CHICKEN-NOODLE CASSEROLE

1 medium-size chicken
1 pound egg noodles
1¼ tablespoons butter
¾ cup breadcrumbs
1 tablespoon all-purpose flour
½ cup milk

▶ Stew chicken until tender. Replenish water while cooking to produce 6 or 7 cups of broth. Remove chicken to a cutting board to dice; do not drain pot. Take out and reserve 2 cups broth. Add noodles to remaining broth in pot; cook gently until noodles are tender and broth is absorbed.

Preheat oven to 350º. Melt butter; stir in breadcrumbs to coat. Place diced chicken in a large baking dish. Stir flour and milk into reserved 2 cups broth, and pour broth mixture over chicken. Spread cooked noodles on top. Cover with buttered breadcrumbs, and bake for 20–30 minutes or until brown.

Note: This can be prepared early in the day, placed in the refrigerator, and put in the oven just in time to heat through and brown before serving.

CLARA'S CREAMED VEAL WITH BISCUITS

Jenna's husband, Doug, had inadvertently started flipping homes. It wasn't something he'd set out to do, but they'd been living in an apartment since they got married, and they'd decided to see if they could find a good home at a low price. Doug was a handyman and work had been slow, so he was willing to buy a nice little house in a revitalized neighborhood, even though it would take considerable work to make it livable.

Doug's gamble paid off. Once he was done and they were talking about moving and buying new furniture, a buyer came forward before they actually took residence and offered them twice what they had paid for the house. It was enough to cover all the remodeling they'd done, too, and still leave them a tidy profit. So Doug started flipping homes.

About four or five houses into this new enterprise, Jenna fell in love with the home Doug had recently bought. It was a cute little home, built in the 1930s, and it was in a good neighborhood. No revitalizing was needed: The area was already nice, and the home itself really didn't need much work. Doug agreed and they decided that, this time, they'd keep the house. Besides, the market had soured to the point that flipping homes wasn't quite the best career choice anymore.

They moved, and Jenna spent a lot of time going all through the house, cleaning it up. Most homes of that age seem to always come with old boxes of junk left by former owners, tucked away in some forgotten corner of a closet or the back end of the attic. This home was no different. They found quite a few boxes of old papers and magazines in the basement— enough that they couldn't put them all out for the trash pickup on the same day. So over the course of the next few weeks, they put out a few boxes until they were down to the last three. Jenna felt like celebrating as she drove off to work and saw them on the curb—the last three boxes of junk finally out of their hair.

At lunch, Jenna came home and was dismayed to find another box still in the house, sitting right on the kitchen table. Clearly, Doug had forgotten to take it down to the curb that morning, but when he got home, he swore that he had taken every last box down. He said he'd even celebrated a bit himself when he plopped the last one on the curb. Still, the next week Jenna took it to the curb herself, but when she came for lunch later that day, there it was again, sitting squarely on the kitchen table.

Jenna was incensed. She just knew her husband was playing a prank on her, even though he swore up and down that he was not. This time, he put the box in his truck and said he'd dump it at work. The next day, Jenna came home and found the same box back in the same spot as it had been every week. She called Doug; he'd forgotten to toss it in the dumpster, but he knew it was in his truck.

Only when he checked, it wasn't. It was sitting at home on the kitchen table. That was when Jenna called me. When I got out to the house, I didn't immediately see any earth-bound spirits, so I went to look at this magical box. Jenna said she'd already gone through it and it didn't have anything but water-logged magazines, decayed papers, and dead bugs in it. The moment I touched it, however, a ghost came rushing up to me out of nowhere. She was pudgy and round and very red-faced, and she told me that the box contained her recipes.

The ghost's name was Clara. She'd been a first-generation immigrant from Poland who had lived in the house originally. She was quite adamant that "the skinny girl" (Jenna) should use her recipes. They could pitch the rest of the box, but not her recipe book. I carefully sifted through the junk and finally fished out the book she'd described to me. I told Jenna and Doug what Clara wanted and why she kept bringing the box back in, but when I opened the recipe book, I had to laugh—the whole thing was written in Polish!

"Okay, Clara," I said. "I'm sure I can find someone to translate this. Why don't you just give me your absolute best recipe so I can give it to them before you cross over?"

"The best one . . ." Clara intensely considered. "That would have to be the creamed veal with biscuits."

CLARA'S CREAMED VEAL WITH BISCUITS

2½ cups sifted all-purpose flour, divided

2 teaspoons baking powder

½ teaspoon salt

4 tablespoons shortening

3¼ cups milk, divided

3 pounds veal or leftover roast

1 tablespoon butter

1 cup meat stock

Salt and black pepper to taste

½ cup chopped celery

½ cup chopped onion

1 cup button mushrooms

1 green bell pepper, minced

¼ cup pimientos, minced

▶ Combine 2 cups flour, baking powder, and ½ teaspoon salt. Cut in shortening. Add ¾ cup milk, stirring until a soft dough forms. Turn dough out onto a lightly floured surface. Roll dough to ½-inch thick; cut with a biscuit cutter.

Preheat oven to 350º. Roast veal for 1 hour; cool and cut into cubes. Increase oven temperature to 400º. Add remaining ½ cup flour, butter, meat stock, and remaining 2½ cups milk to a saucepan; cook over medium heat until thickened. Add salt and pepper. In a separate pan, parboil celery, onion, mushrooms, and bell pepper; drain and stir into stock mixture. Stir in veal cubes and pimientos. Transfer veal mixture to a buttered baking dish. Place biscuits over top, and bake for about 15 minutes.

COMPANY ROULADE OF BEEF AND PARSLEY OR CHIVE BUTTER

I was at a book signing in Arizona; afterward, I had arranged to do some work for Eric and Tina, who lived nearby. As is true in any public place, there are usually quite a few earthbound spirits milling around, and the book signing was no different. I often do a little talk before the signing, and I always make sure to tell people—and the spirits in the room—that if they ever lose their White Light after they die, they just need to head to a funeral home, wait for a funeral, and use that White Light to cross over. I like to think that at least one or two of the ghosts in the audience do just that once I'm done talking!

As I was speaking this particular time, though, I noticed an incredibly sullen ghost in the audience, actually standing near Eric and Tina. This spirit didn't laugh when everyone else laughed; she just sat there looking thoroughly miserable. I kept my eye on her during the rest of the signing to see if she was with anyone and was surprised to see her leave with Eric and Tina. She hadn't come in with them, so I wasn't sure she was the spirit they had called me about.

Turned out I was right: The ghost they had called me about was named Heidi, and she'd stayed at the house when they left to attend my signing. Heidi had followed Eric, a social worker, home from work, and she did not like Tina at all. She was always getting right up in Tina's face—even though she knew she couldn't

see her—and was just generally draining her energy. There was much to her story, and she crossed over without much convincing. That left only the sullen ghost from the bookstore.

"And who are you?" I asked her. "I saw you at the bookstore."

She nodded. "My name's Caroline. I heard you at your talk, and I heard you talking to these two"—she nodded toward Eric and Tina—"so I thought I'd come over and see what it was all about."

"You couldn't go and find a funeral home, like I said?" I wondered. She shrugged. "Why are you so sad?" I asked her, changing the subject.

"Oh, I've always been like this. Everyone just called me 'the crabby lady.' I was always mean and always sad. I don't know why."

Since she was nothing to Eric and Tina, I offered to make the White Light again so she could cross over, but she sort of shrugged and said she wasn't sure she wanted to cross over now, otherwise she would've gone through with Heidi. I let it go and sat down to dinner with Tina and Eric.

While we were eating, Caroline paced around the table looking at our plates, then said to me, "That doesn't look very good." I tried to ignore her—the food actually tasted quite good—but she continued. "I used to cook. It was the only time I was ever happy. I

I got the two recipes from her— after telling Tina and Eric what I was up to—then told her that if she went into the White Light she wouldn't be crabby anymore, and she could probably cook again, as well, if she wanted to.

used to make these *perfect* little parsley-butter squares to go with fish."

Her face actually broke into a smile as she thought about it, so I decided to take another shot at getting her to cross over. "You know, I wouldn't mind a good recipe for those butter squares," I said to her. "I'm always looking for something to go with my fish—would you give it to me?"

Well, Caroline's face lit up. She'd be glad to give me the recipe! So now that I had her talking, I asked if she had any good beef recipes she'd like to share. She thought about it for a second or two, then nodded and said she had a great recipe for roulade of beef, made with beef and spinach and sausage. I got the two recipes from her—after telling Tina and Eric what I was up to—then told her that if she went into the White Light she wouldn't be crabby anymore, and she could probably cook again, as well, if she wanted to. That got her, and she did eventually cross over.

COMPANY ROULADE OF BEEF

1½ pounds round steak
1 cup raw spinach, chopped
¼ pound sausage
1 cup breadcrumbs
1 egg
¼ teaspoon nutmeg
All-purpose flour
Cooking oil
1 cup diced carrot
1 onion, chopped
1 tomato, chopped
½ cup water

▶ Preheat oven to 300º. Cut steak into ¼-inch-thick slices about 4 inches wide and 6 inches long. Mix together spinach, sausage, breadcrumbs, egg, and nutmeg; spread spinach mixture on slices of meat. Roll up slices and tie with kitchen twine. Coat in flour and brown in hot oil in a cast-iron skillet. Transfer meat to a baking dish. Stir carrot, onion, tomato, and ½ cup water into skillet; cook slightly, then pour mixture over meat. Bake, covered, for 1½ hours.

PARSLEY OR CHIVE BUTTER

4 tablespoons butter
1 tablespoon parsley or chives
Few drops fresh lemon juice
Salt to taste
Lemon slices

▶ Cream butter and parsley. Sprinkle with lemon juice and salt, and shape into squares. Chill and serve on lemon slices with broiled or fried fish.

DIVINE BUTTERMILK CHICKEN

Fran and her husband, Hank, didn't just feel like they were being watched all the time; they felt like they were being scolded. I had heard of similar feelings before, like feeling you were being judged, but scolded was an odd word I'd not heard before, so I asked her to elaborate.

"Well, it only happens when we want to do something that, you know, some people might think is bad," Fran explained. "Like, if we want to play cards, the cards will be missing. Or if Hank wants a beer, he'll go the fridge and all the caps will be turned so the beer is flat. Or if we want to watch an R-rated movie, the TV just won't work or the movie won't play. And certainly we aren't, well, you know . . . intimate anymore."

I'd heard enough, so I stopped her and asked if she knew who the former homeowners had been. She did: They had been a preacher and his wife, so Fran couldn't understand why any ghost would be in the house.

"Well, it's not just *any* ghost," I said. "It's the preacher's wife."

"His wife?" Fran asked, stunned. "Why on Earth would she stay here?"

Nora, the preacher's wife, crossed her arms defiantly. She had already made it pretty clear to me that she was the kind of woman who was used to telling other people what to do, how to act, and how to behave, but she wasn't used to be questioned herself. Fran knew from the neighbors that Nora had been highly regarded in the neighborhood but that she was also thought of as, in a word, "severe." Over the years, the congregation had shrunk, and then when Nora died, her husband, James, the preacher, moved away.

"So why did you stay here?" I asked, echoing Fran's question.

"I thought I could help James with the congregation," she said.

"You know, you'd have been able to help your husband better if you'd gone into the Light," I told her.

That didn't sit well with her, coming from me—she didn't like being caught not practicing what she preached, so she sort of clammed up and didn't respond.

"There is one thing, though," Fran suddenly said. "Our neighbor is always going on about Nora's blessed chicken. She'd make it whenever a neighbor was sick and bring it to them, and they swear it made them feel much better."

Nora actually chuckled at that and shook her head. "Not blessed chicken," she corrected. "*Divine* chicken. And it was just a name. Really it was just buttermilk chicken, but it did make people feel better."

"How about you give them the recipe?" I suggested. "To say you're sorry for being so disruptive toward them? To make amends?"

"All right," Nora agreed.

She had already made it pretty clear to me that she was the kind of woman who was used to telling other people what to do, how to act, and how to behave, but she wasn't used to being questioned herself.

DIVINE BUTTERMILK CHICKEN

½ cup butter
1 cup buttermilk
1 egg, slightly beaten
1 cup all-purpose flour
1 cup ground pecans
1 tablespoon paprika
1 tablespoon salt
1 teaspoon black pepper
¼ cup sesame seeds
2 (2-pound) chickens, cut into serving pieces
GARNISHES: fresh parsley sprigs, cherry tomatoes

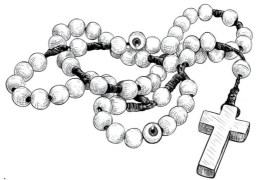

▶ Preheat oven to 350º. Melt butter in a shallow 13x9-inch baking dish. Mix buttermilk with egg in another shallow dish. Mix flour, pecans, paprika, salt, pepper, and sesame seeds in a third shallow dish. Dip chicken pieces in buttermilk mixture and then in flour mixture. Place chicken, skin side down, in prepared baking dish. Turn chicken to coat with butter and place skin side up. Bake for 1¼ hours or until chicken is tender and golden brown. Garnish, if desired.

ED'S VIENNA STEAK AND POTATOES

Earthbound spirits don't often find good ways to communicate with the living. That's what can frustrate them, which is why they resort to things like blowing out light bulbs and moving car keys and things like that—it's little things they can do to get noticed. They are little attempts to communicate, to say, "Hey! I'm here! Look at me!" But to us, the living, they're just annoying and, sometimes, a bit scary.

Del and Sarah were not unique in being frightened by what was going on in their house, but they were unique in that they had a ghost who had figured out a way to talk to them. The problem was, neither Del nor Sarah could figure out what the ghost was trying to say.

They had called me because of an incessant tapping coming from the kitchen. They'd been all over the house a hundred times since it began, and they were quite sure there was nothing rubbing or banging on anything else. Besides which, it always came from the kitchen and it was always rhythmic. Not like a drumbeat, but like a tapping that had *purpose,* not just the random sounds of a branch scraping on something in the wind. That had me excited. Spirits actually finding a way to "speak" was a rare treat.

This particular ghost was an older gentleman named Ed who said he'd known Del in Vienna. Del didn't have an accent, and my face must have shown my distrust because Ed added that they'd both been stationed at an army base there. I checked that fact with Del, and he agreed that he had been stationed in Vienna.

"Well, that's where this Ed guy knows you from," I said, but Del shook his head.

"I don't remember any Ed," he admitted. Ed rolled his eyes, but he was smiling.

"No wonder he isn't getting my messages!" he said.

"Yeah, about that. Can you show me what you've been doing?"

"Sure," he said, and took a huge nail out of his pocket, one of those big stainless-steel nails builders use to hammer together studs when they're framing a house. He took this nail and started tapping it on the counter in this strange stuttered cadence.

"There it is!" Del and Sarah both gasped. "Do you hear it!"

"Oh, I hear it," I said and told them what Ed was doing. "So what is it?" I asked Ed. "Why are you doing that?"

"Del should remember," Ed replied cryptically. "I taught him for his test in Vienna."

I relayed this to Del and his face lit up with a "bingo!" moment. "Morse code!" Del cried. "Ed taught me Morse code when we were in Vienna!"

"There!" Ed said. "That's why I came to him. I knew he'd get it one day!" I didn't have the heart to tell Ed that, without me, Del most likely would never have gotten it.

Del and Sarah were not unique in being frightened, . . . but they were unique in that they had a ghost who had figured out a way to talk to them.

"So what do you want to say, now that you can talk to me?" I asked. "Del called me and got me out here."

Ed short of shrugged and laughed to himself. "Nothing, I guess. I just wanted to see if I could talk to them."

"Are you kidding me?" I asked. He shrugged again and laughed it off.

"You know, Ed," Del said at that moment. He didn't know where to look to speak to the ghost, of course, so I sort of pointed at the counter to let him know roughly where Ed was standing. "I don't think those classes helped me too much after all. I can only remember 'S.O.S.' now!"

Ed laughed about that. Then I asked Del if there was anything else he wanted to say or if there was anything Ed could tell him.

"There is, actually," Del replied. "I went over to his house one time, and his wife made the *best* Vienna steak I've ever had. I *still* think about that steak. Can he tell me her secret to cooking it?"

"Secret?" Ed blurted. "I'll give him the whole recipe!"

ED'S VIENNA STEAK AND POTATOES

4 (½-pound) Delmonico (or club or sirloin) steaks
1 teaspoon salt
½ teaspoon black pepper
4 medium-size Idaho potatoes
Cooking oil (for deep-frying)
4 large onions, sliced
3 tablespoons butter

▶ Pound steaks very thin and season with salt and pepper. Peel potatoes and cut crosswise into ¼-inch-thick slices. Deep-fry potato slices in hot oil (370º) until golden, about 15 minutes; remove from oil and keep warm. Place steak in hot oil, and cook over very high heat for about 10 minutes or until delicately browned on each side and rare inside. Sauté onions in butter in a large skillet until transparent. Place steaks on a hot platter; cover with cooked onions and surround with fried potatoes.

FLAMING CHICKEN BREASTS GRAND MARNIER

Sherry and her husband, Scott, loved to entertain. They'd bought the house they lived in specifically for that purpose. It had a wide, open floor plan; massive windows; and a beautiful deck. The only mark against it was that the former owner had died in a fire in the house not too long before they bought it.

The house had been built in the 1930s, and it had been nicely rebuilt after the fire to match the original style. Sherry and Scott were told about the fire, but the floor plan and location won them over, not to mention the price. With its history and the remodeling that still had to be done, they'd gotten it for a song.

What they hadn't expected was the pervasive smell of smoke, but what puzzled them was that it only happened every few months. They also had trouble with the appliances and had started to doubt that modern electronics manufacturers could make anything worthwhile anymore. And if they were having a big party—a grand old night of entertainment—something would always go wrong. They were in their 50s and they knew how to entertain, but little problems always seemed to crop up, and something would get spilled or burned or otherwise ruin a perfect evening.

On top of all that, they sometimes heard a baby crying, and even Scott agreed that the house just felt uncomfortable, but they attributed that to knowing about the history of the house and the fact that they'd always

liked to hear a good ghost story. When I got there, I got to tell them that now they had one of their own to tell.

The problems were being caused by Norma, the former owner who had died in the house. Usually if a home is remodeled, that's what upsets the earthbound spirit attached to a place, but that wasn't Norma's problem. What she didn't like was the food they served at their parties.

"And they just don't give it their *all*," she explained to me. "When you host a party, you have to give it everything you've got. They need to plan their parties better."

I asked her if there was anything specific she would like me to suggest to Sherry and Scott, and Norma sort of grinned wryly. "Well, I would suggest this flaming chicken dish I used to make, but . . ."

"But?" I prodded.

"But it's the dish that killed me!"

Norma explained that her Flaming Chicken Breasts Grand Marnier was her signature dish. She didn't cook it all the time—that would get terribly boring—but as soon as word got out that she was making it, everyone she invited showed up for the evening.

"It's a show," she explained. "It's an art. You make it right in front of your guests."

On the night she died, Norma had been making this dish. It was a warm August evening, and she had the windows open, the sheer curtains billowing placidly in the breeze. Right in the middle of the "flaming" part of her recipe, one of the curtains had billowed into the flames and caught fire immediately. The decorations quickly followed, and in the blink of an eye the fire was out of control. Everyone had managed to get out of the house—including her—when she realized her cat was nowhere to be seen. I rolled my eyes—I can't tell you how many earthbound spirits I've met who died saving a pet. I've had pets all my life, too, and I know they're like little people, but you have to consider the payoff to going back into a burning home.

Anyway, Norma had found her cat hiding in the pantry under the stairs, and she would most likely have made it back out with her pet, except the pantry door shut and got stuck behind her. No doubt the heat from the flames expanded the wood or something, but try as she might, she just could not get it open again. So in the end, Norma and her cat both died in the pantry.

"But they really should try that dish," she said. "They'll be the talk of the town! No one will ever want to host again because they'll never be able to outdo them!"

"Okay, I'll give them the recipe," I agreed. "But you have to do one thing for me."

"What?"

"Go and find your dead cat and take it with you. It sounds like a baby crying when it mews!"

FLAMING CHICKEN BREASTS GRAND MARNIER

6 boneless chicken breasts or
    3 whole breasts, split
Salt and black pepper to taste
All-purpose flour
3 tablespoons olive oil
1½ pints orange juice
4 drops Tabasco sauce
1½ teaspoons ground cloves
¾ teaspoon ground cinnamon
¾ teaspoon powdered ginger
½ cup raisins (white or seedless)
½ cup slivered blanched almonds
½ cup Grand Marnier, divided
1 orange, sliced

▶ Sprinkle chicken thoroughly with salt and pepper; toss in a paper bag with flour. Heat olive oil in a cast-iron skillet. Add chicken and brown lightly. Drain off any excess fat, and scrape browned bits off bottom of skillet.

Combine orange juice, Tabasco, cloves, cinnamon, and ginger; pour mixture over chicken. Simmer for 15 minutes. Add raisins, almonds, and ¼ cup Grand Marnier. Continue simmering for 15 minutes more or until sauce has thickened and chicken is done. Add sliced orange, rind and all, and simmer for 3 minutes. At serving time, flame remaining ¼ cup Grand Marnier in sight of your guests. (Heat liqueur slowly just before flaming it, pour over chicken breasts, and light with a match.)

FLORENCE'S FRENCH PORK PIE

Thelma called me because her husband was driving her crazy and, as she said, "I just know he brought a ghost home with him!" The way she said it, you'd think he'd gone down to a ghost bar to hang out and picked up a ghost to bring home!

"Why do you think that?" I asked her, and Thelma explained that her husband, Ron, had recently retired. Now he spent all his extra time going to flea markets, garage sales, and rummage sales to find what he called "treasures," which he'd clean up and sell through online auctions. I had to agree that such activities would greatly increase his chances of getting a ghost attached to him.

In fact, there was a woman ghost in the house and, to be honest, had Thelma been able to see this woman, she would have been jealous as well. The woman ghost's name was Florence, and she was, to put it simply, beautiful. Striking, you might say. She was very distinguished-looking, but she was the type of woman who didn't need to spend hundreds of dollars on hair and makeup to look good. When I asked her if she'd come home with Ron because of something he bought, she said she had.

"I've been dead a number of years," she said graciously. "He bought a portrait of me that was supposed to stay in my family. I stayed long enough to see who would take it." Florence looked wistfully into the distance before

continuing. "I don't know how long I've been with it now. No one ever took it. They just moved it from attic to attic, in and out of storage, until finally it ended up in the shop where that man bought it."

Florence was very upset by how the painting had been treated over the years, and she was also very sorry for having disturbed Thelma and Ron. Ron was there, and he listened to her story as I retold it, nodding his head every now and again.

"I know exactly the portrait," he said when I was done. He disappeared into his "warehouse" (the old guest room, now stuffed with junk) and came back out with a gorgeous painting. It was beautiful even without the subject, but the image of Florence as a young woman in her 20s made it almost breathtaking. She had not been a late bloomer who aged into beauty—she had been beautiful her whole life, and she'd aged very gracefully. I couldn't understand why anyone would want to get rid of the painting, especially if the subject was a family member.

"It's a great painting," Ron said. "That's why I got it. I've been trying to research it, but I can't quite make out the signature. Does Florence know who painted it? It seems so well done, I imagine it should be in a museum!"

Fortunately, Florence did remember the painter's name. It didn't ring any bells with me or Ron, but I suggested he look into it before he did anything with the portrait. Ron wondered

In fact, there was a woman ghost in the house and, to be honest, had Thelma been able to see this woman, she would have been jealous as well.

if he should try to track down any of Florence's family to see if they wanted it back, but Florence said he shouldn't.

"They don't deserve it," she stated. "They've already thrown it away. I want Ron and Thelma to benefit from it now, as long as they promise to not just throw it away again."

They promised, and then Florence said there was one other thing she wanted them to have. Tucked in the back of the frame they would find a recipe for pork pie. It was a very old and secret family recipe that had been passed down through generations. Her mother had told her to hide it, so she'd put it in the painting, certain it would be safe and stay in the family.

Thelma did follow up with me later. Ron had researched the painter's name he'd been given and had finally got in touch with an organization that collected and kept track of his works. As it turned out, the painting was worth $4,000, and they were very happy to have found it!

FLORENCE'S FRENCH PORK PIE

CRUST

1 teaspoon salt

3 cups all-purpose flour

1 cup shortening, divided

⅔ cup water

FILLING

2 pounds pork, trimmed of fat and cut into ½-inch cubes

1 pound ground beef

1 cup hot water

¼ teaspoon nutmeg

¼ teaspoon allspice

2 teaspoons salt

½ cup chopped onion

¼ teaspoon black pepper

3 cups breadcrumbs

▶ To make crust, stir salt into flour, and cut in shortening, ½ cup at a time. Mix well and stir in ⅔ cup water. Roll out pastry on a lightly floured surface into 2 (10-inch) circles.

Preheat oven to 325º. To make filling, mix together pork cubes, beef, 1 cup hot water, nutmeg, allspice, salt, onion, pepper, and breadcrumbs.

Fit 1 pastry circle in bottom of a 10-inch pie plate. Spoon filling into crust, and top with remaining pastry circle. Cut a few slits in top crust to allow steam to escape. Bake for 1½ hours or until pie is nicely browned.

GRANDMA'S CUBAN CHICKEN

Luis called me in somewhat of a panic. He had recently emigrated from Cuba, his mother was coming to visit him, and he wanted me to be there when she arrived.

"But what does this have to do with me?" I wondered.

"There are things going on in this house, and I think it's my grandmother doing it," he replied.

"And your grandmother is dead?"

"Yes."

At least that much made sense, and I could tell there was a ghost in the house, so I agreed to go out and visit with him when his mother arrived. I've said it before, but it's absolutely true that a lot of times when a person has a hunch about who a ghost is, they're correct. I think this has to do with the same energies I pick up on. I just pick up on them in such a complete way that there are no hunches about it with me: I see, hear, and talk to them. We can all do this on some level, I believe, but we are trained by society to ignore these hunches and gut feelings, and most people have gotten so good at it that they've learned to absolutely dismiss anything out of the ordinary.

Not Luis, though. He felt it was his grandmother, and he was right. She had died quite suddenly back in Cuba, so he'd not had the chance to travel to her and say goodbye. She was supposed to be visiting along with his mother, so after she died, she decided to visit by herself anyway, and then she just stayed.

"But only to see my daughter again," she concluded. "America is too big. I don't like it."

It was a nice—though touching—family reunion. Luis and his mom and her sister were all there, and they got to share their last goodbyes with Grandma Claudia. They went through the usual list of things when a sudden death has separated the family: who gets what, which knickknacks to get rid of, where the necklace is that you said I could have—all the kinds of things you'd expect. What I didn't expect was Luis's request.

"Grandma?" he asked. "Can you tell Mom how to make that chicken? Because she just cannot make it like you did."

Mom wasn't so pleased with that question, I assure you, but after a brief skirmish about who was the better cook, I finally got them all to calm back down.

"I'll get the recipe," I offered. "Then you can each make your own version, as well as Grandma Claudia's, and then you can decide which is the best."

I've said it before, but it's absolutely true that a lot of times when a person has a hunch about who a ghost is, they're correct. I think this has to do with the same energies I pick up on.

GRANDMA'S CUBAN CHICKEN

1 small chicken, cut up
1 clove garlic
2 tablespoons olive oil
1 cup chopped tomatoes
2 tablespoons chopped onion
1 tablespoon green bell pepper
1 small piece bay leaf
3 cups boiling water, divided
2 cups rice
1½ teaspoons salt
1 tablespoon bacon fat
½ cup cold water
GARNISHES: peas, olives, diced carrots, asparagus spears

▶ Preheat oven to 350º. Place chicken in a roasting pan and bake for 1 hour. Meanwhile, sauté garlic in olive oil in an oven-safe skillet until browned; stir in tomatoes, onion, bell pepper, and bay leaf, and cook until softened. Remove and discard bay leaf; mash tomato mixture to a pulp. Add 1 cup boiling water and strain.

Cut chicken from bones, add to skillet, and cook for 30 minutes. Wash rice and add to skillet. Add salt and remaining 2 cups boiling water; cook until liquid is absorbed. Place skillet in oven and bake, uncovered, for 15 minutes. Add bacon fat; stir with a fork. Add ½ cup cold water; return to oven for 20 minutes. Serve on a platter and garnish, if desired.

HAM-PANCAKE CASSEROLE

Yvonne heard the telltale patter of little feet in the hallway, heading for her room. Sure enough, seconds later, the bedroom door glided all the way open, and in came Lanie and Laurie, her 3- and 5-year-old daughters. They'd lived in this house two years now, and Yvonne couldn't remember a single night when the girls had slept in their own room.

Ed, Yvonne's husband, grunted and rolled over when the girls clambered into the bed. He surfaced long enough to register that Lanie, the youngest, was crying, and that got him fully awake.

"What is it, honey?" he asked.

"She pulled my hair again," Lanie grumbled.

"Who did? Laurie?" Both girls shook their heads. Ed glanced at his wife. They knew what was coming next, and they'd had about enough.

"No! That girl did it! The girl in our room!" Lanie cried. Ed hugged her and tried to calm her. It was the same old story by this time: "That girl"—whoever she was because no one but the girls could see her—had pulled their hair, pinched them, or tugged their feet, or was jumping on the bed or banging in the closet. Yvonne and her husband had heard the noises themselves from time to time. As for the rest, who could argue? The girls were clearly not making it up.

"It's not right," Yvonne whispered to her husband. "It's not right that they're scared of their own room."

"All right," Ed replied, finally agreeing to a request Yvonne had made several times before. "Go ahead and call that lady you heard about."

When I got to the house, I was surprised to see that it was so new. Yvonne and Ed had had it built, in fact—they were the first owners. Yvonne asked if it was possible that it had been built on an ancient burial ground, and I couldn't help but chuckle. People always assume that, thanks to the movies, but I have never, ever heard of a house with problems because it was built on an old burial ground.

"No, it's not that," I said. "There's a woman here named Grace who says you bought some of her china at a secondhand store, and she came with it."

"Oh, she doesn't want me to have it?" Yvonne asked.

"No, it's not that," I replied, relaying Grace's responses. "She saw a little girl ghost pulling Lanie's hair and she thought she'd come along to help out."

"Oh my God!" Yvonne gasped. "So there *is* a little girl!"

By this time the girl in question had come to see what all the fuss was about. She looked to be about 9, with straight brown hair and mean eyes. By her clothes, I'd guess she had died in the 1940s. She was pudgy, but it was baby fat, not because she was overweight.

"I don't have to listen to you, just like I don't have to listen to *her*!" this girl announced with a slight head waggle in Grace's direction. Her name was Jane, and all her short life she had been picked on by her older brother and ignored by her mother in favor of her baby sister. And now that she was stuck here, she'd decided to exact her revenge on the two little girls who lived in the house.

"But why stay?" I wondered. "Why not go and bother someone else?"

"These two can see me," she replied with an evil smirk. "Besides, I like to watch their mother cook pancakes. I loved pancakes."

"Wouldn't you rather go into the light and be with your mother?" I asked her.

"No! She never liked me! It was Grandma who made me pancakes."

"She'll be there too," Grace replied for me. "If you come with me, I'll make sure you find her." Grace gave me a helpless look—it was all she could do, I knew. Grace had told me that the girl just would not listen to her. But maybe there was something in Grace's tone this time that convinced her, or maybe it was because she realized she could finally cross over with my help, because Jane nodded and said she'd go.

"That reminds me, though," Grace said. "My children loved pancakes too. I used to make them this really great ham-pancake casserole. I don't suppose Yvonne would like the recipe, as an apology for all the trouble?"

"I don't know about her," I said. "But with a name like that, I'll take it if she doesn't!"

HAM-PANCAKE CASSEROLE

2 medium-size sweet potatoes, peeled, thinly sliced, and divided

3 cups (about ¾ pound) cooked ham, divided

3 medium-size apples, peeled, cored, sliced, and divided

½ teaspoon salt

¼ teaspoon black pepper

3 tablespoons brown sugar

¼ teaspoon curry powder

½ cup water or apple juice

1 cup pancake mix

1 cup milk

½ teaspoon dry mustard

2 tablespoons melted butter

▶ Preheat oven to 375º. In a 2-quart baking dish greased with butter, layer half of potatoes, half of ham, and half of apples. Combine salt, pepper, brown sugar, and curry powder in a small bowl. Sprinkle half of brown sugar mixture over layers in dish. Repeat process with remaining half of potatoes, ham, apples, and brown sugar mixture. Pour ½ cup water over all. Cover baking dish and bake for 40 minutes or until sweet potatoes are tender.

Beat together pancake mix, milk, mustard, and melted butter. Remove casserole from oven, and pour pancake batter over top. Bake, uncovered, for 20 minutes or until pancake is puffed and golden.

HANK'S RABBIT PIE

I know there's a cliché about old cowboys never dying, but I wonder if anyone really knows how true it is? I certainly didn't, at least not until I found myself in Arizona on a sprawling cow ranch. It was operated by Liz and Bobby Lee ("Not Bobby," he explained before he had to correct me, "Bobby Lee"), and they had recently turned it into one of those vacation ranches for city folk. It was still a real working ranch, though, and those city slickers did real ranch work for fun.

The problem was, those vacationers started coming up and saying they were scared. Liz and Bobby Lee had built four or five rustic cabins for the guests to stay in, and they were complaining about the strangest things. Someone was knocking on the windows at night or banging on the walls. Someone was locking people in the outhouse. Someone was spooking the horses. At first, they put it off to an especially rowdy—and prank-prone—group of vacationers, but then they noticed the same complaints and stories coming from group after group of guests.

When I got out there, it's no exaggeration to say the place was full of ghosts. Most of the earthbound spirits I ran into were benevolent and perfectly happy to leave when I asked them to. Then I came across Hank. Hank was angry, and he was the one causing all the trouble. He'd sit and listen to the vacationers tell ghost stories around the campfire; he'd get ideas,

then he'd do to them what they'd been scaring each other about over dinner. Like banging on the walls or pulling people's hair.

Hank was upset about the strangers on his ranch—not that it had been his ranch. No, it had been in Liz's family for years, but Hank had worked on the ranch his whole life, so he felt entitled and he didn't trust "these kids" who were running the place now (no matter that Liz and Bobby Lee were both in their 50s). Then it came out what was really bugging him.

"She got rid of me!" Hank spat, pointing a disgusted finger at Liz.

I told Liz what Hank had said, and she sort of chuckled. "Hank worked on this ranch for a long time. He was our cook, and he tended the chuck wagon when we went out on roundups. But I didn't get rid of him. I *retired* him."

Hank waved her off with a disgusted swat at the air and turned away. Liz didn't see him, of course, so she went on. "He was too old. He could barely stand, and he certainly couldn't survive too many more bumps on the chuck wagon!"

"You know what really gets me?" he suddenly yelled, turning back to glare at Liz. "That *gal* they got in here to replace me!"

"He doesn't like your new cook," I said to Liz.

"Cassie? What's the matter with Cassie?" she wondered.

"She changed my pie!" Hank bellowed. "She made my pie *horrible*! She put *olives* in it!"

Someone was knocking on the windows at night or banging on the walls. Someone was locking people in the outhouse. Someone was spooking the horses. At first, they put it off to an especially rowdy—and prank-prone—group.

"He's going on about a pie that she ruined," I passed along to Liz.

"Pie?" Liz considered, then realization dawned on her face. "His rabbit pie! Yeah, no one could *ever* match Hank's rabbit pie!"

"That's right!" he agreed vehemently. "That Cassie done *ruined* it."

"Look, if we promise to use his recipe—and only his recipe—from now on, will he go away?" Liz asked. Hank thought about this for a second or two, then slowly nodded his head, and that's how I ended up with a recipe for rabbit pie.

HANK'S RABBIT PIE

¾ cup all-purpose flour, plus more if needed

1 teaspoon salt

1 rabbit, cleaned and cut up

2 tablespoons chopped onion

2 tablespoons bacon fat

3 cups soup stock

Bay leaf

Pinch of mace

1 teaspoon vinegar

¼ pound ham, cut into strips

2 cups potatoes, diced

Dough for biscuits (see Clara's Creamed Veal with Biscuits, page 60)

▶ Preheat oven to 350º. Stir together flour and salt in a shallow dish. Dredge rabbit in flour mixture. Brown rabbit and chopped onion in bacon fat in a large skillet. Transfer rabbit mixture to a baking dish. Heat stock in skillet and pour over rabbit. Add bay leaf, mace, and vinegar. Bake for 1 hour. Remove and discard bay leaf.

Place ham and potatoes in skillet. Add boiling water to cover, and cook for 10 minutes; drain. Add ham mixture to baking dish with rabbit; return to oven.

Increase oven temperature to 450º. Roll biscuit dough out into small, thin pieces; place on top of rabbit. Bake for 15 minutes.

HAWAIIAN PORK CHOPS WITH HONEY BANANAS

Hollywood has done a really good job of giving everyone the wrong impression of ghosts, over and over again. For example, everyone who has a ghost assumes their home was built over a forgotten burial ground. In all my years, I have never come across a home where that was true. The other belief is that run-of-the-mill ghosts can hurt you. They cannot. Yes, there are other forces I've come across from time to time, and they would appear to be able to act in a physical way, but they are not earthbound spirits, they're something else entirely. They're also extremely rare and don't cause the same kind of effects as regular ghosts. Still, when I tell someone there's a ghost in the house, they start to freak out and assume that chairs are going to start flying through the air or that their stove is going to explode. Even with the other entities I've run across, that stuff just doesn't happen. It's typically little things, like a push on the back when you're walking down stairs or a scratch on the leg. But it wasn't until I got to Hawaii that a client told me her home was being haunted by a deity.

"It's a volcano goddess," Tessa told me very sincerely, her eyes wide and scared. She was Hawaiian, born and raised, but her husband, Hank, had moved to the islands from Kentucky when he was a boy. He shrugged at me as if to say, "Sometimes these island stories are true."

"It's not a goddess," I assured Tessa. "For one thing, it's a man—"

"Could be a volcano god," Hank suggested. "They have those too." For a second there I'd thought he was going to be on my side, and I just gaped at him in disbelief. The ghost's name was also Hank—Hank Senior. He called the other Hank, his son, Junior. Hank Senior had apparently been around for several years, moving from house to house and island to island to visit all of his kids, but now he was just going on and on about pork chops.

"It's not a god," I stated simply. "It's a man, and he's telling me I have to try some kind of Hawaiian pork chops while I'm here! Does that sound like a volcano god to you?"

Tessa sort of chuckled with mild embarrassment and glanced at her husband, who mumbled a few words of how it *could* have been a god, and they didn't know because they couldn't see him. Then he stopped mumbling and furrowed his brow.

"Pork chops?" he said.

"Yes," I replied. I wanted to make sure the ghost was telling me the truth, so I added, "And to be honest, Hank, he looks a lot like you. Is your father still alive?"

"No," Hank gasped. "Oh, that makes sense! He *loved* his Hawaiian pork chops! He'd tell everyone they were an island delicacy."

"They are!" the ghost cried out happily. "Look, let me tell you how they're made."

I wanted to make sure the ghost was telling me the truth.

HAWAIIAN PORK CHOPS WITH HONEY BANANAS

6 thick pork chops
Salt and black pepper to taste
2 cups brown sugar
½ cup unsweetened pineapple juice
½ cup honey
2 teaspoons dry mustard
6 whole cloves
12 whole coriander seeds, crushed
6 orange slices
6 lemon slices
6 lime slices
6 Maraschino cherries
Honey Bananas (recipe below)

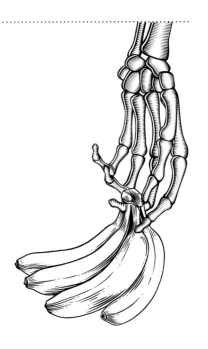

▶ Preheat oven to 350º Brown pork chops in a skillet, seasoning with salt and pepper, then place in a shallow baking dish. Combine brown sugar, pineapple juice, honey, mustard, cloves, and coriander seeds in a bowl. Spoon about 3 tablespoons sugar mixture over each chop. Bake, uncovered, for 1¼ hours or until done, basting now and then with rest of sauce. With a toothpick, peg an orange, lemon, and lime slice on every chop, and top with a cherry. Baste with sauce; bake for 10 minutes. Serve with Honey Bananas.

HONEY BANANAS

6 bananas
Lemon juice
2 tablespoons butter
¼ cup honey

▶ Peel bananas and dip in lemon juice. Melt butter in skillet and stir in honey. Add bananas and cook over low heat, turning gently, until hot and glazed. Do not overcook; it takes only a few minutes.

HERMAN'S SECRET-TOUCH VEAL PAPRIKA

Brian ran a freelance software-development and computer-repair business, so he could make his own hours, but he still didn't like leaving the office in the middle of the day. The truck drivers he'd hired to transport his latest antique car home were insistent because it looked like it might rain. They thought it should be moved into his barn-garage so the soft-top roof of the Packard didn't get water damaged. He grudgingly agreed. Restoring antique cars was his hobby, but he wasn't sure he could do much to repair a damaged roof.

When he got there, he looked the car over again. He'd actually been outbid for it at the auction, but the higher bidder had been unable to produce the funds, so it went to Brian for *his* highest bid. He stopped short and sniffed the air. He could smell cigar smoke.

"Did you smoke in this car?" he asked the truck driver. He shook his head and mumbled that he'd quit smoking years ago.

"Besides," he said. "I couldn't get in that car with all those boxes, even if I wanted to!"

"Boxes?" Brian said and took a closer look through the grimy windows. Sure enough, there was something in there. He opened the door and found the seats stuffed with boxes, all labeled with the same name: Herman.

"What the heck is all *that*?" Brian asked the truck driver. He was just getting into the cab, ready to leave.

"I don't know," the driver said. "The guy at the sale said it had belonged to the car's owner, so he threw it in with the car."

"Great," Brian said. "So now I have to toss out the junk they couldn't sell."

Over the next few weeks, Brian spent time going over the Packard's engine to get an idea of the extent of the restorations, and every time he was out in the garage working on the car, he felt like he was being watched. Most times, he also smelled cigar smoke—not a huge amount, just a whiff, as if whoever was smoking had just left the room a few minutes before. It was enough to get him to call me.

When I got there, it was no huge surprise to find a ghost named Herman. The car had been his, and all the junk they'd piled into it had been his. Brian had since moved the boxes out of the car, and we started to go through them. One of the boxes was full of recipes, and when I asked Herman about it, he explained that he had been a semiprofessional chef. He hadn't run a business, but he catered for friends and friends of friends. I picked up one folder—sort of an odd blue folder that almost looked tailor-made for the contents—and Herman shot over.

"Put that down!" he ordered me. "Those aren't for you! Those are *secret* recipes. He can have them," he added, motioning at Brian. "I know he likes to cook too. Those are for him, not you."

Every time he was out in the garage working on the car, he felt like he was being watched. Most times, he also smelled cigar smoke.

"Okay," I agreed, handing Brian the folder and telling him what Herman had said. Then I turned back to Herman and asked him if he had a recipe for veal paprika. "I've been looking for a good recipe for so long," I said. "And you have so many, I figured you might—"

"How did you see that?" he demanded. "How did you see that recipe through that folder?"

"I didn't see anything," I said slowly. Brian opened the folder and his face broke into a stunned smile.

"The first recipe is for veal paprika!" he said.

"Bah!" Herman spat. "You might as well have it now! Go ahead and take it—but not the others. I mean it! Those are for *him only*."

Once Herman had crossed over, Brian actually made me copies of all three of the top-secret recipes, but I only took the veal paprika.

"I promised Herman that I wouldn't take the others," I explained. "And I keep my promises."

"Well that one's yours, then," he said to me. "You can do whatever you want with the veal paprika."

HERMAN'S SECRET-TOUCH VEAL PAPRIKA

3 slices bacon, diced
2 tablespoons shortening
1 medium-size onion, chopped
1 clove garlic
½ teaspoon black pepper
1 tablespoon paprika (good quality)
1 pound veal stew meat, cubed
Water to cover (about ½ cup)
½ green bell pepper, diced
1 tomato, diced
Chopped fresh parsley
Salt to taste
1 tablespoon all-purpose flour
½ pint sour cream
Hot cooked noodles or dumplings

▶ Fry bacon in a skillet until crisp; remove to paper towels and crumble, reserving drippings in pan. Add shortening, onion, and garlic to drippings. Fry onions very slowly until transparent. Add black pepper and paprika; stir for 30 seconds. Add veal and crumbled bacon, cooking until veal is browned. Add ½ cup water, bell pepper, tomato, and parsley. Cook slowly, covered, until veal is tender. Add salt to taste. Cool mixture—*this is the secret*.

Blend flour with sour cream. Add flour mixture to veal mixture, blending thoroughly. Slowly heat through; serve over cooked noodles or dumplings.

JUST PEACHY CHICKEN

When I got to Lida's house, I felt like I'd walked onto the set of an old movie. Lida lived in a nice, big old house in Atlanta with her sister, Bida, and my visit had prompted all the best place settings they could muster. There were finger foods, pastries, cookies, coffee, iced tea, and lemonade—a good old-fashioned spread of Southern hospitality.

The house itself was like a movie set too. The only word to describe it was sprawling, and the yard was littered with beautiful peach trees. The sisters led me onto the veranda, where the food was all laid out, and explained to me that the house had been their parents' originally, but since neither of them had ever married, they'd both just stayed in it.

"I think it's Mother," Lida said of the ghostly trouble they'd been having. "There's no one else it could be. We've both read your books, Mary Ann, and we know it's always a relative."

"That's not true," I cautioned. "Often as not, it's an old friend or even a complete stranger. Have you dreamed of your mother since she died?"

"Oh, yes," they both said, as if that cinched it. Their faces fell when I explained that dreaming of someone like that, after they've died, means they've crossed over.

"Well, maybe they were just dreams?" Bida suggested.

"Did they feel like they were *just* dreams?" I clarified. Bida slowly shook her head.

"No, ma'am. They felt . . . *real*."

At that moment, in waltzes this ghost, all confident and full of herself, examining the food and smirking at her own private jokes.

"And who might you be?" I asked her. She stopped and looked up at me with a politely charmed expression on her face.

"I heard you were coming. I'm Hennie."

"It's . . . Hennie?" I said to Lida and Bida, and both women gasped dramatically. Bida even fanned herself with her hand.

"*Hennie!*" Lida finally declared. "What is *she* doing here? She *knows* she's not welcome in this house!"

Hennie was loving it. She shared with me how much fun it was for her to watch the sisters bicker over things she'd done, like leaving a door open that was supposed to be closed or moving sewing needles or keys. From the sisters I gleaned that half a century before, when all three women were in their teens, Hennie had somehow come between Bida and her beau. The kicker is, none of the women got him in the end—Hennie had died an old maid, just as Lida and Bida most likely would. Not that it mattered. They were still incensed that Hennie would *dare* to set *foot* in their house.

Hennie started to defend herself, but I cut her off and told her I didn't really want to get involved. My job was simply to make sure she stopped bothering the sisters, and that's all I was going to do. I was certainly not going to

In waltzes this ghost, all confident and full of herself.

referee a 50-year-old grudge match. Hennie was completely unapologetic for the trouble she'd caused, saying that the sisters were mean to her when they were young, so why should she care that she got back at them when they were old? One thing Hennie was especially happy about was that the sisters had never figured out her mom's peachy chicken recipe.

"Oh, they keep trying," Hennie giggled. "But they do it all wrong, and they'll never figure it out."

I have to be honest, I didn't care so much about Lida and Bida getting that recipe, but they made it sound so good that I wanted it. So I suggested that Hennie give it to the sisters, as sort of a final sendoff before she crossed over. She had no reason to keep it, except to be even more spiteful.

"They wouldn't want it," she decided, waving me away dramatically. When I asked them, Lida said she didn't want it, but Bida said she did. After some cajoling, Lida finally agreed that it would be nice. Before "the trouble," they'd actually been quite friendly and often ate supper at each other's houses.

"And that peachy chicken her mom made? It's just the best there ever was," Lida admitted.

JUST PEACHY CHICKEN

1 cup orange juice
1½ cups sliced peaches
1 teaspoon nutmeg
1 garlic clove, minced
2 tablespoons brown sugar
2 tablespoons vinegar
1 teaspoon sweet basil
½ cup all-purpose flour
1½ teaspoons salt
Black pepper to taste
6 small chicken legs
6 small chicken breasts
6 small chicken thighs
Corn oil

▶ Combine orange juice, peaches, nutmeg, garlic, brown sugar, vinegar, and basil in a saucepan. Cook over low heat for 10 minutes.

Meanwhile, mix flour, salt, and pepper in a shallow dish. Dredge chicken in flour mixture. Brown in hot oil in a cast-iron skillet.

Remove chicken from skillet and drain, reserving 2 tablespoons drippings and brown bits in skillet. Return chicken to skillet and pour peach mixture over top. Cover and simmer for 20 minutes.

LOTS-OF-SPICES FRIED CHICKEN

"I want you to slap that boy right upside his head!" Delia said to me. I looked at the ghost over my glasses with my best you-gotta-be-kidding-me expression.

"I'm not doing that," I said. "But why are you so upset?"

"Ozzie went off and married that girl without ever letting me meet her!" she declared.

"So you knew Ozzie?" I assumed. She nodded and explained that she was his great-aunt and that everyone in the family had met his wife, Christine, except her. I passed this along to Ozzie, who looked flabbergasted.

"Aunt Delia?" he said. "I didn't mean anything by it, I swear. Christine and I were in school, and you lived so far away. We tried to get out there, but then you . . . ." He trailed off. Delia crossed her arms and nodded with admonishment.

"Uh-huh," she agreed. "But then I died, so this is my fault. Well, now you know why I've made everyone so scared, you ungrateful—"

I frankly tuned her out and turned back to Ozzie and his wife and asked them what had been happening in the house. Christine said she could smell cooking oils from time to time, when no one was cooking anything. And whenever they had friends over, their friends would invariably bolt back into the room at some point like they'd seen a ghost. Some would tell them they'd seen exactly that: an old woman standing in the hallway. Some out-of-state friends had even spent the night in their car because they were afraid to stay in the house! The neighbors also said they often saw a woman looking out of the upstairs windows when they knew Ozzie and Christine were both at work—they'd even gotten a picture of her once. It was the picture that finally prompted Ozzie to call me.

Delia had calmed down by this point, and I managed to guide the conversation to more constructive goodbyes and last requests and reminiscences. Then Ozzie got sort of a faraway look, like he was unsure if he should say or ask what was on his mind.

"What is it, Ozzie?" Christine asked him.

"Well, there was this chicken that Aunt Delia made . . ."

Christine and I both chuckled, and I had to admit to them how many times people want to get a favorite recipe from a dead relative.

"So you can get it?" Ozzie asked excitedly.

"If she'll give it to me," I replied, turning to Delia.

"Of course he can have it," she said with a wide smile. "Even though he is a mean little—"

I didn't bother listening to the rest until Delia started giving me the recipe!

Whenever they had friends over, their friends would invariably bolt back into the room at some point like they'd seen a ghost. Some would tell them they'd seen exactly that: an old woman standing in the hallway.

LOTS-OF-SPICES FRIED CHICKEN

4 eggs
1 cup whole cream
2 cups all-purpose flour
½ teaspoon powdered ginger
1 teaspoon poultry seasoning
2 teaspoons garlic powder
1 teaspoon paprika
3 tablespoons salt
2 tablespoons granulated sugar
4 pounds cut-up fryer chicken
2–8 cups shortening or cooking oil

▶ Preheat oven to 275º. Whisk eggs and cream together in a large bowl. In a large brown paper bag, combine flour, ginger, poultry seasoning, garlic powder, paprika, salt, and sugar; shake bag vigorously. Dip chicken pieces in egg mixture, coating each part well, then place in paper bag. Shake until all pieces are coated. Add shortening to a large skillet or electric frying pan. (Use enough oil so pan is a little less than half-full to prevent splashing.) Brown chicken pieces, one side at a time, turning and watching. Add oil, as needed. When chicken is golden brown, transfer pieces to a baking sheet in center of oven; bake for 30 minutes or until chicken is crisp. Serve as soon as chicken is tender, if you prefer it juicy.

LOTTIE'S POLISH SAUSAGE WITH SAUCE

I have pretty strict rules for attending funerals because they aren't the place for me to be the center of attention. I will not go unless an immediate family member invites me. I also won't do any kind of communicating with the spirit except in a private room with just the family member who invited me—it just turns into a circus otherwise.

Cassie invited me to the funeral of her Aunt Lottie. She had a few specific questions for her—nothing major, just things she had to know—and after the funeral Cassie invited me back to the church for lunch. Already feeling like a bit of a crasher, I tried to decline, but Cassie wouldn't hear of it.

"Besides," she said. "This is a really unique potluck. Everyone made one of Lottie's own recipes for it!"

When Lottie heard that, she looked at me and grinned mischievously. "I heard what you said about the Light," she said to me. "But you know I'm going to have to stay and see what everyone made."

"All right," I said to Cassie. "I'll come for a bit." Then I added mentally to Lottie, "And to make sure you go where you're supposed to."

At the potluck, I got a little bit of everything and sat down to eat with Cassie. The Polish sausage had looked good, but when I tasted it, it really wasn't. I kind of pushed it aside and ate around it. Lottie noticed this and came over to investigate.

"You don't like Polish sausage?" Lottie asked me.

"No, I do," I said. "I'm afraid I just don't like this recipe very much. It's a bit too sour."

Lottie set her mouth and asked grimly, "Find out from Cassie who made it."

I told Cassie quietly what was going on and Cassie went off to find out. A few minutes later, she came back with the chef in tow.

"Barbara made this?" Lottie asked. "Well no wonder, then! Barbara doesn't know how to cook anything that you don't get out of a can!"

Cassie hadn't told Barbara anything, so I played it cool and asked Barbara if she could remember the recipe. Barbara said she made it exactly like her Aunt Lottie used to make, but Lottie was standing their shaking her head in vehement disagreement.

"My Polish sausage was *not* sour," Lottie said to me. "She probably used too much vinegar."

Barbara actually still had the notebook she'd written it down in to prepare for the potluck, so she dug it out of her purse and read it off to me. Lottie was shaking her head again.

"She forgot to write down some stuff," Lottie noticed. "Here, I'll give you the real recipe—you'll see!"

After Barbara left, I took down Lottie's recipe, and later I did make it, just to see. It was absolutely delicious and not at all sour, just as Lottie had promised.

When Lottie heard that, she looked at me and grinned mischievously. "I heard what you said about the Light," she said to me. "But you know I'm going to have to stay and see what everyone made."

LOTTIE'S POLISH SAUSAGE WITH SAUCE

2 cups beer
2 cups water
1½ pounds Polish sausage
2 onions, sliced
1 tablespoon butter
1 tablespoon all-purpose flour
½ teaspoon Maggi Seasoning Sauce*
2 tablespoons vinegar
1 teaspoon–1 tablespoon granulated sugar or brown sugar
Boiled potatoes

▶ Place beer and 2 cups water in a large pot. Add sausage and onions, and simmer for 20 minutes. Brown butter in a large skillet, and blend in flour; slowly add 1 cup liquid strained from meat and stir until thoroughly blended. If sauce is too thick, add more liquid. Add Maggi sauce, vinegar, and sugar to taste. Remove sausage to a cutting board. Slice sausage, pour sauce over it, and serve with boiled potatoes.

*Maggi Seasoning Sauce is a low-sodium condiment similar to soy sauce. If it's not readily available in your area, it can be found easily online.

LOUISIANA BEEF STEW

To be quite frank, I'm amazed at how stupid some earthbound spirits are. Well, that might not be fair—they aren't stupid, but they certainly stick around for stupid reasons. One of the messages I always leave my clients with is quite simple: You can't do anything if you stay here. You can't help your loved ones raise their kids, you can't help your surviving family find the box of money you hid, you can't make anyone hear your apologies, and you certainly can't win over an old flame. The best thing you can do for everyone involved, including yourself, is cross over. At least you'll then be able to visit people in their dreams.

Unfortunately, Rose never got this message. She was haunting her brother-in-law, Clarence, whose wife had passed away three years before from cancer. When Clarence called me, he said he'd been catching a glimpse of a woman in the house, but that he didn't think it was his wife, Violet. I agreed with him that it was unlikely because cancer patients rarely stay earthbound, especially if they'd had a long battle.

"It was," Clarence assured me. "Violet spent her last months here at home, but they basically turned the place into a private hospital."

I went out to see him. He lived in Louisiana, and I had fit in the visit while I was in the area for other reasons. He was 65, but he still worked, and he took the afternoon off to meet me at the house. While we sat at the kitchen table drinking lemonade and discussing what

had been going on, I saw the woman ghost off down the hall, sort of trying to peek in at us. That was unusual. In most homes, the spirit zips right into the room with me to see what's going on, especially once they find out that I can see and hear them. But not this woman.

"Well, there is a woman here," I said to Clarence. "But she won't come into the room. She's hanging out in the room just down the hall there."

"That was Violet's room," Clarence said quietly. "That's where we put her—where they set up the hospital room."

"I'll have to go down to her," I decided and started to get up. At that point, the woman came trundling down the hall to me.

"I'm coming! I'm coming!" she said. She was plump, but not heavy, and pleasant to look at. I couldn't imagine her being much of a bother.

"Who are you?" I asked.

"Oh, I don't think Clarence would like to know that."

"Did you know Clarence?" I asked, thankful once again that when I communicate with ghosts it's all done in my head so I don't have to speak out loud.

"Oh, yes," she said. "Violet, too, of course."

Now I was getting suspicious. "Were you and Clarence having . . . an affair?"

"No, no!" she blushed, then added. "I *wish*!"

Finally, I got out of her that her name was Rose. She was Violet's sister and, according to

I saw the woman ghost off down the hall, sort of trying to peek in at us. That was unusual. In most homes, the spirit zips right into the room.

her, Clarence had dated her first, then Violet had taken him away. Rose had never married. After Violet died, she started coming around to visit Clarence again, hoping he'd come back to her, but he didn't. Then, when she died herself a year ago, she stayed behind for another chance at Clarence.

"Oh for God's sake!" Clarence cried when I told him this. "She never gives up!"

Rose looked heartbroken, and I felt bad for her, but she certainly wasn't going to be staying with Clarence any longer. I explained this to her gently.

"Well, he should at least give me credit for my beef stew!" she decided obstinately. "Ask him about it!"

I did, and Clarence readily admitted that Rose's beef stew was the best he'd ever had, even better than Violet's. "I don't know what she did to it, but Violet never could get it right."

Being curious myself, I suggested to Rose that she give me the recipe for Clarence, so he'd always have something to remember her by. Naturally, she thought that was a magnificent idea!

LOUISIANA BEEF STEW

3 tablespoons all-purpose flour
1 teaspoon salt
½ teaspoon celery salt
¼ teaspoon garlic salt
¼ teaspoon black pepper
½ teaspoon ginger
3 pounds beef chuck,
    cut into 2-inch cubes
2 tablespoons cooking oil
1 (16-ounce) can tomatoes
3 medium-size onions, sliced
⅓ cup red wine vinegar
½ cup molasses
½ cup water
6–8 carrots, cut diagonally
½ cup raisins

▶ Combine flour, salt, celery salt, garlic salt, pepper, and ginger; sprinkle over beef. Brown beef in hot oil. Transfer meat to a Dutch oven; add tomatoes, onions, vinegar, molasses, and ½ cup water. Bring to a boil, cover, and simmer for about 2 hours. Add carrots and raisins, and simmer for 30 minutes or until carrots are tender.

NUTTY DILL CHICKEN PIE

One of the most memorable homes I've cleared would have to be the houseboat on Lake Mead in Nevada. Cecilia lived on the boat with her husband, Jared. They were both retired and thought you couldn't get much closer lakefront property than actually living on the lake.

They'd bought the houseboat used from an older woman who'd had a similar idea with her husband. The previous owners had lived on it for years, but, after her husband died, it was too much to maintain alone, and the wife had to sell it. Once they moved in, Cecilia and Jared gave it a thorough cleaning and found several items of the woman's stowed away in cubbyholes. So they called her daughter, Carol, who had brokered the sale, to see about returning them to her, only to find out about her passing. Shortly after moving off the boat, the woman had died.

"Did you find a recipe book?" Carol asked, and was overjoyed to learn that it was, indeed, one of the things they had found. "Oh, thank goodness—I was going crazy trying to find it in all her things!"

Cecilia had actually already been flipping through the recipe book. A lot of the recipes seemed quite unusual and looked like they would be pretty good, so she'd decided to start copying them down in the evenings, before they called Carol to return the belongings (and after they were sure they'd found everything that had been hidden away). That first night,

she'd started feeling sick to her stomach, though, and decided to turn in early. She was still sick for the next few days and never really felt completely better. She was run-down and cranky and nauseated in a way she'd never felt on a houseboat before. To top it off, the toilet kept flushing by itself—not leaking, but actually flushing—and the water bills for a houseboat were never cheap to begin with.

By the time I was able to get out there, Carol had already been by and had picked up the box of her mother's belongings, but her mother, Terri, was still there.

"What are you doing here?" I asked her.

"I was worried about the boat," she said. "And I never wanted to leave it to begin with."

She was also upset with her children, who had been told to cremate her and spread her ashes over the lake. Carol had called to arrange that, only to be told by park officials that she wasn't allowed to. So they'd buried Terri instead of sneaking her ashes out to the middle of the lake and spreading them. But the thing that had really got her upset was when Cecilia started copying down her recipes!

"Those were my *special* recipes!" Terri said. They weren't secret, exactly, because she did give them out to people, but she always left out some ingredient or other so it would never be perfect. She hadn't even written them down in the book completely because she remembered which ingredients she'd left out!

The previous owners had lived on it for years, but, after her husband died, it was too much to maintain alone, and the wife had to sell it. Once they moved in, Cecilia and Jared gave it a thorough cleaning and found several items of the woman's.

After owning up to it, Terri had to agree that it was kind of silly. It's not like she was making any money off her recipes, so there was no real reason to keep them secret, except out of spite. Terri felt bad and said that she wanted to make amends. Her best recipe had been for a dill chicken pie, and not even her daughter had the right recipe because she'd not written it down correctly in the book.

"I'll give it the right way to Cecilia," she said. "But she can't give it to Carol."

"Why not?" I asked, not sure why she'd not want her own daughter to have the right recipe.

"She buried me!" Terri cried. "That's what she gets for burying me!"

NUTTY DILL CHICKEN PIE

¼ cup butter
¼ cup all-purpose flour
1 cup light whipping cream
½ teaspoon salt
¼ teaspoon black pepper
1 cup chicken broth
¼ teaspoon dill
1 teaspoon chopped fresh parsley
2 cups diced cooked chicken
1 cup sliced mushrooms
½ cup toasted slivered almonds
Pastry for single-crust 9-inch pie

▶ Preheat oven to 450º. Melt butter in a large skillet; stir in flour. Gradually stir in cream and cook, stirring constantly, until smooth and thick. Add salt, pepper, broth, dill, and parsley; cook until smooth and thick. Stir in diced chicken, sliced mushrooms, and almonds. Pour chicken mixture into a deep 9-inch pie plate and cover with pastry. Slash top of dough for steam to escape. Place on a baking sheet and bake for 10 minutes. Reduce oven temperature to 350º and bake for 15 minutes.

OVEN-BARBECUED CHICKEN

Some earthbound spirits stay around just to make sure people stay in line. They rightly figure that once they're gone, people might not keep up the traditions they had kept so carefully in life, so they stick around to make sure people do things right. What I've learned is that when it comes to barbecuing in Texas, what's "right" isn't just a tradition, it's a fact, and it was why Grandpa John was causing trouble at Bobby Joe's restaurant.

Bobby Joe was doing okay, but he was close to having to shut the place down. He had massive ovens and pits out back for spit-roasting, and he always got great reviews, but no one ever seemed to come back. Without any regulars, he wasn't sure he'd be able to keep his head above water for much longer.

His sister, Sally, called me. I'd done work for her before, when she'd lived in Arizona, but now she'd moved back to Texas and she recognized the signs: The stoves would turn off for no reason, food would burn when it never had before, the light bulbs kept burning out, and even some of the guests had been overheard saying they felt *weird,* like someone was watching them.

Of course, someone was: Grandpa John. He was upset because Bobby Joe had taken his trusted barbecued chicken recipe and changed it.

"*Ruined* it," he added emphatically.

"What's wrong with it?" I asked. I'd had it for lunch before Bobby Joe had closed up to prepare for dinner, and I thought it was delicious.

"Barbecued chicken shouldn't have griddle marks on it," Grandpa John explained. "He's grilling that chicken, and you don't *grill* barbecued chicken! And Bobby Joe knows better. I never served it that way when he was growing up."

"Okay," I said. "I don't see how else you grill chicken without grilling it, but . . ." I passed along what Grandpa John had said, and the two siblings looked at each other.

"I told you," Sally finally said. "I told you that's not how Grandpa John made that chicken."

"But people *expect* the grill marks!" Bobby Joe protested. "It's *barbecued!*"

"It's not the grill that matters!" Grandpa John shouted—Texans get pretty fired up about their barbecues. "It's the *sauce* that matters, Bobby Joe! No one wants burn marks on their chicken! Now you do it right, or you won't do it at all."

I relayed the threat to Bobby Joe and told him I couldn't force a ghost to cross over, and it didn't sound like Grandpa John had any intention of leaving if he didn't get a promise out of his grandson. Bobby Joe looked at me sort of sheepishly and grinned like a kid caught pulling his sister's hair.

"I don't think I can make it exactly like Grandpa," he admitted. He glanced at Sally,

Some of the guests had been overheard saying they felt weird, like someone was watching them.

and she looked away guiltily too. "We sort of tweaked his sauce recipe, and now we don't know where the original is."

"Oh, sweet lord," Grandpa John sighed. He looked at me and shook his head slowly.

"Will you give me the recipe to give to them? The sauce recipe and exactly how to cook this chicken in the oven instead of on the grill?"

"Yes," he replied without hesitation, which sort of surprised me. But family usually wins out, and Grandpa John added, "If he promises to make it right. I want him to be successful, and I really think this will help him with that."

Bobby Joe swore up and down that he'd fix the sauce and cook the chicken right and do whatever else Grandpa John thought he should do, so I got the recipe and passed it along to him. He called me a few months later to let me know how it went, and he said I wouldn't believe it.

"People are coming from *miles* around now to eat here! And they all want that oven-barbecued chicken!"

OVEN-BARBECUED CHICKEN

2 pounds fryer chicken,
    cut into quarters
Salt and black pepper to taste
Hot water
3 medium-size onions, sliced thin
Barbecue Sauce (recipe below)

▶ Preheat oven to 300º. Place chicken in a single layer, skin side up, in a roasting pan. Sprinkle with salt and pepper. Pour in hot water to cover bottom of pan. Arrange onion slices over chicken, tucking some in under wings and legs. Bake, uncovered, for 30 minutes. Turn chicken over and bake for 30 minutes. Remove from oven and pour off all but ¾ cup pan liquid. Turn chicken skin side up, and pour Barbecue Sauce over top. Bake for 1 hour, basting frequently.

BARBECUE SAUCE

1½ cups tomato juice
¼ teaspoon cayenne pepper
2 teaspoons salt
¼ teaspoon black pepper
¼ teaspoon dry mustard
4½ teaspoons Worcestershire sauce
1 bay leaf
1 teaspoon granulated sugar
½ cup apple cider vinegar
3 peeled garlic cloves, minced
3 tablespoons butter

▶ Combine all ingredients in a saucepan. Bring to a boil and simmer for 10 minutes. Remove and discard bay leaf.

OYSTER-AND-SAUSAGE CASSEROLE AND TUNA-NOODLE LUNCHEON CASSEROLE

Anita was worried about her husband, plain and simple. She had died in a car crash just six months before her husband, Raymond, called me, and she was still worried about him. They were a young couple, in their 30s, and they didn't have any kids. Anita had stuck around for him.

"He needs to move on," she told me when I got there. "We were married five years, but he needs to start dating again."

I glanced at Raymond. The reason he'd called is because he'd kept seeing his dead wife in the house.

"Well, you know, your being around isn't helping that," I stated simply. "I think it's honestly you who needs to move—to cross over—so he can get used to being without you. You know he sees you sometimes, right?"

She nodded sheepishly. "I thought so. And I know he's happier and even healthier when I'm not around. That's why I mostly stay with him at work now."

That made sense. Raymond worked outside all day as a landscape designer and maintainer for a zoo. As best as I can describe it, the energy an earthbound spirit uses can get sort of trapped, like perfume. When you're outside, it can dissipate pretty quickly, but inside a house, the energy can get bottled up until it starts affecting people and even things like the electricity.

"She says she stayed around because she was worried about you," I told Raymond. "But she was most worried that you wouldn't, you know, move on. And she wants you to know you should."

He sort of chuckled and said, "The funny thing is, I feel uncomfortable doing that because I keep seeing her."

I gave Anita a knowing look. She nodded with acceptance, then said, "He should date that woman at work, Jill."

"Excuse me?"

"Yes. And there's two lovely women right here in the neighborhood. They're both single and pretty, and I've been watching them—they'd both make lovely wives for Raymond."

I couldn't believe it! Now I was cast in the role of passing on dating advice to a husband from his dead wife's ghost! But that's what I was there for, so I sighed and passed along the messages. He turned up his nose at the idea of two of the women, but the other one he was amenable to. Then Anita started into a litany of other messages for Raymond and everyone else in her family. She'd had a lot of time to think about this, and because she'd died so suddenly, there was a lot she'd left unsaid. Raymond got it all down, and it was finally time for Anita to cross over.

"Oh, one more thing," she said. "Tell him that while I certainly don't mind him

As best as I can describe it, the energy an earthbound spirit uses gets sort of trapped, like perfume. When you're outside, it can dissipate pretty quickly, but inside a house, it gets bottled up until it starts affecting people and even things.

remarrying, he's not to give her my wedding ring. That was ours, and I want him to give it my goddaughter when she's old enough."

"Fair enough," Raymond agreed when I passed it along.

"Oh!" Anita cried. "And one other thing! Well, two, actually. Can you give him my recipes for two casseroles he just *loved*? I've watched him try to make them, and he just ruins them every time."

"Yes, all right," I said. I was beginning to think she'd never run out of reasons to stay, so I took down the recipes and then she did finally cross over.

About three years later, Raymond followed up with me. He was newly remarried. It wasn't to one of the women Anita had picked out, but it was the sister of one of them!

OYSTER-AND-SAUSAGE CASSEROLE

1½ cups sifted all-purpose flour

3 teaspoons baking powder

½ teaspoon salt

1 tablespoon shortening

½ pint oysters

6 tablespoons oyster juice or milk

Butter

8 small pork sausages, pricked

▶ Preheat oven to 450º. Stir together flour, baking powder, and salt. Cut in shortening. Drain and chop oysters; add to flour mixture with oyster juice or milk (or a combination). Spread oyster mixture in a greased (with butter) shallow pan. Place sausages on top. Bake for about 20 minutes.

TUNA-NOODLE LUNCHEON CASSEROLE

1 package wide egg noodles, cooked

3 cups milk

2 tablespoons all-purpose flour

1 tablespoon melted butter

2 hard-boiled eggs, chopped

¾ (4-ounce container) pimiento cheese

1 (5-ounce) can tuna

½ cup plain breadcrumbs

▶ Preheat oven to 325º. Boil noodles in salted water for 20 minutes; drain. Whisk together milk, flour, and butter. Layer half of noodles, eggs, cheese, and tuna in a casserole dish; top with half of milk mixture. Repeat layers. Sprinkle breadcrumbs on top and dot with butter. Bake for 30 minutes or until brown.

PICNIC HAM LOAF

I try really hard not to butt into other people's business. When I'm out clearing a house for someone, I just relay what the earthbound spirits are saying and try to reserve my judgment (at least for the living—I've told a few ghosts what I think, though!). And especially when I'm out in public, I try to just let everyone around me be, whether they're living or dead. Yet despite my best efforts, sometimes people have other plans. Frank and Donna were one such couple.

In the summers, my husband, Ted, and I like to go to amusement parks and take a picnic lunch. We don't do much these days but ride the "old folks" rides, but we love the carnival atmosphere of amusement parks, and we like to watch the kids carrying on and having fun. We met Frank and Donna on one such outing.

The picnic pavilion was crowded that day, and we ended up having to sit right next to someone no matter where we sat. We ended up near two couples who looked to be around 70. They seemed to be having fun until the one man said, "I like fried chicken and all, but I wish I knew how Ellie made those sandwiches."

Oh my. This was clearly a long-standing bone of contention. The woman sitting across from him had instant fire in her eyes, and the other couple sort of paled, looked away, and tried to pretend nothing was happening.

"I am *so sorry* I didn't know Ellie, Frank," the woman with fire in her eyes said in a very cutting tone of voice. "I'm sorry I didn't get her recipe, and I'm sorry you don't like my sandwiches. So if you don't *want* them, don't *eat* them."

I had seen a ghost hovering near the group, and when I looked over at her now, she was grinning from ear to ear. "You're Ellie, aren't you?" I asked her mentally. She nodded.

"I'm sorry, Donna," Frank was saying. "It's just that picnics always remind me of those meatloaf sandwiches."

"And *her*," Donna decided. Frank looked like he was going to quibble that point, then decided it wouldn't be worth it. I turned back to Ellie and asked who she was, and she explained that she was Frank's first wife and she had been sick for quite some time before she died.

"Do you know what he's talking about?" I wondered. She nodded and grinned again.

"My meatloaf sandwiches," she said proudly.

"Meatloaf sandwiches?" I asked. "What's so special about meatloaf sandwiches? Everyone makes sandwiches out of leftover meatloaf."

"Not like mine," Ellie said. "I don't use ground beef, and mine is actually better cold. It's *perfect* for sandwiches."

I had to know how she made meatloaf without beef, and she was very forthcoming with the recipe, which uses only ham and pork. I jotted it down; then I wondered if I should butt in with Frank and Donna. The couples were now playing cards and seemed content, but I wondered how long it would be before the same argument might replay itself again. I

When I'm out clearing a house for someone, I just relay what the earthbound spirits are saying and try to reserve my judgment.

certainly wasn't going to tell them about Ellie, however—that wouldn't have done any of us any good—but I felt like I could offer them some future peace and quiet.

Finally, I sort of caught Donna's eye and said bashfully, "I wasn't listening in before, but I heard you talking about meatloaf sandwiches . . .?" I thought Donna might well reach out and slap me. Clearly, this was not a topic one brought up. Ever. But I was in it now, so I kept going.

"Well, my . . . *aunt* used to make this really unique meatloaf that she only ever used for sandwiches. It was actually better cold than hot. I thought you might like to try it." Now Ted was glaring at me, too, and Donna just huffed and turned up her nose.

"I don't think so," she said definitively, so I dropped it. Ted and I finished eating. Then, while we were packing up to go, Donna edged over and nodded to me slowly.

"You know, maybe I will try that recipe," she said. "If it shuts him up, it'll be worth it."

Considering the true source, I have a feeling it most likely *did* shut Frank up!

PICNIC HAM LOAF

1½ pounds fresh pork, ground by the butcher

1½ pounds smoked ham, ground by the butcher

2 eggs

1 cup breadcrumbs

1 cup milk

Dash of black pepper

2 tablespoons brown sugar

1 tablespoon yellow mustard

▶ Preheat oven to 350º. Combine pork, ham, eggs, breadcrumbs, milk, and pepper in a large bowl. Mix with hands, and pack meat mixture into a loaf pan. Stir together brown sugar and yellow mustard, and spread on top. Bake for 1 hour. Serve hot or cold on sandwiches.

PINOCHLE CASSEROLE

Earthbound spirits affect people in lots of different ways. There are the more obvious ones, such as light bulbs that are constantly burning out and other electrical problems, even up to radios and TVs that seem to have minds of their own. There are the subtle ones, such as headaches, sleepless nights, and a general malaise. Then there are the strange effects the spirits of the dead sometimes have on the living, like with Kay, who suddenly couldn't get enough pinochle in her life.

Kay and her husband, Ernie, had played pinochle for years, at least two nights a week, so it wasn't odd that Kay wanted to play. In fact, they played competitively in a local club, and just recently that had taken up two more nights a week. On Saturdays, they played for fun with friends, meaning at least three, sometimes four, nights a week they were out playing cards. That didn't sit well with their 15-year-old daughter, Ally. She thought they were gone too often, and Ernie had to agree. Kay, on the other hand, did not. She wanted to find more games, if she could.

This had been going on for about six months by the time the couple called me out to the house, and the stress of it, though not great, was what Ernie attributed his headaches and sleeplessness to. He finally sat Kay down and told her straight that she had to cut back. It was all Kay needed. She let out a sigh of relief and shook her head.

"I don't know what's gotten into me," she admitted. "I just suddenly can't get enough. It's like someone's almost *forcing* me to play more . . . ." Kay trailed off, her eyes widening. She knew about me and about ghosts, and the subtle signs all around them—the flickering lights, the headaches, the almost-constant runny noses and colds—finally added up.

The problem, it turned out, was Eileen, and her influence on Kay. Eileen had also been an avid pinochle player and instructor. Her husband had actually divorced her over pinochle because she spent more time playing pinochle than with him! She'd come home with Kay and Ernie from one of the clubs they played at because she knew she could influence Kay, and she wanted one last student before she left for good.

"She has a tell," Eileen said to me, as if that would explain and excuse her behavior.

"A *what?*"

"A tell. Everyone at the table knows what she's going to do. She twirls her hair when she's going to bid for trump."

"Okay," I agreed. I didn't know pinochle from go-fish, but I assumed this would make sense to Kay, and it did when I told her what Eileen had said.

"Another thing," Eileen added. "Tell her to stop going to that club down the road. Sarah and Megan down there cheat. They have all these signs and conversational cues to each

The flickering lights, the headaches, the almost-constant runny noses and colds—finally added up.

other—like when Megan mentions her daughter's grades or schoolwork, that tells Sarah what she should do."

Kay didn't believe that at all, but three months later, she called and told me it had been absolutely true—Megan and Sarah *were* cheating. She'd also wanted to let me know that she'd dropped down to only two nights a week, and one of those was just for fun. She'd found a new club for the competitive play, one that Eileen had suggested—they played less often, and they didn't cheat.

Eileen had also given her one other tip: There was a casserole recipe she should make on card nights because it was simple and everyone loved it. Kay had a report on that too.

"She was absolutely right—it's both easy and delicious!"

"And how do you feel now?" I asked her. "Do you still feel like you have to play more and more and more?"

"Nope, that all went away after you helped Eileen cross over," Kay replied. "Ernie's headaches went away, the lights don't flicker, and, while Ally's still a teenager, she doesn't seem quite as moody as before."

PINOCHLE CASSEROLE

2 onions, chopped
1 garlic clove (plus more, if desired)
1 tablespoon olive oil
1½ pounds ground chuck
2 tablespoons melted butter
1 medium-size head cabbage, chopped
Salt to taste
1 (10¾-ounce) can tomato soup, undiluted
Hot cooked noodles or rice

▶ Preheat oven to 350º. Caramelize onion and garlic in olive oil in a large skillet. Add ground chuck and cook until meat crumbles and is no longer pink. Brush a baking dish with melted butter. Place one-third of meat in bottom of dish and then add one-third of cabbage. Sprinkle with salt. Repeat layers twice. Spread soup over top. Cover with lid and bake for 1 hour. Increase oven temperature to 450º, and bake, uncovered, for 30 minutes or until all liquid is absorbed. Serve over noodles or rice.

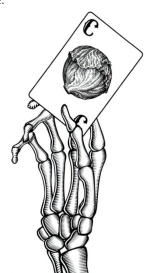

PORK TENDERLOIN IN SOUR CREAM

For every ghost I've encountered that stayed earthbound for silly, petty reasons, I've probably run into one who I can't believe stayed earthbound for any reason. Joe was one of those. His wife, Millie, was still alive, and after five minutes in the room with her, I couldn't imagine why Joe hadn't just run as fast as he could into that White Light when he died. I can only imagine he'd stayed for his daughter, Ellen.

Ellen was the one who had called me. She'd been seeing a male ghost in the house, and she was quite sure it was her father. He had died two or three years before, after a time of declining health. Both he and Millie had moved in with their daughter when they were in their 70s, and Ellen was about 50. That had been about 10 years before, when Joe had developed lung problems that prevented him from working. Millie had continued to work and Ellen worked as a schoolteacher; while they were out, Joe would putter around and clean, and he'd always prepared a nice big meal for them when they got home.

Millie disagreed with this assessment.

"He was useless," she crabbed. "I taught him how to cook and he never did it right. And he couldn't even lift a finger to clean anything."

"That's not true, Mom," Ellen said patiently. "Dad was a good cook, and he was very helpful."

Millie harrumphed, and Ellen went on to explain that Joe later had a stroke that left the right side of his body paralyzed, so for the last few years, it was true that he wasn't able to clean or cook anymore. Ellen said how much she missed his cooking, but reading between the lines, I'd say she just missed her dad.

"I never actually got to say a real goodbye," Ellen concluded.

"Nonsense!" Millie spat. "He wouldn't have said goodbye anyway!"

At that moment, a male ghost walked into the room. It was Joe, but Ellen couldn't see him right then. She'd only caught glimpses of him from time to time. Ellen repeated how much she missed his cooking, and Millie repeated how she'd taught Joe how to cook.

"What's the recipe for pork chops then, Mom?" Ellen asked, now getting a bit perturbed. Millie waved her off and turned away. "See? You don't know, Mom, because you didn't cook them!"

"Does she want that recipe?" Joe asked. "Let me give it to her."

I sat and copied it down for Ellen and then gave it to her. She was overjoyed when I handed her the paper. You'd have thought I'd given her the secret location to a stack of gold!

"Bah!" Millie spat again. "Your father wasn't so great. You don't know!"

"Would you like to cross over now?" I asked Joe, since he and Ellen had finally managed to have their last goodbyes.

"Yes," he said without hesitation.

At that moment, a male ghost walked into the room. It was Joe, but Ellen couldn't see him right then. She'd only caught glimpses of him from time to time. Ellen repeated how much she missed his cooking, and Millie repeated how she'd taught Joe how to cook.

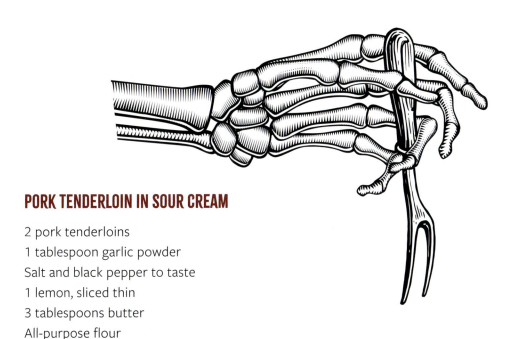

PORK TENDERLOIN IN SOUR CREAM

2 pork tenderloins
1 tablespoon garlic powder
Salt and black pepper to taste
1 lemon, sliced thin
3 tablespoons butter
All-purpose flour
4 tablespoons sour cream

▶ Preheat oven to 400º. Place pork in a roasting pan. Rub meat well with garlic powder, sprinkle with salt and pepper, and cover with lemon slices. Roast, basting frequently with butter, then with pan drippings, for 30 minutes or until meat begins to brown. Dust meat with flour, add sour cream, and continue basting until meat is thoroughly brown and tender, about 45 minutes–1 hour, depending on size and thickness of meat. Care should be taken, however, not to overcook the meat or it will be too dry.

QUICK BEEF STROGANOFF

Lucy called me because she didn't just suspect she had a ghost, she'd actually seen him. She didn't recognize him, but she described him as a repairman. He had been wearing a gray one-piece uniform with the name "Guy" on the patch, but she couldn't remember seeing a company or logo or anything. I thought it quite strange because, usually, earthbound spirits are dressed in the clothes they were wearing when they were buried, so that would mean he'd been buried in his work clothes!

When I got out to Lucy's house, Guy was there. He told me he'd been a sort of general repairman, but his specialty was stoves. He had not died repairing anything—he just really liked the uniform!

"So, what are you doing here?" I asked him. "Did you do repair work for Lucy?"

"Nope," he said simply. Then he mumbled something I didn't hear and looked away. I could tell by his body language that he wasn't proud of the last bit, but if he thought I was just going to let it slide, he was mistaken. I always want to know why an earthbound spirit is hanging around.

I pressed him on it, and he finally admitted that he just went from house to house, checking up on the occupant's cooking. If he didn't like the way they cooked, he'd mess up their stoves.

"That's true!" Lucy agreed, when I shared this with her. "Florence next door? Her stove suddenly died, and I had to make her a couple of meals. Then right after that, *my* stove died. I've had a repairman out three times to fix it!"

"You know," I said to Guy. "That's not very nice at all. These people have to pay for that, just because you don't like their cooking."

"No, no," he disagreed, shaking his head. "I only do it to stoves that are still under warranty or if the person has a contract with a repair shop that they're paying for anyway. I won't do it if it's going to cost them."

"Well, I don't know," I said slowly. "What makes you such a food critic, anyway?"

He told me that, aside from being a repairman, he'd also been an amateur chef when he was alive. He told me that what annoyed him most about Lucy's cooking wasn't her recipes—he said her recipes were all quite good—it was what she did to them.

"She just can't make a recipe straight. She always has to substitute things and cut ingredients, and she just messes them all up," he complained. "If she'd just follow the recipes, then her cooking would be a lot better! And the microwave—sheesh! I hate it when people use a microwave to *cook!*"

I told Lucy all the things he'd said, and she sort of shrugged them off. "I have to cut the ingredients down," she said. "I live alone—I can't make a recipe that serves six people! And I don't use the microwave for anything but warming up coffee." She stopped and thought

I could tell by his body language that he wasn't proud of the last bit, but if he thought I was just going to let it slide, he was mistaken. I always want to know why an earthbound spirit is hanging around.

for a second, then added, "There is one recipe I know I do mess up, though. I really want to get it right, but I just can't. Have you ever tried to make—"

"Beef stroganoff," Guy finished at the same time as Lucy. "Yes, she does mess that up, and it's *not* that hard to make."

"It is pretty hard to get it right," I said to Guy in Lucy's defense.

"Nah!" Guy denied, waving me off. "Let me give you my recipe—it's so easy!"

QUICK BEEF STROGANOFF

1 pound lean beef filet

1 tablespoon paprika

3 tablespoons olive oil

4 ounces sliced mushrooms

1 cup white cooking sherry

½ cup beef stock or canned condensed beef broth

1 cup sour cream

1 teaspoon lemon juice

Salt to taste

Cooked white rice or noodles

▶ Slice beef into ¼-inch-thick strips; sprinkle with paprika. Heat oil in a skillet, and then sauté beef quickly (2–4 minutes). Remove meat from pan. Add mushrooms and sauté for a few minutes; remove from pan. Add sherry to pan and cook until liquid is reduced by half. Add beef stock and let boil briskly, uncovered, for 5 minutes.

Stir in sour cream, lemon juice, and salt. Return meat and mushrooms to pan, and bring just to a boil. Spoon over rice or noodles.

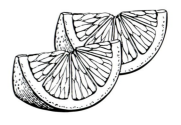

REAL SOUTHERN-FRIED CHICKEN WITH CHICKEN-MILK GRAVY

Annie had two strikes against her already, at least in her mother-in-law's eyes. For one thing, she was from the North, and good ol' Arkansas boys like her son, Vern, did not marry Northerners. And two—and perhaps most important—she was a horrible cook, and her son should not have married a woman who couldn't take care of him.

"Okay," I said to the earthbound spirit. "So you're Vern's mother, then?" She nodded. "And what's your name?"

"You can call me Miss Elma."

I looked over at Vern—ever the skeptic—and told him who it was and what I should call her, and he went white as a sheet. For her part, Annie looked as uncomfortable with the news, but for different reasons.

"I knew it," Annie said. "She *never* liked me!"

Vern and Annie were actually a really good couple. They were both quiet and unassuming. Vern was a private accountant—he'd worked from home and had cared for his mother until she died—and Annie had moved to Arkansas for a job with a charitable organization. Their paths had crossed when Annie needed an accountant and had found Vern.

"She did like you," Vern said quietly. Miss Elma stood stoically and mumbled, "She's not who I would have picked."

Vern had gotten everything when Elma died. He had three older sisters, and the youngest was nine years older than him. Miss Elma had doted on Vern—her baby and her only boy—and Vern had returned the favor. He'd never left home, had set up his business there, and had cared for his mother until she died.

"I told them before I died that Vern got everything," Miss Elma said. "He cared for me and gave up his life for me—but now, to see him throw it away with that woman! She doesn't even do anything anymore!"

Which wasn't true. It was true that she'd been able to quit her job after marrying Vern, but she filled her time with volunteer work instead. She was actually a full-time volunteer. In hindsight, I wonder if some of her volunteerism was driven by her wanting to get out of the house. She told me she'd never felt comfortable there, like she was being watched—and worse, being judged. But she loved Vern and he loved her, so there was really nothing Miss Elma could do to get between them.

When I explained that to her, she huffed at me and said, "You *could* tell her to learn to cook! She doesn't even know how to make real fried chicken!"

Annie disagreed. She said she made fried chicken all the time and that Vern liked it. Vern agreed with that, but you could tell he was holding something back, not wanting to upset Annie. Fortunately, Miss Elma explained his reticence with her next outburst.

She told me she'd never felt comfortable there, like she was being watched—and worse, being judged. But she loved Vern and he loved her, so there was really nothing Miss Elma could do to get between them.

"She doesn't make *real* fried chicken, and that's his favorite food! There are *no* breadcrumbs in real fried chicken!"

"Well, why don't you give me the recipe for your fried chicken, and I can give it to Annie?"

"Oh, I don't know about that," Miss Elma said slowly, shaking her head. So I went for the heart.

"Don't you want Vern to be happy? And wouldn't *your* fried chicken make him happy?"

She hemmed and hawed for a few seconds, then said, "Well, it's not just the chicken. It's the gravy too."

"So why don't you give me the gravy recipe as well?"

Finally, she agreed.

REAL SOUTHERN-FRIED CHICKEN

1¾ pounds chicken
Salt and black pepper to taste
All-purpose flour
Shortening, such as Crisco
Chicken-Milk Gravy (recipe below)

▶ Cut chicken into serving portions, season with salt and pepper, and dredge in flour. Melt enough shortening to cover bottom of a large skillet (about 2 inches deep). Add chicken and brown quickly on both sides (about 15 minutes total). Reduce heat, cover, and cook slowly for another 15–20 minutes or until tender. Serve with Chicken-Milk Gravy.

Note: No breadcrumbs are used in this fried-chicken recipe.

CHICKEN-MILK GRAVY

1–2 teaspoons all-purpose flour
Milk

▶ Remove fried chicken and set aside. Pour off grease, leaving browned bits in bottom of skillet. Add flour gradually, and stir over low heat until browned. Add milk slowly and stir until gravy reaches desired consistency.

ROAST LAMB IN WINE

Lala told me up front that her real name was hard for Americans to pronounce, so I should just call her Lala. It was true—judging by the message she'd left on my machine, I'd never be able to get her full name right. A recent immigrant from the Middle East, she spoke with a thick accent, so not only did her real name sound completely foreign to me, I also wasn't sure I was even hearing it correctly. One thing that did bridge the culture gap was the earthbound spirit in her home.

Lala told me she'd seen a ghost in her house and she thought she knew who it was. Lala and her husband, Renni, had left the Middle East to give their kids a chance at a better life. That was the official story, anyway. After chatting with her, though, it came out that there had been other reasons to leave, and if the ghost was who she thought it was, then one of the reasons they left had followed them to America.

"It's my mother-in-law," Lala told me with conviction. "She had other plans for who Renni was to marry, so she doesn't like me at all."

The ghost was standing in the room with us and I looked over at her. So far, she had refused to talk to me, but now she slowly shook her head no; she was not the mother-in-law.

"I don't think it's her," I told Lala. "She won't talk, but she's indicating 'no.' Is there anyone else who died recently?"

Lala couldn't think of anyone. She was clearly frustrated and shaken up by the whole

thing, not to mention this had been one of my "secret" visits, where the husband didn't know I was coming out. That happens a lot, when wives feel they have to keep it secret from their husbands. I don't try to pry into their business and just go along with them, and I have met my share of ardently skeptical husbands who are just plain rude to me. So when a wife says I have to visit when the husband is gone, I go along with it.

Lala then started to tell me how her husband was a doctor and that she, too, had been in the medical field in her home country, as what we would call a medical assistant. She was trying to get certified to continue working in America, but she kept failing the exams.

"I was very good at my job," she said sadly. "And I *know* the right answers, but when I get there to take the test, I can't concentrate and my mind goes blank."

I told her that earthbound spirits can often have exactly that kind of influence over people, enough to make them uneasy or nervous and so prone to making mistakes. At this point, the ghost started to laugh, not in a humorous way like someone just told a good joke, but in a mean way, like she'd just pulled off a prank meant to humiliate someone.

"Are you doing this?" I said to the ghost. She stopped laughing instantly and looked down. No one likes to be caught being mean. "Look," I said to her. "You obviously have something to work out with Lala, so why don't you tell me your name and we can set it straight?"

The ghost looked up at me grudgingly, then finally said, "Vespa."

I asked Lala if the name Vespa meant anything to her and she gasped and shook her head. "No, no," she said. "It can't be Aunt Vespa! She would never do this to me. She was older than mother, like a second grandmother to me!"

After some more personal questions to make sure the ghost wasn't lying, Lala had to finally accept that it was her "second grandmother." At first, Vespa had seemed very bitter and angry, almost jealous. I didn't think it had anything to do with Renni, although that was the excuse—that Lala had married the wrong man. I got the impression that she was more jealous that Lala had found a way to move to America, leaving everyone else behind.

They did manage to make up, and Vespa even apologized. I asked Lala if there were any last-minute things she wanted to know because I was about to make the White Light and send Vespa on her way.

"There is one last thing," Lala admitted. "My roast lamb never comes out right. Can she tell me how she cooked hers? It was always so good!"

Thankfully, Vespa was more than happy to share her recipe.

ROAST LAMB IN WINE

3–4 pounds breast of lamb
2 tablespoons butter, divided
1 onion, sliced
2 carrots, diced
½ celery root, diced
½ parsley root, diced
1 leek
1–2 stalks celery with leaves
Salt and black pepper to taste
2 cups soup stock
1½ cups dry white wine
1 tablespoon all-purpose flour
3 egg yolks

▶ Sear meat in 1 tablespoon butter in a large pot; add onion, carrots, celery and parsley roots, leek, celery stalks and leaves, salt, and pepper. Braise, tightly covered, adding soup stock a little at a time, for 1 hour. Add white wine and simmer for 1 hour. Remove meat and cut into pieces.

Melt remaining 1 tablespoon butter in a small bowl; stir in flour, adding a little pan sauce and stirring to dissolve lumps. Stir butter mixture into sauce. Return meat to pot. Lightly beat egg yolks in a small bowl, adding a little pan sauce, 1 spoonful at a time, so eggs will not curdle. Stir egg mixture into pan sauce and serve immediately. Sauce should be thick and have a distinct wine flavor.

RUB-DOWN CHICKEN

Wayne was worried about the kids in the apartment block. It wasn't a big block, only eight units, but it was owned by the university in town and all the residents were college kids. He was concerned that they didn't eat well—mostly chips and bologna and those flavored noodles you just add water to. Cheap food—cheap and unhealthy. By the looks of him, Wayne didn't have room to talk.

"That's how I died," he admitted. "I didn't eat right, and it killed me."

Lydia had called me originally to come out and see if there was anyone in the building. I told her that, living in an apartment block, she could count on it. What intrigued me the most was that she and the other residents had all smelled food cooking, even when none of them was cooking, and it always smelled like chicken. Now, spirits that have crossed over will often make their presence known with a smell, usually a fragrance they always wore—something that would remind people of them—but I'd never heard of a spirit using food, certainly not one who hadn't crossed over. Earthbound spirits, if they brought a smell, usually smelled like rotten eggs or backed-up sewers.

"No, no," Lydia said. "This smells *really* good. I mean, we get together and cook every once in a while, but we smell this when we aren't cooking, and it smells *so* good!"

When I got out there, the building was relatively full of ghosts, as I had expected. There

were about five or six of them, feeding off the high energy and stress of the college kids. Most of the ghosts were benign. A couple had been causing problems, scaring people and dragging their energy down, which made them sick, but they were all happy to cross over. Wayne held back, though. He didn't look mean, but he clearly had something he wanted to say first, which is when he told me he was worried about the kids.

"Is that you making the food smells?" I asked him.

"Yes. It's my mother's rub-down chicken. These kids should eat it—it'd be good for them."

Wayne had worked in a fast-food restaurant that had been at the location where the apartment block now stood. It had been torn down to put up the apartments, but not soon enough for Wayne. He'd eaten fast food exclusively, and he swore it had killed him. He was very overweight and said he'd been diabetic, so I couldn't argue with him.

"I just think they should eat that chicken," he said again.

"Do you have the recipe?" He nodded and gave it to me, and I had to laugh.

"Wayne, there's a *ton* of butter in this recipe—are you sure this is any better than what they're eating now?"

"The butter cooks out!" he protested. I could tell this was his private solution—his way to make some small amends before he crossed

There were about five or six of them, feeding off the high energy and stress of the college kids. Most of the ghosts were benign. A couple had been causing problems, scaring people and dragging their energy down, which made them sick.

over—so I passed it along to Lydia and told her what Wayne had said.

"Where would I get oiled paper?" Lydia wondered, looking over the recipe.

"You can use butcher paper," Wayne said to me. "That's what I did. Or foil would work, too, probably."

Lydia said she'd give it a whirl, and Wayne finally crossed over.

RUB-DOWN CHICKEN

2 small fryer chickens
Butter
1 clove garlic, chopped
Fresh parsley, finely chopped
Cracker crumbs
Cooking oil

▶ Preheat oven to 350º. Cut small fryers in two. Dot with pieces of butter. Rub chopped garlic and parsley into butter pieces on chicken. Rub chicken with cracker crumbs; dab with more butter. Coat a 14-inch-square piece of parchment paper with oil. Wrap paper around chicken, folding over so steam cannot escape. Put wrapped chicken in a roasting pan with a little oil or water. Bake for about 45 minutes.

SHRIMP-AND-BROCCOLI CASSEROLE FOR TWO

The most memorable thing about Lynn's vacation was what she and her husband, Keith, brought home with them. It wasn't anything particularly exotic—they'd only been to Pensacola, Florida, for their honeymoon—and it wasn't anything as ordinary as a bad sunburn. It was unique, and if Lynn had been able to see her, she certainly would never have let her in the house. The newlyweds had unknowingly brought home a ghost named Lilly—a young, tan, and quite vivacious ghost.

Lilly had followed them all the way home because she liked the look of Keith, and she was trying to get his attention. Her attempts only sapped Keith's energy, however, and he started to experience bad headaches and sleepless nights, which only served to make him more irritable. In fact, he tossed so much at night that Lynn took to sleeping on the couch—which may have been the ghost's plan all along.

Some nights, Keith said, he swore the cat had jumped up on the bed next to him, in Lynn's spot, but when he'd roll over to shoo the cat away, there was nothing there. More often than not, he'd also see Lynn walking by out in the hallway—it seemed like every time he woke up, she'd walk by in one direction or the other. Except Lynn said she'd slept quite comfortably all night on the couch and hadn't gotten up once.

Soon enough, Lilly decided to share her attention, perhaps deciding that her best shot was not to go after Keith directly, but to get rid of the competition. One morning, as Lynn was sitting in the kitchen reading the paper, she heard Keith walk into the room behind her.

"You want breakfast?" she asked casually, but he didn't reply. She turned to see why he was being so quiet and found the room empty. While she was turned around, a mug fell from the counter behind her and smashed on the floor. She shrieked and jumped, expecting to see the cat looking back at her nonchalantly, and though the cat was there, it was not looking nonchalant. It was staring with wide eyes at the air near the counter, far away from where the mug had fallen. Keith came running into the kitchen at that moment to see what had happened.

"We need to talk," Lynn decided evenly. So they did, and they found their stories similar and eerie. In fact, the whole time they chatted they both swore they could *feel* someone watching them.

When I got there and told them who it was, where she came from, and why she was there, Lynn was understandably indignant.

"Who does she think she is?" she protested. "I mean, what does she have to say for herself?"

Lilly looked guilty and offered a weak apology. Her husband had been a driver at the race track they'd visited while they were in Florida, and he'd died in a crash there. After the accident, she'd been so distraught and lost that

Some nights, Keith said, he swore the cat had jumped up on the bed next to him, in Lynn's spot, but when he'd roll over to shoo the cat away, there was nothing there. More often than not, he'd also see Lynn walking by out in the hallway.

she'd taken her own life. When she saw Keith, she said, she just "took a shine" to him.

"I didn't really mean anything by it," she explained. "I loved my husband, but since I was stuck here, and Keith sort of reminded me of him . . . you know, they both love shrimp."

"Pardon?" I checked. "Shrimp?"

"Yes," Lilly agreed. "Keith loves shrimp and so did my husband. Lynn's always trying to find new shrimp recipes so she doesn't have to make the same thing over and over—she's very good to him." She stopped for a second to think about something, then nodded and said, "You know, I have a recipe for a shrimp casserole that my husband just *loved*. Can I give it to you?"

And so she did!

SHRIMP-AND-BROCCOLI CASSEROLE FOR TWO

1 package frozen broccoli, cooked
1 small onion, chopped
2 tablespoons chopped fresh parsley
¼ teaspoon basil
¼ teaspoon dill seeds
¼ teaspoon marjoram
3 tablespoons French dressing
½ cup ketchup
2 tablespoons lemon juice
1 pound shrimp, cooked and cleaned
Salt, pepper, and paprika to taste
2 tablespoons butter, cut into tiny pieces
3 tablespoons sherry
3 tablespoons grated American cheese

▶ Preheat oven to 350º. In a baking dish, arrange a border of cooked broccoli. Combine onion, parsley, basil, dill, marjoram, and French dressing in a small bowl; pour over broccoli. Stir together ketchup and lemon juice; toss shrimp to coat with ketchup mixture. Sprinkle with salt, pepper, and paprika, and place in center of baking dish. Dot shrimp with butter pieces. Sprinkle sherry and cheese over top. Bake, uncovered, for about 30 minutes.

SMOTHERED ROAST BEEF WITH MADEIRA SAUCE

I can't count how many "imaginary friends" of kids I've been asked about only to discover that "invisible friends" might be the better term, because they're far from imaginary. Children seem to see and hear ghosts pretty well, but they learn to ignore them because the grown-ups keep telling them to stop making things up or stop being silly. Wendy and her husband, Tom, didn't do that with their daughter, Katie. What worried them—and what made Wendy call—was that Katie's imaginary friend was a woman, a "grown-up," named Lana.

Katie was 8 years old, and she spent a lot of time out in her playhouse in the backyard, cooking with this imaginary friend. Katie's playhouse was bigger and more elaborate than some actual houses I've seen! Well, not quite, but it was designed as a miniature of the family's real house, and it even had running water to a little kitchen that also had a little fridge in it (one of those small fridges most college kids have in their dorm rooms). It was no surprise that Katie loved playing out there!

Katie had actually had imaginary friends before, which is why it didn't bother her parents at first. Right around when she started kindergarten, they all seemed to go away, and her parents assumed the phase was over. But recently, they'd come back—or rather one had, this woman named Lana.

Lana was real and she was a grown-up. She was very pretty, with long blonde hair and a beautiful flowing white dress. A little girl wouldn't have to use any imagination to think she was a princess—or an angel. In fact, Lana actually used that to her advantage. When she'd first started hanging out with Katie, she pretended to be an angel.

"You didn't!" I admonished her.

"Well, I didn't actually say I *was* an angel," Lana clarified.

"But you didn't say you weren't either?" I assumed. Lana just looked down at her feet with guilt. I have to be honest, I was not a fan of this ghost at all. She was clearly manipulative and had told Katie that she wasn't allowed to tell anyone about her; that she was Katie's secret. It's never right to tell a child she has to keep a secret like that, especially from her parents. After getting the whole story from Katie and Lana, I knew this was one ghost I would have to get to cross over one way or another.

"So why are you here?" I asked her, no longer even pretending to be polite. "What do you want with this little girl?"

"She reminds me so much of my Betsy," Lana explained. "My daughter, Betsy. We both died in a car crash."

"So why did you stay? Why didn't you go into the Light to be with your daughter?"

"I didn't see her there," Lana replied.

That was my hook, then. I assured her that children rarely stayed earthbound because they had guardian angels—*real* angels, I added pointedly—who helped them, so if she really wanted to see Betsy, she had to cross over.

Now, this whole time Katie had been watching us talk. She could see and hear Lana just as well as I could, but she couldn't hear what I was saying to Lana because I was just thinking the words. But once Lana agreed she would cross over, Katie started to protest.

"Who's going to cook with me now?" Katie wailed. Wendy was dumbfounded. She said they cooked all the time.

"Not *packaged* food," Katie said. "Miss Lana and I make *real* food!" No one pointed out to her that the "real" food she cooked with Lana was actually completely imaginary, out in a fake kitchen with a fake stove. Instead, Wendy asked her daughter what she liked cooking with Lana and told her they could make it when Lana was gone.

"How about roast beef?" Katie suggested, her face lighting up. The little girl was clearly still her mother's child, despite Lana's influence.

Wendy sort of grimaced and looked at me. "I don't know how to make roast beef," she admitted. "I'm not even sure I have it in a cookbook!"

"Look," Lana said, "I have a recipe I can give her, if she'll take it."

Thankfully, Lana did cross over. Katie was sad, but once everything was explained to her, she was happy that Betsy would get to see her mommy again.

SMOTHERED ROAST BEEF

3–4 pounds rib roast, boned
2 tablespoons butter
½ cup soup stock
¾ cup Madeira or ½ cup red wine
Salt and pepper to taste
Pinch of marjoram
1 tablespoon all-purpose flour
Madeira Sauce (recipe below)

▶ Sear meat on all sides in 2 tablespoons butter in a large skillet. Stir in soup stock, ¾ cup Madeira, salt, pepper, and marjoram; simmer, tightly covered, for at least 2 hours or until meat is tender. Sprinkle in 1 tablespoon flour. Cook, basting and stirring occasionally, for a few minutes or until pan sauce is thickened. Slice roast thin, and serve with Madeira Sauce.

MADEIRA SAUCE

2 tablespoons butter
2½ tablespoons all-purpose flour
1½ cups beef broth
½ cup Madeira
Salt to taste
Freshly ground black pepper to taste

▶ Melt 2 tablespoons butter over low heat. Add 2½ tablespoons flour and stir until smooth. Stir in broth slowly and cook until thickened. Stir in ½ cup Madeira, salt, and pepper; simmer for 5 minutes.

TAMALE CASSEROLE

Bertha had been dead for about seven years by the time Inez called me out to her house, but she still hadn't reached that despondence I see in so many ghosts. Bertha attributed that to the fact that she liked Inez and her young boys, Charlie and Joey.

"But you're scaring them," I pointed out. Inez told me that the boys kept seeing a woman in the house, usually in the kitchen. One time Charlie had even thought he smelled food cooking. They were afraid to go upstairs alone, and a team of wild horses couldn't have dragged them down to the basement. Bertha shrugged apologetically but didn't actually apologize. Her expression was the same one I imagine she'd wear at a surprise party, waiting for the guest of honor to show up. She looked happy and expectant somehow.

"Say 'tamale tamale tamale' to Inez," Bertha urged me, chuckling a bit.

"Okay," I replied hesitantly, turning to Inez. "There is a woman here. And she wants to say 'tamale tamale tamale' to you."

"Oh my *good*ness!" Inez gasped with excitement. "Bertha?" Bertha grinned widely and nodded emphatically.

"That's her," I said. "So you knew her?"

"Sure I did!" Inez answered. "She was a cook at the boys' school."

"That would explain why she's wearing a hairnet and apron," I mentioned, but Inez was on a roll.

"I volunteer there all the time—it's a private school—and Bertha and I used to chat a lot. She was only 45 when she died. It was quite sad. Never married."

Bertha's expression darkened briefly, but she managed to smile again. "I never needed anyone," she explained proudly. "I had all those kids at the school—why would I need my own? Of course, Inez was the only mother who was ever nice to me."

"She used to give me the best recipes to try at home," Inez said.

"Then ask her about the tamale casserole," Bertha shot back. "Ask her why she never made that, if they were all so good!"

I asked Inez for her, and Inez laughed out loud. "I lost the recipe!" she cried. "I wanted to make it, but I just couldn't find it! And you'd already given it to me twice!"

"I'll give it to her again," Bertha said. "This time she better not lose it!"

I told Bertha I'd only pass along the recipe if she promised to cross over when I made the White Light. She readily agreed. In fact, I got the impression she may have been hanging out for no other reason than to make sure Inez made that tamale casserole one way or another!

They were afraid to go upstairs alone, and a team of wild horses couldn't have dragged them down to the basement. Bertha shrugged apologetically but didn't actually apologize. Her expression was the same one I imagine she'd wear at a surprise party, waiting for the guest of honor to show up.

TAMALE CASSEROLE

2 pounds ground chuck
1 large onion, chopped
1 (16-ounce) can whole tomatoes
1 (16-ounce) can whole-kernel corn, drained
2 tablespoons chili powder
Salt and black pepper to taste
1 (6-ounce) can pitted black olives, drained
3 cups milk
2 cups cornmeal
Butter
1 cup grated cheddar cheese

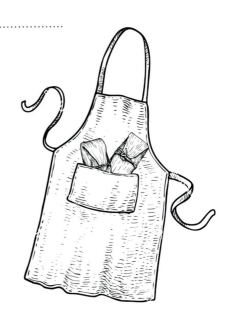

▶ Preheat oven to 325º. Cook meat and onion in a large skillet over medium heat until meat crumbles and is no longer pink. Stir in tomatoes, corn, chili powder, salt, and pepper; reduce heat and simmer for 30 minutes. Remove from heat and add olives. Cook milk and cornmeal in a large saucepan until thickened. Spread cornmeal mixture on bottom and sides of a greased (with butter) 3-quart baking dish. Add meat mixture; top with cheese. Bake for 30 minutes.

TOLEDO LEBANESE MEATBALLS

Remodeling a house can often increase any ghostly activity. You might have had a ghost with you for years and not noticed it, then suddenly when you start to remodel, things start to happen. In some cases, the remodeling actually offends the earthbound spirit, but in other cases it just disturbs it. The latter is what happened to Agnes and Arnie.

The couple had bought a home in an old ethnic neighborhood in Toledo, Ohio. Like most cities of a certain size and age, Toledo had ethnic communities that had slowly faded away and fallen into disrepair. Agnes and Arnie were in their 50s, without children, so they were more concerned about finding a nice home they could fix up and use to entertain than they were about good schools. The neighborhood they ended up in had once been the "Little Lebanon" of Toledo, though by now it was a mixed bag of ethnicities and the city was offering incentives to have it revitalized.

Agnes told me she had never felt like she was alone in the house, but she wrote it off to being in a new home in a new neighborhood—just that generally unsettled feeling you always get after a move. She started to wonder more about it when they began to remodel and nothing would go right. Shelves would end up so crooked it seemed impossible, accidents would cause whole panels of new drywall to be replaced, and carefully cut counters or cabinets would end up just a bit too wide or otherwise unusable.

Agnes didn't call me, however, until they heard a woman crying. Not the loud, ghostly wails of a Hollywood movie, but the distinct, quiet sobs of someone crying to herself in private. When I got there, I discovered a woman named Leena who had not crossed over. Leena was Lebanese and had lived in the house her whole life. She'd never married and, being the end of her family line, had been left caring first for her grandmother and then for her mother as they aged and died.

Leena had been upset by the remodeling. She thought it looked quite nice, but she was sure her mother and grandmother would disapprove, which upset her. It wasn't enough to make her stay, though, not now that I was there and could help her cross over. Her only other gripe was the cooking Agnes did when she entertained.

"I guess she thinks herself a great cook," Leena said dismissively. "But she just makes hors d'oeuvres and finger food." She paused and rolled her eyes, "And her Swedish meatballs are horrible! She calls them her specialty, but *nothing* is as good as real Lebanese meatballs."

"I'd like to test that theory and see how they stack up to *Italian* meatballs," I told her with a laugh. She chuckled and gave me the recipe, then said that she wanted to do something

Agnes told me she had never felt like she was alone in the house, but she wrote it off to being in a new home in a new neighborhood—just that generally unsettled feeling you always get after a move. She started to wonder more about it.

for Agnes and Arnie, to pay them back for the trouble she'd caused.

"There's a secret room in the basement," she said. "They haven't found it yet, even with all the changes they've made."

So I took Agnes and Arnie with me, and we all followed Leena into the basement. She explained to me where it was and how to access it. The room was really just a big closet where they'd hidden away valuables, and there were still several boxes of jewelry in there.

"They can have it all," Leena said. "It was mostly my mother's and grandmother's, but they're both long gone, and there's no one else left in the family to give it to."

Sometimes you get more than a recipe out of earthbound spirits!

TOLEDO LEBANESE MEATBALLS

½ cup chopped onion
3 tablespoons butter, divided
1 pound ground beef
1 egg, beaten
2 slices bread, soaked in ½ cup milk
1 teaspoon salt
1/8 teaspoon black pepper
1 cup dry breadcrumbs
2 cups plain yogurt
Hot cooked rice or wheat pilaf

▶ Sauté chopped onion in 1 tablespoon butter in a large skillet over medium heat until transparent; cool. Combine onion, meat, egg, bread, salt, and pepper in a large bowl. Shape meat mixture into 1¼-inch balls (or smaller for hors d'oeuvres), then roll in breadcrumbs.

Brown meatballs slowly in remaining 2 tablespoons butter in same skillet over medium heat. Drain off all but 2 tablespoons fat. Gently spoon yogurt over and around meatballs. Simmer for 20 minutes. Serve hot with rice or wheat pilaf.

VEAL SCHNITZEL

I am often amazed at how the smallest of injustices can make people stay behind instead of crossing over. That's one of the reasons I do so many public talks: to try and educate people about what I've learned of life after death and how you really do just have to let go of this plane of existence when the time comes. Once you cross over, you can move much more freely between planes, though I really don't think you'll want to.

My own grandmother Maria could also see and talk to spirits, but unlike me, she could only communicate in dreams and only then with spirits that had crossed over. The one thing that my grandma told me over and over that I should tell any earthbound spirits I came across is that, once you cross over, you no longer care about the petty little problems that seem to be calling you to stay on our plane. You can find the peace and tranquility that you'd expect.

Bert had never received this message, however. Or if he had, he'd ignored it. Bert stayed earthbound because his friend Stella had stolen his recipe for veal schnitzel. You read that right: He gave up the peace and tranquility of crossing over—not to mention the chance to reunite with all of his deceased friends and family—because a friend was going around claiming credit for a recipe.

I ran across Bert in Chicago while visiting some friends, Charlene and Arnie. They also had some friends from Europe in town for a visit, so they'd put together a small dinner party for all of us. Stella and Frank were the couple from Europe, but unbeknownst to them, there were three in their party because Bert, the ghost, came right along with them.

When I'm in a situation like that, I usually keep my mouth shut. We were all there for dinner and company, not to talk about ghosts. Charlene's house is on the lake overlooking Navy Pier, and it was a beautiful night—I was not going to spoil it by asking Stella and Frank who could be attached to them. Bert had other plans, though.

About halfway through the meal, Stella suddenly asked Charlene if we were eating her recipe for veal schnitzel, and Charlene admitted that we were. Then Bert started yelling and shouting and doing everything he could to be heard, screaming, "That's *not* her recipe! That's *my* recipe! She took that recipe from me!"

Fortunately, when I speak to earthbound spirits, it's all mental for me, so I don't actually have to talk out loud. I looked at Bert and asked him to stop screaming about the recipe. He froze in mild shock, then pretty quickly recovered.

"You can see me?" he said and walked right over to me and gave me an earful about how Stella took his veal schnitzel recipe and had been going around ever since telling everyone it was her recipe.

"This is a pretty unique recipe," I said aloud to Stella. "Usually schnitzel has eggs on top—"

At that moment, both Stella and Bert said at the same time, "Fried eggs are for breakfast." Bert gave me a told-you-so look, so I thought I'd try and get her to admit it.

"Where did you get the recipe?" I asked her, and she sort of clammed up and sat up straight.

"It's not to share, if that's what you're asking. It's my secret recipe."

I wanted to point out that she'd obviously shared it with Charlene, but Bert was screaming about it being his recipe again, so I thought I'd have a little fun.

"Maybe I can guess it," I said to Stella, then added silently to Bert, "Tell me the recipe, so I can repeat it out loud." Bert grinned and told me what was in it, and I repeated it aloud for everyone to hear. Stella's face dropped, and her mouth opened wider and wider.

"How did you do that?" she gasped when I was done.

I shrugged. "Oh, you know, I like to eat."

After Stella and Frank had left, Charlene jumped on me: "How did you get that recipe? Who's here?" So I told her the story of Bert, and Charlene said that what he'd told me was actually a little bit different from the recipe Stella had given her.

"Stella probably gave it to you wrong on purpose," I suggested. "People get really hung up on their 'secret' recipes!"

VEAL SCHNITZEL

4 veal cutlets

6 tablespoons butter, divided

1 cup beef stock

10 medium-size fresh mushrooms, sliced

6 eggs

1 tablespoon chopped chives

1 teaspoon salt

¼ teaspoon black pepper

▶ Pound veal cutlets thin. Sauté veal in 4 tablespoons butter in a large skillet over medium heat until golden on both sides and cooked through. Remove veal to a warmed serving dish; keep warm.

Stir stock into pan gravy, and cook until smooth and slightly thickened; keep warm. Sauté mushrooms in remaining 2 tablespoons butter in a separate large skillet for about 4 minutes. Beat eggs with chopped chives, salt, and pepper. Stir egg mixture into mushrooms. Cook over medium heat, stirring like scrambled eggs, until done. Pour egg mixture over cutlets.

And that was the weirdest thing of all. She didn't want anything, really. There was no forgotten will or hidden treasure. There were no loose ends—her health had declined quite quickly after she got an infection after a fall, but not so quickly as to leave anything unsaid.

—Almond Soup

 # DESSERTS

ALMOND SOUP

"Pink Grandma needs to talk to Grandma downstairs," little Meg said to her mom one day.

"What did you say, honey?" Peggy wondered, a chill creeping up her back and tickling her neck. The hair on her arms even bristled. She hadn't heard the phrase "Pink Grandma" since she was her daughter's age—since she was 7 herself.

"That's what she said," Meg said evenly, not too concerned and not picking up on her mother's fear. "The lady over there said to tell you that Pink Grandma needs to talk to Grandma downstairs."

Peggy took her daughter's hand without another word and led her downstairs to her parents' apartment. The two families split a house, with Peggy and her daughter on the second floor and Peggy's parents living on the first floor. Her parents were always home, and today was no different, so Peggy and Meg went right in, and Peggy told her mom what Meg had just said.

"Pink Grandma?" Peggy's mom, Margaret, repeated. "But that's what you and your sister called *my* mother."

"I know," Peggy agreed. It was something the girls had come up with to differentiate between their mother's mother and their father's mother: Pink Grandma for mother's mother and Blue Grandma for father's.

"Do you call me that to Meg?" Margaret wondered; Peggy shook her head no.

"I haven't said that for 20 years, not since she died."

"Don't worry," Margaret said reassuringly. "I know who to call."

It never fails to amaze me how frightened some people are to think that their relatives are haunting them. I'm sure any haunting is unnerving, but you'd think that when you were given proof that it was just a loved one, that would make it better. Well, it didn't make it any better for Peggy, but then that might have been nothing more than a mother's protection kicking in.

"She has been here for *months*," Peggy explained to me dramatically. "At least, I've heard little Meg talking to someone for some time now."

Sure enough, when I looked over to where Meg was coloring, I could see her gazing off into the distance, but she wasn't lost in thought. As I watched Meg, I could see that she was watching Pink Grandma—and I could also see that there was nothing sinister about the ghost. In fact, she was very conscientious. I think she'd been around for much longer than just a few months because she explained to me how she knew she should have left when she noticed Meg getting sick or more grumpy than usual. Pink Grandma knew it was because of her, because she was draining the girl's energy just with her presence.

"But look at her," Pink Grandma offered lovingly. "Wouldn't you want to be with that little angel?"

"Yes, I would," I agreed. "It also helps that she's the only one who can see and hear you."

"Well . . ." she stalled bashfully. "Maybe."

"So why's she here?" Peggy wanted to know. "What does she want?"

And that was the weirdest thing of all. She didn't want anything, really. There was no forgotten will or hidden treasure. There were no loose ends—her health had declined quite quickly after she got an infection after a fall, but not so quickly as to leave anything unsaid. No, she had hung around because no one else knew how to make her almond soup, and she wanted to make sure someone had the recipe. She was also adamant that only Margaret should make it.

"Almond soup?" Peggy asked incredulously. "She's haunting us over a soup recipe?"

"Hey," I replied. "Not all hauntings are like you see in the movies. In fact, most of them are over pretty boring things, like almond soup."

Peggy didn't like that any better, and she urged me to take down the recipe and get rid of the ghost. Of course, once I'd given the recipe to Margaret, Pink Grandma was quite willing to step into the Light and move on.

ALMOND SOUP

½ pound sweet almonds
10 bitter almonds
7 cups milk
Granulated sugar to taste
½ cup cooked white rice
2 tablespoons seedless raisins

▶ Blanch and peel almonds. Grind or chop them, and then mash to a paste with a little milk. Put through a fine sieve, using a little hot milk to help with the process. Scald remaining milk, then combine with almond paste and stir thoroughly. Add sugar to taste and let mixture bubble up once. Add cooked rice and raisins, and serve immediately.

BANANA PIE WITH ORANGE CRUST

Ted and I often spend a few weeks every winter on Marco Island in Florida. A friend of ours has a condo down there that we use, and we love it. The island is basically a retirement community, and they do practically roll up the sidewalks at 8 p.m. It's very quiet, very relaxing, and the perfect place to get away from the cabin fever of an Ohio winter.

We've been vacationing there for years, so we've become acquainted with the owners of the restaurants we frequent most often. At one spot in particular, the owner, Peggy, always makes an effort to walk over to our table and chat with us. This was the case one of the last times we were down there, and she came over to tell us that we had to try a special dessert that they rarely made but currently had available. It was from a recipe they'd inherited with the restaurant from the previous owners.

"It's a banana pie with orange crust," Peggy said. Ted's eyes got wide and he started licking his lips—that was right up his alley. I'm not a huge fan of sweets myself, so as she described the pie, my thoughts wandered and my eyes drifted over the room. Restaurants usually have many earthbound spirits in them, simply for the fact that there are so many people who work and eat at them. As I looked around, though, I saw one ghost in particular who seemed very interested in what Peggy was saying. He was a smaller man who had come out of the kitchen when she started talking about

the pie; then he hovered around us as she went to get Ted a piece.

Ted tried the pie and loved it. In fact, he wanted the recipe, which doesn't often happen, so when Peggy came back to see how it was, I asked her if she'd give us the recipe. I figured it obviously wasn't a signature dish, since she said they rarely made it, and we lived in Ohio, besides, so it wasn't like we'd be able to compete, even if we did own a restaurant.

But Peggy just shook her head. "No, I don't think I can," she explained. "It's one of our specialties."

"Was it a secret recipe?" I guessed, since most restaurants don't serve their specialties only rarely. Peggy shook her head no.

"I've seen it in cookbooks, actually. Well, *versions* of it, but not the same one, exactly. This one was given to us by Bernie, who worked here with the previous owners."

Now as she was speaking, I saw this small male ghost still hovering about us, and he rolled his eyes and started shaking his head in disbelief. I let our conversation with Peggy end; then when she walked off, I looked at the ghost.

"Are you Bernie?" I guessed. He looked mildly surprised but quickly recomposed himself.

"Yes, yes I am."

"So that was your recipe?"

"No, not really," he admitted. "She doesn't make it right. I can give you the *real* recipe, if

Restaurants usually have many earthbound spirits in them, simply for the fact that there are so many people who work and eat at them. As I looked around, though, I saw one ghost in particular who seemed very interested in what Peggy was saying.

you want, then you can give it to whoever you want. Secret!" he laughed. "It was never a secret when I made it! The secret is that she *changed* it! And made it worse," he added with a wink.

I took down the recipe and asked Bernie if he was ready to cross over. He actually declined; he wanted to stay and watch the business some more. The funny thing is, the next time we were down there the restaurant had changed hands again, but Bernie was still there. When he saw us come in, he came right over to us.

"Are you ready to cross over now?" I guessed. He smiled widely and nodded.

"Did you like the pie?" he asked before he left.

"It was delicious," I assured him. "Better than Peggy's, just like you said!"

BANANA PIE WITH ORANGE CRUST

CRUST
1 cup sifted all-purpose flour
½ teaspoon salt
1 tablespoon granulated sugar
2 teaspoons grated orange rind
⅓ cup shortening
3 tablespoons fresh orange juice

FILLING
2 ripe bananas
1 cup granulated sugar
⅛ teaspoon salt
½ teaspoon lemon juice
2 egg whites
Whipped cream

▶ Preheat oven to 500º. To make crust, combine flour, ½ teaspoon salt, 1 tablespoon sugar, and orange rind in a large bowl. Cut in shortening. Reserve ⅓ cup flour mixture. Add fresh orange juice to remaining flour mixture; stir until a soft dough forms. Roll dough out into a circle on a lightly floured surface; fit into a 9-inch pie plate, and prick with a fork. Bake for 10 minutes; let cool.

Reduce oven temperature to 350º. To make filling, mash bananas in a large bowl until a liquid consistency is reached. Add 1 cup sugar, ⅛ teaspoon salt, and lemon juice. Beat egg whites until stiff, and then fold into banana mixture. Transfer filling into cooled piecrust. Top with reserved flour mixture. Bake for about 25 minutes. Cool and serve with whipped cream.

BOILED CAKE

Selma had been caring for her 8-year-old granddaughter, Lindsey, since the girl was 4. She never told me why, and I didn't think it right to pry. When Selma called, she made it clear that she was calling out of concern for Lindsey, as her religious upbringing made it hard for her to believe. I just went along with her, not wanting to get into a discussion on the numbers of priests I've helped in my day. It wasn't that important to prove myself to her, when what she was really trying to say was how deep her concern for her granddaughter was.

"What's been happening?" I asked. Selma explained that she was one of the parish cooks, who worked at the church and made all their bake-sale wares and the pierogies to sell and whatnot. She explained that Lindsey always went down to the church with her and usually sat coloring or drawing quite happily.

"But lately," Selma said. "She's been talking to someone."

"Like an imaginary friend?" I guessed. Kids often have imaginary friends, and in my experience, as often as they really are imaginary, they are also earthbound spirits.

"Lindsey's always had imaginary friends," Selma said. "This is different."

"How so?"

Selma paused, and I could tell she was gathering the words to explain something she didn't herself believe—or, more likely, didn't *want* to believe.

"The other day," Selma explained. "Lindsey said, 'Grandma, the lady standing over there wants to know why you don't make the boiled cake anymore.' Well, we laughed it off, of course—you don't *boil* cake, we told her, you *bake* it. But she just shook her head and said, 'No, the lady says you boil it. Her name is Verna.'"

One of the other women in the kitchen got really quiet at that point and told everyone to stop laughing for a second. This woman, Loretta, went over and asked Lindsey what the lady's name was again.

"Verna," Lindsey said.

"That's right," Loretta replied, looking around at her friends with wide eyes. "Verna used to work with me here, and she did make a boiled cake."

"With only fresh currants," Lindsey added. Loretta nodded, and Selma called me.

Now, I've said it before and I'll say it again: Kid ghosts playing with kids is one thing, but grown-up ghosts bothering kids is just a bit weird, bordering on mean. Adult ghosts haunting children will always get me to come out and see what's going on.

When I got to the church, it was exactly as Lindsey had told them: Verna, one of the old cooks, was there, and she was telling me she had a recipe for boiled cake. With Lindsey there, who could see Verna as well, the ladies really didn't need me to take down the recipe,

I just went along with her, not wanting to get into a discussion on the numbers of priests I've helped in my day. It wasn't that important . . . when what she was really trying to say was how deep her concern for her granddaughter was.

but I was able to help Verna cross over, so it was certainly not a wasted trip.

"Do you see other ghosts?" I asked Lindsey. She nodded.

"Not here at church, but a lot at school. They don't bother anyone, though."

"That's good," I told her. "And just so you know, they can't hurt you, okay?"

I only hoped she'd have the same kind of support for her abilities that I did growing up. It's a rare and special talent, and I'd hate to see it suppressed. Selma seemed quite convinced, though, and I had a feeling she was the kind of grandmother who would nourish and help Lindsey's talents, no matter how strange they seemed to her.

Selma also now believed in boiled cake!

BOILED CAKE

2 cups granulated sugar

2 cups water

2 cups raisins

2 cups currants

1 cup butter

1 teaspoon cloves

1 teaspoon cinnamon

1 teaspoon baking soda

3 cups all-purpose flour

▶ Preheat oven to 350º. Stir together sugar, 2 cups water, raisins, currants, butter, cloves, cinnamon, and baking soda in a large saucepan. Bring to a boil; remove from heat and let cool. Stir in flour. Transfer mixture to a well-greased (with butter), floured 9x12-inch baking pan. Bake for 1 hour.

BROWN SUGAR REFRIGERATOR COOKIES AND CREAM CHEESE COOKIES

Long before the mass-produced cookie brands started selling "ready to bake" cookies in tubes, mothers and grandmothers had been doing the same thing for generations. They called them "refrigerator cookies" because you'd mix all the ingredients together and have the cookie dough ready to bake—but instead of making two dozen cookies right then, you'd roll up the dough and put it in the fridge. Then, when you wanted fresh cookies, you'd just cut off enough dough for as many as you wanted and pop them in the oven for a few minutes. That way, you always served cookies that were fresh from the oven.

Carl remembered those cookies well. Whenever he went to his grandmother's house as a kid, she'd always have fresh cookies. Sometimes he'd even help cut them off the roll and put them on the baking sheet.

"In fact, I think the ghost must be an old woman," he said. His wife, Lori, rolled her eyes. Usually, it's the man who's the skeptic, but in this family, it was the wife.

"Why do you think that?"

"Because I keep smelling that liniment smell, just like Grandma used to have. She had arthritis, and she used to rub that liniment on her elbows and knees." I knew exactly what he meant—that strong smell you get from rubbing lotions for muscle or joint pain—and

by the look on her face, Lori knew what he meant too.

"Lori, have you smelled anything?" I asked her. She sighed and nodded slowly.

"Yes. I know what he means. I always seem to smell it when I bake. At holidays, when I do a lot of baking, it gets really bad. But only ever in the kitchen." She glanced at her husband for confirmation, and he nodded.

"What else have you noticed?" I asked, and Carl said that small items would go missing, only to turn up days later in odd places.

"But we have two teenage boys," Lori said by way of explanation. "It is likely they're just playing tricks on us."

"Not according to the ghost who's here," I replied. "She says her name is Sadie—was that your grandmother's name, Carl?"

"No," he said thoughtfully. Neither of them could remember ever knowing a woman by the name of Sadie.

"They have my grinder," Sadie offered. "The young lady uses it to grind nuts. It's one of those that you attach to your tabletop. She picked it up down the road at the secondhand shop."

I passed along this information, and Lori's face went white. Between us, reader, I love that moment of realization when the skeptic gets the proof they need to know there really is someone there I'm talking to.

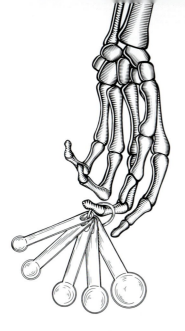

"I know what cookies he's talking about too," Sadie said kindly. "Let me give you the recipe."

I took it down, and Carl looked it over, nodding and smiling as he did so. "Yes! This looks just like the recipe she used to make! She called them Brown Sugar Refrigerator Cookies."

"My grandma's specialty was cream cheese cookies," I offered. "Boy were those good. Carl, do you mind if I copy down that recipe for myself as well?"

Carl had no problem with that, and as I was copying it down for myself, Sadie spoke up again and said that she also had a recipe for cream cheese cookies. She didn't have to ask me twice to take down that one too!

BROWN SUGAR REFRIGERATOR COOKIES

1 cup shortening
1¼ cups brown sugar
2 eggs, well beaten
1 teaspoon almond extract
⅔ cup blanched shredded almonds
3 cups sifted all-purpose flour
2 teapoons baking powder
⅛ teaspoon salt

▶ Cream shortening in a large bowl; gradually add brown sugar. Stir in eggs, almond extract, almonds, flour, baking powder, and salt, mixing well until a soft dough forms. Shape dough into a compact roll and wrap in waxed paper. Chill overnight or until needed.

Preheat oven to 375º. Cut dough into thin slices. Grease baking sheets with shortening. Transfer slices to prepared pans, and bake for 8–10 minutes.

CREAM CHEESE COOKIES

⅓ cup butter
½ cup granulated sugar
2 egg yolks
¼ pound cream cheese
½ cup sour cream
3½ cups sifted all-purpose flour
2 teaspoons baking powder

▶ Cream butter in a large bowl; add sugar and egg yolks, 1 at a time. Mix in cream cheese until mixture is smooth. Stir in sour cream, flour, and baking powder, mixing well until a soft dough forms. Cover dough and chill for 3–4 hours. Preheat oven to 350º to 375º. Roll dough out thin on a lightly floured surface. Cut as desired, and bake on ungreased baking sheets for about 12 minutes.

CHOCOLATE TAPIOCA PUDDING

Earthbound spirits often frighten children because, in our culture, we are raised to believe ghosts are scary. In my experience, very few ghosts are truly scary. I've run across some that are funny-looking or mean, but they're still no more scary than they would have been alive. In fact, they're perhaps less scary, if anything, because they can't physically injure anyone. Still, children in our society are raised to associate ghosts with fear, and so when a child can see and hear spirits just like I can, it can often scare them. This was certainly the case with little Jake, age 5, though the spirit in his house looked anything but frightening. Comical might be a better word to describe him, and that's sort of how he acted: like a clown.

I met Ryan, Jake's father, at his house. When I first started doing this, it was hard to find a man who'd even be in the same room with me, even if they agreed that something odd was happening. Recently, more and more men have been calling for my help. I take that as a good sign. Hopefully, it means our society is becoming more open to the truth I witness firsthand every day.

Ryan was a little freaked out, though. Not so much for himself as for young Jake.

"We like to fish," he explained to me. "I take him out to the pond every so often—there's always people out there fishing—and he has fun trying to cast with his toy rod. But ever since we went out there a few weeks ago, Jake's

been acting kind of funny. He keeps going on about fish eyes and how we're trying to make him eat fish eyes!"

"That is a bit strange," I agreed. "Did anything unusual happen at the pond that day?"

Ryan thought for a few seconds, then nodded slowly. "There was a guy next to us, he caught a huge fish, which is strange for that pond. Jake went over to look at it, and you know what? He said the guy had been talking about eating fish eyes!"

"Interesting," I said. "There is a ghost here, and he's dressed up like a fisherman, complete with the vest, cargo pants, and the floppy hat with lures pinned to it."

"Are you kidding?" Ryan gasped. I shook my head.

"Nope. He says his name's Phil. It was his son who caught that big fish."

"You know, what made me finally call you is because a few weeks ago we were eating tapioca. Jake was loving it, then he suddenly started screaming his head off that we were making him eat fish eyes!"

As Ryan said this, Phil started laughing as if he'd just told the funniest joke ever.

"Did you tell him that?" I asked him angrily.

"Oh, it's fine," he chuckled, waving me off. "It'll toughen him up. I used to tell my own kids the same thing when they ate tapioca!"

"You think that's funny? Scaring a little boy like that?"

I've run across some that are funny-looking or mean, but they're still no more scary than they would have been alive..

Phil's chuckles subsided, and then he shrugged and looked at me sheepishly. "I don't know. I guess my kids didn't find it very funny either." He sighed, then his face brightened and he snapped his fingers. "You know, we can fix this! My youngest boy reacted a lot like that little boy, so I just gave him chocolate tapioca instead of plain; that way, it didn't look like fish eyes anymore. I had to make it myself—it's really easy. Let me give you the recipe."

I took down the recipe and told Ryan what Phil had said. He still wasn't amused, but he took the recipe from me. A few weeks later, he followed up and said that his wife had explained to Jake that calling tapioca "fish eyes" was just like gummy worms: they weren't really worms, they were a treat. Then she'd made the pudding and let Jake help, so he could see that they weren't really fish eyes, and it seemed to work. In fact, now they actually did call it "fish eyes pudding" instead of tapioca.

I imagine Phil's son had been trying to tell Jake that story the day he caught the big fish, but why Phil decided he had to go home with Jake and rub it in is beyond me!

CHOCOLATE TAPIOCA PUDDING

⅓ cup quick-cooking tapioca

2 squares (2 ounces) unsweetened chocolate, cut small

½ cup granulated sugar

¼ teaspoon salt

4 cups milk

1 egg, beaten

1 teaspoon vanilla extract

Whipped cream

▶ Combine tapioca, chocolate, sugar, salt, and milk in upper part of a double boiler. Cook, stirring frequently, for 15 minutes or until tapioca is clear. Gradually add egg, and cook for 3 minutes. Cool slightly; add vanilla. Chill and serve with whipped cream.

CHOCOLATE TORTE

My friend Louise was 40 when she had her first child, so they'd gone all-out for the baby shower, hosting it at an upscale restaurant in Akron, Ohio. I wasn't at all surprised to see earthbound spirits there—between there being 80 guests and it being held in a public restaurant, a few spirits were to be expected. What I didn't expect to see, as I was waiting in line at the buffet, was a pair of ghosts arguing by the dessert table, one of which was Louise's Aunt Meg. I hadn't seen Meg in years, and I wasn't even sure that I knew she'd died, but there she was, arguing quite heatedly with a man I didn't recognize who was dressed like a chef.

As I got closer, I pretended not to see Meg—this wasn't the time or place for me to be talking with Louise's deceased relatives—but she tried to catch my eye, knowing full well what I could do. I won that battle, but as I ate, I could see Meg watching me from across the room. Finally, she wandered over just as if she were still alive and struck up a conversation.

"Meg," I said. "It's good to see you, but you *know* what I always tell people about crossing over when they die, so why are you still here?"

Meg shrugged. "I just don't like to give up control of things, I guess. And I died too young—I wanted to see more of the world."

"So what were you arguing with that chef about?" I asked.

"Oh, he made the chocolate torte all wrong!" she said in a huff. One thing everyone knows

about Louise is how much she loves chocolate, and the torte had been Meg's recipe that they'd asked the pastry chef to make for the shower.

"*He* made it wrong?" I clarified. "The *ghost* you were talking to made the torte wrong?"

"Well, not *him*," Meg replied. "Obviously *he* didn't make it, but his nephew's in the kitchen, and when I commented on it, his uncle started defending him, saying that's how torte is made. He was supposed to use *my* recipe, and that is *not* how you make torte!"

"I hate to say it, Meg, but I tried that torte and it's very good. What could possibly be wrong with it?"

Meg went on to explain how to make it in great detail, even asking me to write it down so I could take it back to the kitchen and show the chef how to make it correctly. The problem, according to Meg, was that he'd used bulk liquid chocolate instead of grated chocolate. That, she said, ruined the whole dessert.

"His name's Davis," she concluded, waving over at the ghost chef. "Go and tell him to make it right!"

"Go and tell the ghost to make the torte?"

"No," she chided me. "They're both named Mr. Davis—go and tell Mr. Davis in the kitchen how to make it right. You have the recipe. . . ."

I grudgingly got up and walked over to the kitchen. The deceased Mr. Davis was standing at the kitchen door, watching his nephew, so I asked him about it, but he wanted nothing to

I wasn't at all surprised to see earthbound spirits there— between there being 80 guests and it being held in a public restaurant, a few spirits were to be expected. What I didn't expect to see . . . was a pair of ghosts arguing by the dessert table.

do with me. "He makes it the right way!" was all he'd say.

Eventually, I did get the pastry chef to speak with me. I told him that I wanted his opinion on an old family recipe. Whether or not he realized it was the same one he'd been given I couldn't say, but he told me he thought it looked quite good. Then I asked him whether it was okay to substitute liquid chocolate for the grated chocolate.

"Well," he admitted. "The grated would be how you'd want to make it, but with groups of this size, I have to use liquid chocolate."

So Aunt Meg was vindicated, and it just goes to show you that modern convenience isn't always the best substitute when a bit of hard work can yield a better taste.

CHOCOLATE TORTE (UNBAKED)

2 sticks butter

2 cups granulated sugar, divided

½ pound bittersweet chocolate, grated

2 cups (½ pound) walnuts or hazelnuts, finely ground

3–4 tablespoons heavy whipping cream

Chocolate Icing (recipe below)

GARNISHES: almonds, candied orange peel, lemon peel

▶ Cream 2 sticks butter in a large bowl. Add 1 cup sugar and ½ pound bittersweet chocolate, and blend thoroughly. Grease a torte pan (with removable bottom) with butter. Transfer chocolate mixture to prepared pan and chill until set. Combine nuts, remaining 1 cup sugar, and cream in a bowl. Remove chocolate base from pan and spread with nut mixture. Spread with Chocolate Icing, and garnish, if desired.

CHOCOLATE ICING

½ pound milk chocolate or bittersweet chocolate

1½ teaspoons butter

1 cup water

▶ Melt ½ pound milk chocolate and 1½ teaspoons butter over low heat; simmer with 1 cup water until a thick syrup is formed. Spread icing on cake while hot.

CREAM CHEESE PIECRUST WITH STRAWBERRIES

Many people assume I'd have a bad relationship with religious figures, such as priests and nuns, but the truth is, many priests actually call me for help. It might be true that some of the smaller religious organizations might not like me because of what I can do, but what I think of as the mainstream churches don't see much wrong. I am quite sure they wouldn't advise their parishioners to seek out and learn abilities like I have, but they understand that if God has decided to bestow those powers on someone, then far be it from them to argue. I have found that priests and nuns are also more understanding simply because they know all these things to be true: They know there is life after death, they know there is an "other side" that has to be crossed over to upon death, and they know that sometimes people don't cross over. So if they know someone can help earthbound entities cross over, they appreciate the help.

For example, years ago I was called to a Catholic convent. The nuns were getting worried because several of them had seen a man in a dark suit walking around the convent—a man they knew shouldn't be there. They were also having a lot of trouble with the appliances in the kitchen not working, and they were just generally feeling uncomfortable. One of the priests who worked with the nuns had called me before, and he suggested they ask me to come out and visit with them.

Sister Naomi was the one who called me, and she and Sister Paula took me on a tour of the convent when I arrived. We purposely made the appointment during school hours, when most of the nuns were in class, teaching, so the convent was mostly empty during the tour. There was a male ghost there, and he certainly had no affiliation to the church or the nuns. In fact, he readily admitted that he was only there because he thought it was "cool" to scare nuns! That was all I needed to hear from him, and in no time he was gone and wouldn't be bothering the nuns anymore. I could tell there was still someone around, though. I could still feel the energy of an earthbound spirit that had not been the man.

Because a lot of the problems had been happening in the kitchen, I asked my tour guides to take me there, and sure enough, there was another ghost. It was a nun, as least to judge by her dress (this order still wore full habits), and she was surely one of the roly-poliest people I've ever seen! She admitted that it was she, not the man, who had been causing the issues in the kitchen. When I told Sister Naomi and Sister Paula that it was a nun and described her to them, they both looked shocked.

"Is it Mena?" Sister Naomi asked.

"Sister *Philo*mena," the ghost corrected, but she chuckled and said that, yes, she was the sister they'd all called Mena.

"Why is she here?" Sister Naomi wondered, still in shock. "Why in the world wouldn't she cross over?"

They know there is life after death, they know there is an "other side" that has to be crossed over to upon death, and they know that sometimes people don't cross over.

Sister Mena explained that she'd stayed because she wanted to watch over her sisters and make sure they ate well after her passing. She felt her staying was justified, too, because they had almost immediately started using substitutes for ingredients instead of the real thing: powdered milk, margarine, even powdered eggs.

"I wanted them to stop cooking until they started cooking like I used to!" she concluded. "Ask them," she added. "Ask them if they miss my cooking!"

"Of course we do!" Sister Naomi and Sister Paula agreed in unison.

"In fact," Sister Paula said. "What we miss most—what the other sisters are *always* going on about—is the cream cheese piecrust she used to make, with strawberries."

"That's as good a place as any to start," Sister Mena decided. "Let me give you the recipe!"

CREAM CHEESE PIECRUST WITH STRAWBERRIES

CRUST
1 stick butter
1 (8-ounce) package cream cheese
2 cups all-purpose flour
¼ teaspoon salt

FILLING
2 pints strawberries
3 tablespoons cornstarch
1 tablespoon water
1 cup granulated sugar
¼ teaspoon salt
1 tablespoon lemon juice
1 tablespoon butter
Whipped cream

▶ Preheat oven to 400º. To make crust, cream 1 stick butter and cream cheese in a large bowl. Stir in flour and ¼ teaspoon salt until mixture forms a soft dough. Roll dough out into a circle on a lightly floured surface; fit into a 9-inch pie plate. Bake for about 10 minutes.

To make filling, arrange enough berries to make 1 layer in cooled crust. Mash remaining berries in a 4-cup glass measuring cup, and add enough water to make 2 cups. Mix cornstarch with 1 tablespoon water in a saucepan. Stir in berry mixture, sugar, ¼ teaspoon salt, lemon juice, and 1 tablespoon butter. Cook over medium heat until thickened. Cool and pour over berries in crust. Spread top with whipped cream before serving.

DOTTIE'S DATE-NUT BARS

Charity called on behalf of her husband, Alex. That's often the case—even if the man does believe in ghosts, there just seems to be something in men that won't let them call me. Some do call me, of course, but given the choice, they either make their wives do the talking or they ignore the situation altogether. Alex was convinced they had a ghost, though, and he even knew it was his grandmother.

Alex came from a big family, with four brothers and three sisters, and their Grandma Dottie often came up in conversation, especially around the holidays.

"She always did the baking," Alex recalled. "She used to make the best date-nut bars—we all miss having those at the holidays, but no one has her recipe!"

Recently, she'd been coming up more often because several of the siblings, including Alex, thought they'd seen her. Alex's mother also thought she had seen Grandma Dottie. Charity had not seen her, but she said there were a couple of times a month when she'd felt weird and uneasy in the house. Nothing scary, really, just a general odd feeling. It would be there for a few days, then just as suddenly it would be gone.

We were sitting in their formal dining room talking. The ghost hadn't shown herself yet, but I could tell she was there. Ghosts leave energy behind them, like the lingering scent of perfume when someone has just left the room. And just as with leftover perfume, the stronger the "energy," the closer the ghost is. So as we sat there chatting and waiting for the ghost to show up, I looked around and commented on the beautiful china in a nice hutch they had.

"Were any of the teacups Grandma Dottie's?" I asked, and the question brought her out. An older female ghost walked into the room, smirking proudly and nodding.

"Yup," she admitted. "The cup with the fine blue flowers on it was mine. My daughter broke up the set among all the brothers and sisters, so I just go from piece to piece, visiting them."

"Are you Dottie?" I asked. She nodded again and smiled. "Why didn't you cross over when you died, Dottie? Didn't you see the White Light?"

"I saw it," she said, and her brow furrowed at the memory. "But I didn't see my husband in it, so I thought he must have stayed here. I decided to look for him."

"And you never found him?" I assumed. She shook her head no. "Well, if I make the White Light now, will you go into it?"

"I will," she said, straightening up resolutely. "But can you do me a favor?"

"I'll try," I replied.

"Alex mentioned my date-nut roll—they all talk about that recipe. Can you give it to him?"

Of course I could, and I did. When I told Alex what was going on, he was overjoyed—you'd have thought I just gave him the winning lottery numbers!

The ghost hadn't shown herself yet, but I could tell she was there. Ghosts leave energy behind them, like the lingering scent of perfume when someone has just left the room. And just as with leftover perfume, the stronger the "energy," the closer the ghost is.

DOTTIE'S DATE-NUT BARS

1 cup chopped dates
5 tablespoons boiling water
½ cup sifted all-purpose flour
¼ teaspoon baking powder
½ teaspoon salt
½ cup chopped nuts (any kind)
2 eggs, beaten
1 teaspoon vanilla extract
1 cup brown sugar
Butter
Powdered sugar

▶ Preheat oven to 350º. Place dates in a small bowl; pour 5 tablespoons boiling water over dates to soften. Cool. Stir together flour, baking powder, and salt in a large bowl. Stir in nuts and dates.

In a separate bowl, mix together eggs and vanilla; stir in brown sugar gradually. Add egg mixture to flour mixture, stirring well. Grease (with butter) a 7x11-inch baking pan. Spread date mixture to ½-inch thickness in bottom of pan. Bake for 30 minutes. While still warm, cut into 1x2-inch strips. Remove from pan and roll in powdered sugar.

DOUGHNUTS (PACZKIS)

More often than not, earthbound spirits have the best intentions, especially if they are strangers who follow people home. I've come across very few ghosts who latch on to strangers to be mean or annoying. Why would they—any more than a living stranger would just decide to start annoying you? Most people who decide not to cross over make that decision because they think they can help out those they leave behind, so for them to move on later and try to help a stranger makes a certain amount of sense. I have to believe that, on the balance, most people are good at heart, and since they're the same dead as they were alive, that means most earthbound spirits are also good at heart.

I came across a good example of this a few years back, around Lent. There's a very strong Polish tradition throughout the Upper Midwest, and certainly around Cleveland, to serve *paczkis* (roughly pronounced "punch-keys" or "poonch-keys") as a treat before Lent. To put it most simply, paczkis are jelly-filled doughnuts . . . but not exactly. They are heavier than a typical doughnut, sort of like the difference between homemade bread and Wonder bread. Around Lent in Cleveland, you can't go anywhere without finding paczkis!

Lenny called me just after "paczki season" because he had seen a female ghost in the house, dressed like a baker, with the white shirt, pants, and smock. I had done work for him and his wife, Nina, several years before, but they had moved to a new house since then.

"I don't think she came with the house, though," Lenny told me. "The house has felt fine until recently, right around when I saw the woman."

It's not uncommon for a previous client of mine to be able to "feel" a ghost in a house. It's because they lived with that feeling for so long—the energy drain and the sense of being watched—that when it's finally gone after I've cleared the house, then they realize how a house *should* feel. This allows them to be able to tell later when they run across a ghost again, as now they know what it feels like. They get the old feeling back, and they know from experience that it most likely means there's an earthbound spirit around.

When I got to the house, the female ghost was there, as if waiting for me. She was indeed dressed like a baker, and she stood there smiling at me. Her name was Buela, and she'd only been in the home for a few weeks. She had seen Lenny and Nina at the store buying paczkis and felt compelled to follow them home.

"Why?" I wondered.

"Ask him what he asked the girl at the counter that day," she replied instead of answering. I did, and after Nina helped jog his memory, he remembered asking the girl behind the counter if they had any paczkis without the jelly filling.

It's not uncommon for a previous client of mine to be able to "feel" a ghost in a house. It's because they lived with that feeling for so long—the energy drain and the sense of being watched—that....they realize how a house should feel.

"I don't need the extra sugar," Lenny said. "I'm diabetic. But the girl just told me they only made them one way and there was nothing she could do about it."

"There!" Buela said. "That's the problem! But there is something *he* can do about it. I have a recipe for pazckis that he can make himself and leave the jelly filling out."

"You really followed them home to give him a recipe?" I chuckled. Buela nodded and smiled.

"He tugged on my heartstrings," she admitted. "I felt so bad for him, and I just wanted to help. Nobody should have to go without their paczkis at Lent!"

DOUGHNUTS (PACZKIS)

4 cups sifted all-purpose flour
3 teaspoons baking powder
1 teaspoon salt
1 teaspoon grated nutmeg
1 cup granulated sugar
1 egg, beaten
2 cups milk
2 tablespoons melted shortening
1 teaspoon vanilla extract
Powdered sugar

▶ Stir together flour, baking powder, salt, and nutmeg in a large bowl; add sugar. Stir in egg, milk, shortening, and vanilla until a soft dough forms. Turn dough out onto a well-floured surface. Roll to ½-inch thickness, and cut with a doughnut cutter. Fry doughnuts in hot shortening (360º–375º) for about 3 minutes, turning doughnuts as they rise to the top. Drain on paper towels and sprinkle with powdered sugar. Makes 3 dozen.

DREAM BARS

"Can a ghost make you do something?" Randy asked me. "Like, force you to do something for them?"

"No," I told him simply. "They can maybe influence your thoughts and reactions to things, but they can't make you do something you don't want to do. Why?"

Randy glanced at his wife, Violet, then back at me. He shrugged lightly. When Violet had called me, she'd said she felt like there was someone in the house. She felt like she kept bumping into somebody. She also felt like she and Randy were arguing more. They'd only been married two years, but sometimes they squabbled and bickered over the silliest things, like an old married couple.

"I don't know," Randy said, trying to dismiss the notion. "I've just . . . it's that, you know. . . ." He sighed and tried to think of the best way to say it, then took a deep breath. "I just suddenly want *bakery* all the time, like I never have before."

"Bakery?" I wondered.

"Yes. Like cookies and pastries and cakes. Only Violet isn't much of a baker."

He glanced at his wife apologetically. She sort of looked down and twiddled her fingers nervously, but she was also nodding slowly. "It's true. I can only make cookies, and we've actually been fighting about what he wants me to make, and I've been trying to tell him I can't make it. I just don't know how!"

The whole time, a female ghost had been in the room with us, and at that revelation she began laughing with a mean tone. I looked straight at her and asked if she was trying to break up their marriage. She stopped laughing and shook her head no, that she was not.

"So who are you?" I demanded. "What do you want with these people?"

Her name was Isabel. She had actually been attached to Randy's friend Jim, but once Jim's marriage ended, she'd decided to follow Randy home. Isabel was about 30, pretty, and she readily admitted that she "likes men."

"Did you break up Jim's marriage?" I asked.

"Ask Randy," she replied. "I bet he'll tell you they broke up because of her *baking*." She had that gleeful—but mean-spirited—twinkle in her eye again. I asked Randy about Jim, and he said he didn't know why his marriage had ended and wasn't about to ask him. It was none of his business. What he wanted to know, after I'd shared what I knew of Isabel, was what she did when she was alive. Since she kept mentioning bakery, and since Randy often smelled baking in the house, he thought she must have been a baker or something.

"I'm sorry," she suddenly blurted. "I didn't like Jim's wife, but I like Violet. I don't mean to ruin their marriage, it's just so easy. I'm just angry at my fiancé. He was driving and we were fighting, and he crashed the car. I died, but he lived, and that was just *so* unfair." She went on to explain how she had broken up her fiancé's subsequent marriage to a different woman, and after discovering how easy it was, she just began finding handsome young men to follow home. If they were married, she'd break them up by making the men crave her bakery, then she'd move on.

"What kind of bakery?" I asked.

"My Dream Bars," she said with a proud grin. "Coconut, vanilla, brown sugar—they're delicious. It's what Randy wants Violet to make, but he doesn't know what they are and she wouldn't know how to make them anyway. Let me give them the recipe."

I took down the recipe and told Randy and Violet everything she'd said, about how she broke up marriages by making the men crave her Dream Bars. When I offered them the recipe, they both held up their hands and shook their heads—neither of them wanted anything to do with it.

I told Isabel that if she crossed over, she could visit with her loved ones again and that she'd even have more influence over her fiancé. It wasn't true—she might be able to give him nightmares, but that would be it—but she certainly didn't belong on this plane anymore.

Isabel did cross over. Three weeks later, Randy followed up with me. He had talked to Jim, who said it was the weirdest thing, that he and his ex-wife had just started arguing more and more, about him wanting his wife to bake!

DREAM BARS

CRUST

½ cup butter

½ cup brown sugar

1 cup all-purpose flour

FILLING

2 eggs

1 cup brown sugar

1 teaspoon vanilla extract

2 tablespoons all-purpose flour

½ teaspoon salt

1 teaspoon baking powder

1½ cups coconut flakes

1 cup chopped nuts (any kind)

▶ Preheat oven to 375º. To make crust, combine butter, ½ cup brown sugar, and 1 cup flour to form a crumbly mass; pat into bottom of a large baking sheet, covering bottom. Bake for 15 minutes. Cool.

To make filling, beat eggs, 1 cup brown sugar, and vanilla together in a large bowl. Mix together 2 tablespoons flour, salt, and baking powder in a separate bowl; stir in coconut and nuts. Add flour mixture to egg mixture, stirring well. Pour filling onto prepared crust, spread evenly, and bake for 20 minutes. Cool and cut into bars.

EASTER GUMDROP BARS

Children quite often see and talk to earth-bound spirits. I have met too many children to count who could see and talk to ghosts just like I can. The only difference is that they are raised in typical American households, and in typical American households, ghosts are scary and anyone who can do something extrasensory is strange. In this way, our culture subtly teaches children to "turn off" these abilities that I truly believe are innate in all of us. I was lucky enough to be raised in a family that didn't think such abilities were something to forget or ignore. I was also raised to believe that ghosts were very real and not at all scary—at least, no more scary than anyone else is. One thing I learned pretty quickly is that whatever kind of person a ghost was in life, they are still that same person in death. If they were funny and jovial when they were alive, then so is the ghost. If they were sour and bitter, then the ghost is also grumpy.

Debbie knew all of this before she called me, but it still didn't make any difference. I had first done work for her a decade before she called. Now she had a husband and two children, ages 3 and 5, and they lived in a typical American household. Debbie called because the kids were talking to someone, a woman they called Beverley. Debbie was freaked out that her kids could see and talk to Beverley, and she was frightened that there was a strange woman in their house.

Now, to be fair, I don't care what a ghost was like as a person—I do find it sort of creepy when grown-up ghosts play with children they are not related to. I understand why they do it: As ghosts, they quickly realize that no matter what they think, they cannot communicate with most of the people who are alive, so when they come across someone they can talk to, even if it's a child, they jump at the chance to be heard.

Beverley fell into this category. She meant no harm and wasn't trying to manipulate or frighten the children—she just wanted to talk. More to the point, she wanted to make sure one of her best recipes wasn't lost with her death.

Beverley had actually worked at the preschool the kids attended. She had died suddenly of a stroke at the age of 42 and had hung out at school for several years, but she took a shine to Debbie's girls and came home with them. Then, at Easter, she had told the girls to save the gumdrops in their Easter baskets to put in the cake, which they had dutifully explained to their mother.

"*In* the cake?" I checked. Debbie nodded. I looked over at Beverley. "Did you mean *on* the cake?"

"No, no," Beverley said happily. "That was my special recipe for the children at Easter—Gumdrop Bars."

Debbie's daughters had tried to explain that they were like Rice Krispie treats, but they

I was lucky enough to be raised in a family that didn't think such abilities were something to forget or ignore. I was also raised to believe that ghosts were very real and not at all scary—at least, no more scary than anyone else is.

were cake and they had gumdrops inside them. Beverley cut in to explain that her role at the school had been something of a general helper, not a teacher. She helped make the lunches, get the kids ready to go home, and then cleaned up after them. At Easter, she used to bake these special Gumdrop Bars, and the kids just loved them.

I got the recipe from her and she crossed over. Later, Debbie called me back and said she'd gone to the school and asked about Beverley. Beverley had indeed worked there, just as she'd described. So Debbie asked about the Gumdrop Bars, and they knew exactly what she was talking about. They also bemoaned the fact that when Beverley had died, the tradition had died with her.

"I think I might have a recipe for something like that," Debbie had told them.

EASTER GUMDROP BARS

4 eggs
2 cups brown sugar
1 tablespoon cold water
2 cups sifted all-purpose flour
1 teaspoon baking powder
¼ teaspoon salt
1 teaspoon cinnamon
1 cup gumdrops
Butter
Icing (recipe below)

▶ Preheat oven to 325º. Beat eggs in a large bowl, and gradually add brown sugar. Stir in 1 tablespoon cold water. Stir together flour, baking powder, salt, and cinnamon in a separate bowl. Add flour mixture to egg mixture, stirring to combine. Sprinkle gumdrops with a little flour, and stir gently into batter. Lightly grease (with butter) and flour 2 (8x8-inch) square cake pans. Transfer batter to prepared pans and bake for about 30 minutes. Spread with Icing while hot. When cool, cut into squares. (Instead of icing, bars may be cut and rolled in powdered sugar, if desired.)

ICING

3 tablespoons melted butter
3 tablespoons orange juice
Powdered sugar

Whisk together all ingredients, using enough powdered sugar to make icing the right consistency for spreading.

ELDERBERRY PIE

When I'm out traveling, I love to stop at roadside fruit stands and buy fresh fruits and vegetables, right out of someone's field or garden. There is just nothing that compares to the full, fresh taste of fruit-stand wares! Once, when my husband, Ted, and I were driving across Pennsylvania, we found a roadside stand that was really a small grocery store. It not only had fruits and vegetables, but there were also baked goods, jams, jellies, and cheese. A lot of fruit stands have items I can't buy because they need to be refrigerated and we're too far from home for them to last, but I felt sure this stand would have something.

Pennsylvania has a large Amish population, and as I'd suspected, this fruit stand was run by an Amish family. We had parked by a huge bush with massive blackberries on it, and when we got out of the car, something seemed very familiar about them.

"Ted?" I called out to him. "What do you call these berries?"

"I don't know," he replied. "They'll probably kill you!"

"No!" I said and picked a few, popping them into my mouth. I thought poor Ted was going to faint!

"What are you doing?" he demanded. "You don't know what those are!"

"I just forgot their name," I replied with a chuckle. "We used to pick them all the time when I was a kid—don't worry!"

In the store, I asked the woman behind the counter about the bush, and she told us they were elderberries. "But they're not much good for anything," she added with a laugh. "You need so many of them to make anything!"

"Elderberries!" I said, snapping my fingers. "That's right! I guess I don't remember anyone really cooking with them."

"There was one woman in our community who used to cook with them," the woman said. "Her name was Sister Troyer. But they're just so hard to work with, her recipes died with her. You need so many, and they're very difficult to clean and prep to make them good."

As we were talking, I had noticed that the fruit stand had several earthbound spirits in it, but only one of them perked up at the mention of Sister Troyer and came over to listen in on our conversation. After I'd bought my goods and we'd stopped chatting, I moved back into the shop as if I'd forgotten to look for something else. That's when I said to the ghost, "You're Sister Troyer, aren't you?" Thankfully, my conversations with spirits take place in my head; otherwise, the woman at the counter would have thought I was crazy!

"Yes!" she said happily. "And I can tell you, that elderberry pie is not that hard to make—they just don't want to bother."

"Would you give me the recipe?" I asked. "I've always loved elderberries, and you never really see recipes for them."

As we were talking, I noticed that the fruit stand had several earthbound spirits in it, but only one of them perked up at the mention of Sister Troyer and came over to listen in on our conversation.

Sister Troyer was only too happy to share her recipe with someone, so I had her follow us back out to the car where I could write it down. She explained it all very carefully, right down to the fact that it had to be baked in a very hot oven—at 450°—before reducing the heat to 350° for the last 30 minutes.

"You had an oven with exact temperatures?" I asked her. As far as I knew, the Amish had no such things in their homes.

"Several community ovens are used to cook and bake for the shop," she explained. "You wouldn't be able to get the uniformity you need from our home ovens."

"Oh, that makes sense," I agreed. "Would you like me to make the White Light so you can cross over now?"

"You can do that?" she gasped.

So I made the Light for her, and she was very happy to finally be able to cross over.

ELDERBERRY PIE

1 package refrigerated piecrust dough (2 crusts)

3 cups fresh elderberries, cleaned and stemmed

½ cup granulated sugar

1/8 teaspoon salt

2 tablespoons all-purpose flour

3 tablespoons lemon juice

Egg white, whisked (optional)

▶ Preheat oven to 450°. Fit 1 piecrust into bottom of a 9-inch pie plate; fill with berries. Mix together sugar, salt, and flour; sprinkle over berries. Spoon drops of lemon juice over all. Top with remaining piecrust. Bake for 10 minutes. Reduce oven temperature to 350°, and bake for 30 minutes. If desired, during the last 15 minutes of baking, gently brush top of pie with egg white and sprinkle with sugar.

FROSTED PENUCHE CAKE

Little Daisy was 4 years old, and her best friend was her doll, Bella. Daisy and Bella often had tea parties, and Daisy's mother, Veronica, said she always heard her daughter chattering to her imaginary friend. Most of the time Daisy answered for her doll, though she didn't always, but she would still react as if the doll had answered. None of this concerned Veronica until the day she heard Daisy playing and talking to Bella about making cookies.

"Why don't we have cake instead?" a woman replied when Daisy suggested cookies. Veronica went cold, and the hair on her arms and neck stood up. The voice had definitely come from Daisy's playroom and had certainly been in response to the child's conversation, but it had been an adult's voice—not Daisy's voice, but the voice of a grown woman.

"There was no one in there with her, of course," Veronica told me. "The room was empty. I packed up Daisy and we went to my mom's house, and we haven't been back since!"

Veronica's house was beautiful—not the kind of house you just up and left without a very good reason. Suffice to say, it was the kind of home that actually needed hired help to take care of it—it was too big for one person to maintain. Daisy was an only child and very spoiled, but for a good reason: She was also in remission from leukemia. When we went into her playroom, I saw a young woman there, a ghost who looked to be about 30.

"Are you Bella?" I asked. She nodded. She had blonde hair and was dressed in a crisp white blouse and dark slacks.

"Is that Bella, your doll?" I asked Daisy, whom I had asked to be there with us, but she shook her head no.

"That's *Lady* Bella," Daisy corrected me. "My doll is Bella, too, but that's the lady Bella."

"So your name is Bella too?" I said thoughtfully, and the ghost nodded again.

"I came home with Daisy from the hospital. I had a . . . *long* disease," she said cryptically and wouldn't speak of it any further than that. "I liked Daisy, and when I realized she could see me and talk to me, *and* that she had a doll named Bella, it all seemed perfect."

Perfect, I thought, *if you were trying to get into the girl's house without being noticed.* After all, it wouldn't seem strange for a girl to be talking about Bella if she'd always had a doll named Bella.

"But she always plays tea and *cookies*," Bella complained in a snotty tone of voice. "Why always cookies? Why not ever cake? Cookies go with hot chocolate, not tea. Tea goes with cake."

"Do you have a recipe for tea cakes?" I asked her, hoping it would satisfy her enough to cross over. "If I give Veronica the recipe you think goes with tea, will you leave?"

She certainly didn't belong in the house. Not only was she manipulative and attached to a child, she was also attached to a child who

Veronica went cold, and the hair on her arms and neck stood up. The voice had definitely come from Daisy's playroom and had certainly been in response to the child's conversation, but it had been an adult's voice—not Daisy's voice.

was in no condition to have her energy sapped by a ghost.

"That would be acceptable, I suppose," she agreed in the same snotty tone. Fortunately, she did also cross over and leave Daisy and her mother in peace.

FROSTED PENUCHE CAKE

½ cup butter
½ cup granulated sugar
1 whole egg, beaten
1 egg yolk, beaten
1½ cups sifted all-purpose flour
½ teaspoon salt
½ teaspoon baking soda
½ teaspoon baking powder
½ teaspoon cinnamon
½ cup sour milk
½ cup brown sugar
1 egg white, stiffly beaten
½ cup pecans

▶ Preheat oven to 325º. Cream butter in a large bowl, and gradually add sugar. Whisk in beaten egg and egg yolk.

Combine flour, salt, baking soda, baking powder, and cinnamon in a large bowl. Add flour mixture to butter mixture alternately with sour milk. Grease (with butter) and flour an 8x8-inch baking pan. Transfer batter to prepared pan.

Stir brown sugar gradually into stiffly beaten egg white to make a meringue. Spread over batter, and sprinkle with pecans. Bake for about 45 minutes.

FRYING PAN CAKE

I've only ever been camping once. Ted and I took our girls when they were about 2 and 5, and it was a complete disaster. We rented one of those pop-up campers that you tow behind a car, and we set out for a week of camping. The biggest problem was that it rained for the first five days. Compounding that was the fact that I was not much of a campfire chef, especially when all the wood was wet and it was drizzling as I tried to cook. It also didn't help that an earth-bound spirit seemed to be hanging around near the camper in the spot next to us. Whenever I'd start to cook, she'd come over and start snick-ering at me and mumbling about how badly I was doing. I just ignored her.

The people in the next spot had one of those giant silver Airstream campers and obviously used it as a vacation cottage all through the summer. They had a nice stack of firewood under a cover and a long awning that stretched out and covered their picnic table to shelter it from the rain. They were nice enough, a 40-something couple named Holly and Bert. Their kids were older—18 and 19, if I recall—and didn't need to be entertained like ours did.

One night we were all sitting around Holly's and Bert's campfire (since they'd been able to light theirs) after my girls were in bed. We got to talking about cooking over campfires, and Holly mentioned that her Aunt Alice—whom she had gotten the camping bug from—was a wonderful campfire chef. Aunt Alice and her husband had apparently retired and spent the rest of their time traveling all across the coun-try camping, and whenever they were in the state, Holly and her siblings would go and stay with them for a few days.

"And she had the *best* camping recipes," Holly concluded. "I've still never tasted any better."

"Well, at least breakfast is easy," I joked. "You can't really ruin eggs and bacon!"

"Oh, that reminds me!" Holly said excitedly. "She even used to make a *cake* in a frying pan!"

"A cake?" I checked and Holly nodded vehe-mently. Now, while we were talking, I noticed that the ghost I'd seen hanging around started moving over toward us, nodding and smiling the whole time. Once she was close enough to hear the stories better, she stopped and lis-tened. Holly was still going on and on about Aunt Alice's campfire skills.

"She could even make full casseroles," Holly said.

"To be honest," I said pointedly, to get back at the ghost for making fun of me, "if you're just hanging a big pot over a fire, it can't be that difficult. I mean, it's really the pot that's doing the cooking." The ghost frowned at this, just as I'd expected, and started scowling at me. So I met her eyes and said in my head to her, "You're Alice, aren't you?"

If ever a living person scared a ghost, it was right at that moment. Alice jumped back and stood straight, her face panicked and her mouth gaping. "You can see me!" she finally managed to say.

"I can hear you too," I replied. "And I heard all your snide comments about my cooking."

She blinked a couple of times, mumbled a nervous apology, then took in a deep breath and straightened herself up again. "Look, Holly loved this cake recipe she's talking about—really *loved* it. It's actually very easy to make—I don't suppose you could give the recipe to her?"

I'm not a spiteful person, and since I had given her a good shock, I figured fair's fair. So I got some information from her that I couldn't possibly know and used it as a way of introducing Holly and Bert to what I can do. I got the date she died, to begin with. Holly just got really quiet and agreed that it was true, that her Aunt Alice had died on that day.

"And everyone got to the funeral except your sister, Betty," I added.

"How are you doing that?" Holly asked. "Are you psychic?"

"No, Alice is here telling me," I told her, and then explained what I could do. Of course, once they knew and were convinced, Holly had all kinds of personal questions for Aunt Alice—the usual last-minute things people often ask a loved one. With that out of the way, Aunt Alice finally passed on the recipe for the frying pan cake, then crossed over into the White Light. The next night, Holly made the cake, and it really was delicious.

FRYING PAN CAKE

¼ pound butter
1 cup brown sugar
7 slices pineapple
3 eggs, well beaten
1 cup granulated sugar
1 cup all-purpose flour
1 teaspoon baking powder
½ cup pineapple juice
Whipped cream

▶ Preheat oven to 350º. Melt butter in an oven-safe skillet. Stir in brown sugar, cook until blended, and place pineapple slices in skillet. Combine eggs, granulated sugar, flour, baking powder, and pineapple juice in a large bowl, mixing well. Pour batter over pineapple slices. Bake for 40–45 minutes. When done, turn upside down onto a large serving plate. Serve with whipped cream.

Note: To make over a campfire, use a cast-iron skillet and cook for about 40 minutes.

GRAHAM CRACKER CAKE WITH MOCHA FROSTING

Gwen didn't like Grandma Bubba at all. She didn't mind her kids playing with "imaginary friends"—and at ages 6 and 7, they played with a lot of imaginary friends—but she did mind them playing with the one they called Grandma Bubba. What scared her the most was that when her kids talked about Grandma Bubba, they seemed to be talking about the same person. They both described her as round with wild gray hair, and she told them both the same thing: That they shouldn't eat any more graham crackers.

"So I don't think she's an imaginary friend," Gwen said to me. "They've *never* had the *same* imaginary friend before."

I agreed with her and went out to her house, a beautiful old home in the Hollywood Hills, built in the 1930s. Everything in it seemed to be made of ornate, dark wood, which really only made the house dark and dreary. Perhaps if you lived in Los Angeles, you got sick of the sun and needed a cavelike retreat every so often? I don't know, but I've been in a few of those old movie-star houses, and they all seem dark to me. Back in Ohio, we like big windows and lots of light to try to combat the winter grays.

Anyway, there was a ghost there, and the darkness of the house made her appear spooky even to me. It was really just her hair that did it. It was long and gray, but very uncontrolled and naturally curly, so it just stood out in all sorts of odd angles and made her look wild or crazy. Add to that the fact that she refused to be called anything other than "Grandma Bubba" and that she kept saying, in an odd accent, "This is *my* house." It was a wonder the poor kids had slept a wink since she arrived.

As it turned out, sleep wasn't the problem. The problem was graham crackers. Gwen's kids loved graham crackers in any form: cookies, crackers, cereal, candy bars. But since Grandma Bubba had arrived, they'd not only stopped eating graham crackers, they were actually *afraid* to eat them. The kids had a nanny who took care of them while their mother worked, and she confirmed that they had loved graham crackers until Grandma Bubba had come on to the scene.

"Why are you scaring the kids?" I asked the ghost. She straightened up and looked at me defiantly.

"I'm not scaring them," she said. "I love these kids."

In reality, it was very difficult to get answers out of the woman. She seemed very confused and would often not answer my questions directly; instead, three questions later, she would suddenly respond to something I'd asked several questions before. I never was able to piece together how she'd died, and as far as I could tell, she'd been the live-in nanny at the home back in the 1930s when it was first built.

"What's all this about the graham crackers?" I asked her. Eventually, she got around to

Anyway, there was a ghost there, and the darkness of the house made her appear spooky even to me. It was really just her hair that did it. It was long and gray, but very uncontrolled and naturally curly.

explaining that, in her day, graham crackers only belonged in cake. In her confused, slightly scary way, she was showing her concern for the kids. She thought they were eating too many graham crackers. To her, the crackers were a key ingredient in a special cake, not something you ate every day.

"In cake?" I checked, assuming her confusion was getting the better of her again. "I've heard of graham cracker piecrust, but not cake."

"No!" she replied angrily. "Cake! I will *tell* you how to make it!"

Honestly, not jotting down her recipe never occurred to me. She just had that presence about her: She was big and loud, and you tended to feel yourself unwilling to argue with her. I knew why the kids had stopped eating graham crackers so readily!

Thankfully, Grandma Bubba did cross over when I made the White Light. After that, the children went back to eating graham crackers whenever and however they liked!

GRAHAM CRACKER CAKE

⅓ cup butter
½ cup granulated sugar
3 eggs, separated
⅔ cup milk
1 teaspoon vanilla extract
2 dozen graham crackers, finely crushed
1 teaspoon baking powder
½ cup finely chopped nuts (any kind)
Mocha Frosting (recipe below)

▶ Preheat oven to 375º. Cream ⅓ cup butter and granulated sugar in a large bowl; beat egg yolks well and add to butter mixture. Stir in milk and 1 teaspoon vanilla. Combine graham crackers, baking powder, and nuts; add to batter. Fold in stiffly beaten egg whites. Transfer batter to 2 greased (with butter) 8-inch round cake pans; bake for about 25 minutes. Let cool, and spread with Mocha Frosting.

MOCHA FROSTING

6 tablespoons butter
3 cups powdered sugar
5 tablespoons dry cocoa
4 tablespoons double-strength coffee
1 teaspoon vanilla extract

▶ Cream 6 tablespoons butter well. Stir together powdered sugar and cocoa, and gradually stir into butter. Add coffee, 1 tablespoon at a time, to moisten. Add 1 teaspoon vanilla with last addition of coffee.

GRANT'S PEANUT-COVERED SQUARES

One of the quickest and easiest ways to get an earthbound spirit attached to you is to go secondhand shopping and buy an item that once belonged to the spirit. Not that I would advise doing such a thing, of course, but suffice it to say that if the ghost in your house isn't attached to you, then it's probably attached to something you got secondhand. That's why I really did not want to try and help out Missy and Greg—because the first thing they told me was that they were huge collectors of peanut memorabilia. To my way of thinking, they weren't mere collectors, they were obsessed. It didn't stop at Mr. Peanut figurines and old tin trays depicting classic peanut advertisements, but it extended to peanut curtains, peanut place settings, peanut books, and even peanut recipes.

In other words, their house in Georgia was like its own antiques mall: Almost nothing was new, and that meant that almost everything could have a spirit attached to it. Antiques stores are practically clearinghouses for earthbound spirits.

What got me to the house was that the ghost sounded particularly agitated. Missy and Greg told me stories of doors flying open, and that kind of interference does not sit well with me. This was a level of physical interaction.

Amazingly, when I got to the house, there was only one ghost in the whole place. As I stood and looked around at all the peanut-this and peanut-that knickknacks, I was absolutely shocked that there was only one ghost. And on top of that, he didn't look at all violent.

"So what's the deal?" I asked him. "Who are you?"

"Grant," he said quite forthrightly.

"And why are you here?" I asked, looking around the house again. "Which piece was yours?"

"None of it was mine," he admitted. "I came home with them from a sale they were at."

"But they didn't buy anything that had been yours?" I wondered. He shook his head slowly—no, none of the peanut stuff was his. I found that doubly amazing: Only one ghost and he wasn't even attached to any of the items Missy and Greg had bought secondhand?

Grant went on to explain that he had been at the home the sale was held in and that Missy had found some peanut recipes in a homemade recipe binder that she hadn't heard of before. She asked the person running the sale if she could have a few of them and was told the binder was only for sale as a whole, for $10. It was nothing more than a binder full of index cards, so instead of paying $10, Missy had gone off in a corner to "look them over and think about it," then had slipped the recipes she wanted out of the binder and into her purse. That didn't sit well with Grant. True, one of the recipes had been his, but he didn't care about that. Grant was more concerned about punishing them for stealing it.

"Do you know anything about a cookbook?" I asked, hoping they'd make it easy and confess. I could tell by their faces and glances at each other that they knew exactly what I meant, but they played dumb.

"There was a sale with a cookbook," I went on. "More like a recipe book, really. Grant says he made the back door fly open as you left? And your car wouldn't start at first?"

"Oh, yeah . . ." Greg finally said. "I think I remember that sale. But we didn't . . . buy a cookbook."

I looked at them. Missy met my eyes, then looked away. She looked mortified, so I let it sink in for a few seconds. "I'm sorry!" she cried. "I only took one recipe! I wasn't going to pay $10 for *one* recipe!"

Once the cat was out of the bag, it made the conversation much easier. Grant had also made sure the recipe never came out right. Whenever she tried to make it, he'd break the eggs or spill the peanuts they needed.

"That's true," Missy admitted. "I've never been able to make it yet. Please, ask him where I can send the money—I'm *so* sorry!"

Grant shook his head slowly. "Forget the money," he said. "I think they've learned their lesson."

Grant was perfectly happy to cross over after he'd made sure he got his point across, but before he left, I asked him if I could have this recipe that had caused so much trouble!

GRANT'S PEANUT-COVERED SQUARES

4 eggs
1 cup granulated sugar
1 cup sifted all-purpose flour
1½ teaspoons baking powder
¼ teaspoon salt
½ cup boiling water
½ teaspoon vanilla extract
Icing (recipe below)
1 cup ground peanuts

▶ Preheat oven to 325°. Separate eggs, reserving 1 egg yolk for Icing. Beat remaining 3 egg yolks in a large bowl until thick; gradually add granulated sugar. Stir together flour, baking powder, and salt. Stir flour mixture into egg yolk mixture. Add ½ cup boiling water and vanilla. Stiffly beat egg whites and fold into batter. Transfer batter to a greased (with butter) 12x8x2-inch baking pan. Bake for about 30 minutes. Cool and cut into 2-inch squares. Spread Icing on top and sides, and dip in ground nuts.

ICING

½ cup butter
1 reserved egg yolk, beaten
2½ cups powdered sugar
1 teaspoon orange flavoring
Heavy whipping cream (optional)

▶ Melt butter; add beaten egg yolk, powdered sugar, and flavoring. Mix well. (Stir in heavy whipping cream to make icing the right consistency to spread, if desired.) Keep refrigerated.

KEY LIME PIE

My husband, Ted, and I enjoy going to murder-mystery dinners, where you eat and try to solve a mystery that is being acted out live by actors. Ted sometimes gets frustrated with me because there are always earthbound spirits around, and they often try to help the guests solve the mystery by telling them whodunit. The problem, of course, is that I can see and hear them, so they really do help me—or spoil it for me, depending on which way you look at it.

Once we were attending a murder-mystery dinner that was on a train ride through the Florida Everglades. It was a great setting, and the meal, though basic, was pretty good. Dessert was—as you'd expect, being in Florida—Key lime pie. As they brought it around to the tables, I noticed one of the earthbound spirits on the train with us going from table to table, checking everyone's plates. Actually, she was "flitting"—that's the only word I can use to describe it. She never stayed in one place very long, sometimes just long enough for a glance, before she moved over to the next table. She'd been doing this the whole meal, looking concerned if a guest was low on water or needed a clean fork or something. When the dessert started to be passed out, she began to flit even more. She was roughly following the path of the dessert cart, then retracing her steps, and as people began to eat and comment on the Key lime pie, this ghost's smile got broader and

broader. By all accounts, it was the best Key lime pie anyone had ever tasted!

The ghost was probably about 35 when she died, and even though we were in Florida, she looked like a typical California girl—blonde, tall, tan, blue eyes. When she flitted over to our table, I saw that she was wearing a name tag that said "Sunny." That struck me as odd because earthbound spirits typically wear the clothes they were buried in, and I kind of doubted this woman had been buried with her name tag on. Still, stranger things have happened, so I just shrugged it off. What I couldn't as easily dismiss was how upset she looked when she saw my plate.

I don't have a very big sweet tooth. I don't dislike desserts, but I often do not finish them, no matter how good they are. The Key lime pie was very good but also very rich, and it didn't take long for me to have had enough! By the time Sunny got to our table, I had already pushed my plate away, the dessert half-eaten.

"She doesn't like my pie," Sunny said to herself, looking honestly distressed. "I can't believe she doesn't like my pie!"

I didn't want to ruin this poor woman's mood, so I pushed my plate toward Ted and said, "This is really good pie, isn't it? But you know I never finish my piece—do you want the rest?" Ted didn't need any convincing and quickly pushed his empty plate out of the way

That struck me as odd because earthbound spirits typically wear the clothes they were buried in, and I kind of doubted this woman had been buried with her name tag on. Still, stranger things have happened, so I just shrugged it off.

and started on the rest of my piece. I looked up at Sunny and winked.

"You can see me?" she gasped.

"Yes I can," I replied, speaking only in my head, as I always do with earthbound spirits. "It really was good pie. I'm just not a big fan of desserts. Is it your recipe?"

She nodded proudly and smiled again. "It's my family's recipe. My family owned a restaurant, and this was our pie."

"Well, my husband really likes it, as you can see!"

"Would you like the recipe?" she asked me unexpectedly. I glanced at Ted—who was scraping up every last crumb from my plate—and told her that I would love to have it!

KEY LIME PIE

24 vanilla wafers
2 tablespoons butter, melted
4 egg yolks, beaten
2 cans Eagle Brand milk
1 cup Florida Key lime juice
4 egg whites
2 teaspoons granulated sugar

▶ Preheat oven to 400º. Crush vanilla wafers into fine crumbs, and mix well with melted butter. Press crumb mixture into a 9-inch pie plate. Bake for 5 minutes.

Meanwhile, whisk together egg yolks and Eagle Brand milk in a large bowl. Add lime juice, 1 tablespoon at a time, and stir well. Pour lime mixture into prepared crust.

Beat egg whites with sugar until stiff peaks form. Spread meringue mixture on top of pie. (Whipped cream may be substituted for meringue.)

Increase oven to broil. Place pie on bottom oven rack, and broil until golden brown. Remove pie from oven and set aside to cool for 1 hour before serving.

LEMON SOUR BARS

Kathleen and Pamela were the very picture of stereotypical old aunties. One was 80 and the other was 85, both were widowed, and both were just terribly prim and proper. The house was immaculate, right down to the little lace doilies that everything rested on, to prevent the wood from being scratched. The walls were covered with holy pictures and just a few pictures of family. There was a picture of each of their husbands (just one each) and a few table-top pictures of them when they were younger. They offered me tea—coffee would have been unheard of—and pastries.

"It's Caroline," Pamela said to me with a quiet air of certainty, sipping her tea.

"No, no," Kathleen disagreed, tutting at her sister. "It must be one of our husbands, back for a visit."

Pamela shook her head. "The dears just wouldn't *do* that to us. It *must* be Caroline."

"Excuse me?" I cut in. They both stopped and eyed me curiously. "Who was Caroline?"

Caroline was their other sister. She had died 30 years before, in the late 1940s, when they were all in their 50s. None of them had children. The surviving sisters wouldn't say how, exactly, she had died. All they told me is that she'd had "lady problems." I didn't press the issue.

"Well," I told them. "I'm quite sure it's not one of your husbands because the earthbound spirit is a woman."

"Caroline!" Pamela cried, overjoyed partly at the thought of her sister and partly at the thought of being right.

"She's nodding," I agreed. "It is Caroline."

Caroline told me she didn't always stay in the house but that she did like to "look in on them" from time to time. She quickly realized what a drain on their energy her presence caused, and she commented that the drain made them crabby and argumentative. I had to chuckle.

"I'm sorry," I explained to the listening sisters, who couldn't hear a word of what Caroline and I had been saying. "She was just telling me how, when she's around, you two turn into a couple of sour lemons!"

They chuckled politely at first, then both their eyes lit up at the same time, and they both breathed out, "Lemon bars!" together.

"Lemon bars?" I asked.

"Yes!" Kathleen explained. "Caroline used to make these simply *delightful* lemon bars, but since she died, we just haven't been able to figure out what she did to make them so *good*."

Now it was Caroline's turn to chuckle. "They have the recipe," she said. "But the secret is in the *cooling*. They have to let them cool for 15 minutes after they've baked, then pour the glaze over them while they're still a bit warm. Then, once they've cooled completely, they can cut them into bars."

The house was immaculate, right down to the little lace doilies that everything rested on, to prevent the wood from being scratched. The walls were covered with holy pictures and just a few pictures of family.

I told them what Caroline had said, and they both nodded sagely and agreed that their bars did always fall apart, leaving them "in no condition to be served."

Before Caroline crossed over, they did ask me to get the recipe again from her, just to make sure they had the rest of it right. And as a thank-you, they said I could take it too.

LEMON SOUR BARS

1 cup all-purpose flour
2 tablespoons granulated sugar
⅛ teaspoon salt
⅓ cup butter
2 eggs, lightly beaten
1 cup firmly packed brown sugar
½ cup chopped pecans or walnuts (optional)
½ teaspoon vanilla extract
Glaze (recipe below)

▶ Preheat oven to 350º. Mix flour, granulated sugar, and salt together in a large bowl. Cut in butter until mixture resembles coarse meal. Grease (with butter) a 9-inch baking pan. Press flour mixture firmly into pan. Bake for 15 minutes.

Combine beaten eggs; brown sugar; pecans, if desired; and vanilla. Pour egg mixture over hot crust; bake for 30 minutes or until topping is firm. Cool for 15 minutes, then pour Glaze over warm bars. Let cool completely, and cut into squares.

GLAZE

2 cups powdered sugar
2–3 tablespoons fresh lemon juice
1 teaspoon grated lemon rind
1 tablespoon melted butter

▶ Combine all ingredients, and mix until smooth. Pour over warm bars.

MALTED BUTTERSCOTCH BARS

Leslie inherited the old family drugstore from her grandparents when they died, but she had no interest in running it. It was a nice little store, still with the hardwood floors and a fully functioning soda fountain, and the location was perfect—right on an old town square. But Leslie knew she didn't have the time, money, or energy to keep the store going. The era of mom-and-pop drugstores was limping into its final lap, Leslie knew. And she realized, after a few years of trying to figure out what to do, that the best thing was to simply unload the store and sell it to someone who wanted it.

The store was still open, but Leslie nominally ran it. Her grandparents had both been actively involved in running the store right up until the days they died, six months apart from each other. When she was at the store—usually after hours—she would often hear loud crashes from the back room, or if she was in the back, then she'd hear sounds from the front. When she went to investigate, there was never anything out of place. She did start seeing an old woman in the store, however. A couple of times she'd even called out to her to tell her they were closed, but by the time she'd got up to where the woman had been standing, there was no one there and the doors were all firmly locked.

"It's haunted," she said to me. "And I bet that's why I can't sell it."

"That might just be the economy," I pointed out. "There's not really much an earthbound spirit can do to prevent a shop or a house from

selling. Not directly, anyway. I guess they could make people feel uneasy, but I'm not sure that would be enough to deter a serious buyer, especially of a business."

I agreed to go out to the shop and meet with her, though, and there was this old woman ghost there. She was really cagey, acting weird, and giving me a wide berth whenever I came close. She clearly didn't like me being there.

"Is it my grandma, Emma?" Leslie wondered. The ghost shook her head no.

"I'm Queenie," she stated, as if daring me to argue.

"Queenie!" Leslie said happily when I told her. "Oh, Queenie was wonderful!" Back in the store's heyday, Queenie had made all the pies and cakes that the store sold. She'd also made sandwiches for lunches. She made everything off the premises because the store didn't have a kitchen, then brought it in wrapped to sell. As time marched on and health standards changed, there came a day when this arrangement was deemed by the city to be unhealthy. The ruling argued that since Queenie's kitchen could not be inspected, they had no way of telling if the standards were up to code or not. They had to stop selling her food, but they could keep the soda fountain and candy counter.

"Baloney!" Queenie disagreed angrily. "It was old what's-his-name on city council who cooked up the whole story and shut me down. He wanted to open that restaurant on the other side of town, and we were the competition. It was that simple."

"There's not really much an earthbound spirit can do to prevent a shop or a house from selling. Not directly, anyway. I guess they could make people feel uneasy, but I'm not sure that would be enough to deter a serious buyer."

"Queenie was the best baker in town," Leslie agreed sadly. "It's true that without her cooking here, the store took quite a hit. She even invented these malted butterscotch bars that were our specialty. She wouldn't happen to remember the recipe, would she?"

Queenie puffed up proudly and tried not to smile. "Of course I do! And they *were* the best cookie bars anyone ever tasted, I *know* that!"

Queenie passed along the recipe and agreed to let me try it too. Finally, I offered to make the White Light so she could again see Emma and Frank, the couple who had run the store when Queenie had been alive.

"I'd like that very much," Queenie said. Leslie thanked her for watching over the store for all the years since she'd died, then Queenie left us alone. I'm sure it was a coincidence, but six weeks later, the store did finally sell.

MALTED BUTTERSCOTCH BARS

1 cup sifted all-purpose flour
½ cup powdered malted milk
1 teaspoon baking powder
½ teaspoon salt
⅓ cup shortening, melted
1 cup brown sugar
2 eggs
2 tablespoons milk
1 teaspoon vanilla extract
½ cup nuts (any kind)

▶ Preheat oven to 350º. Stir together flour, malted milk, baking powder, and salt in a large bowl. In a separate large bowl, combine shortening and brown sugar. Add unbeaten eggs, and mix well. Add milk, vanilla, and nuts. Stir flour mixture into egg mixture to combine. Grease (with shortening) a 9x13-inch baking pan. Transfer batter into pan, and bake for about 30 minutes. Mark into bars while hot. Remove from pan when cool.

MITZI'S GOLDEN PUMPKIN COOKIES

An old friend of mine named Fran called and invited me to join her for a Thanksgiving meal with her mother, Flossy. I liked Flossy, but since I'd known her, Fran had had to move her into a nursing home, and I really don't like visiting nursing homes. Nursing homes and hospitals are always full of earthbound spirits. It's not just the 10 people sitting in the community area playing cards and watching TV; to me, it's the 10 people plus the 10 other people attached to them. That's a lot of bodies—both physical and not—that I have to try to dodge because I'm not about to start walking through ghosts if I can help it.

"I don't know, Fran," I said slowly when she invited me to go. It was the Wednesday before Thanksgiving, and I could offer the usual excuses about baking and preparations, but Fran would see right through them.

"Come on, Mary Ann. You know my mom would love to see you."

"And . . . ?" I knew that Fran was holding something back.

"And I know why you don't like nursing homes, but I had to buy tickets for this meal and my original guest backed out, so I ended up with an extra ticket."

"All right, I'll go," I agreed grudgingly.

Over lunch, we just chatted and had small talk, and I tried to avoid the eyes of any earthbound spirits for fear of cluing them in to what I could do. We got to talking about holiday cookies, and Flossy asked Fran if she remembered the pumpkin cookies Fran's grandmother used to make.

"The orange ones?" Fran asked, licking her lips unconsciously. "Mary Ann, they were *so* good. They were made with actual pumpkin, not just the spices."

We were at a table that seated eight people, and everyone started chiming in about these orange pumpkin cookies that were like small, cookie-shaped pumpkin pies. Then everyone started wracking their brains for the best recipe, but this being a nursing home . . . well, let's just say no one could quite remember how these cookies were made.

"I know," a ghost attached to one of the other guests at the table said. "They're called *Golden* Pumpkin Cookies." I don't think she expected me to answer, and had it not been for everyone at the table going on and on about how delicious these cookies were, I probably wouldn't have.

"What's your name?" I asked her. She took a step back in surprise but knew that I was talking to her.

"Mitzi."

"Mitzi, can you give me that recipe?"

She did, and I jotted it down quickly while everyone else was still chatting. I offered Mitzi the chance to cross over, but she had no intention of doing so and sort of slunk away from the table, probably afraid I could force her to

Nursing homes and hospitals are always full of earthbound spirits. It's not just the 10 people sitting in the community area playing cards and watching TV; to me, it's the 10 people plus the 10 other people attached to them.

leave. After the lunch, I gave Fran the recipe and told her what had happened. Three days later, she called me back and said she'd made the cookies for her mother. Flossy had loved them and swore they were exactly the same as the ones her mom used to make!

MITZI'S GOLDEN PUMPKIN COOKIES

⅓ cup shortening

1⅓ cups granulated sugar

3 eggs, well beaten

1 cup cooked pumpkin or plain canned pumpkin

1 teaspoon vanilla extract

1 teaspoon lemon extract

1 teaspoon grated lemon rind

¼ teaspoon allspice

1 teaspoon cinnamon

¼ teaspoon ginger

1 teaspoon nutmeg

2½ cups all-purpose flour

4 teaspoons baking powder

1 teaspoon salt

1 cup raisins

▶ Preheat oven to 400°. Cream shortening and sugar in a large bowl. Add eggs, pumpkin, vanilla, and lemon extract. In a separate bowl, combine lemon rind, allspice, cinnamon, ginger, nutmeg, flour, baking powder, and salt. Stir flour mixture into pumpkin mixture until a soft dough forms. Dredge raisins in a little flour; mix into dough.

Grease a baking sheet with shortening. Drop dough by teaspoonfuls onto baking sheet. Sprinkle with sugar and cinnamon. Bake for 15 minutes.

NANA'S LEMON SHORTBREAD PIE

I cannot make any public appearances or write a book without trying to work in at least one warning to stay far, far away from Ouija boards. They might be labeled as "games" in toy stores, but they most certainly are not games. Ouija boards do exactly what they claim: They allow you to communicate with nonliving entities. Sometimes that might mean kind earthbound spirits, other times naughty earthbound spirits, and sometimes something else altogether. I don't run into them often, but there are entities among us that are not the ghosts of people who were once alive. They are entities that were never alive in the first place, and so calling them "dead" isn't really accurate. As with people, some of them appear to be good, while others appear to be bad. From my experience, the good entities—be they ghosts or these other things—don't generally communicate using Ouija boards. If there's a bad entity in a home, a vast majority of the time they were invited there by someone using a Ouija board, and then they long outstayed their welcome.

That was exactly the case with Liza. She was 19 years old and scared to death—I could hear the panic in her voice on the answering-machine message she left for me. She was a newlywed, and she and her husband had just moved into one side of a duplex. It was a new home, with no history, so she didn't think it was the house that was the problem.

"Besides," she said. "I've been feeling like there's someone watching me for about four or five years now."

When I got to her house, she actually had two ghosts attached to her, a woman and a man. The man was the one who had been scaring Liza, and he was, in a word, creepy. At first, the woman wouldn't talk to me, but the man said he'd been with Liza about five years, just as Liza had guessed. Then he grinned mischievously and his eyes twinkled.

"And I have been watching her," he admitted. "I watch her *all* the time. Especially when she thinks she's alone."

"That's enough!" I demanded, cutting him off. "You have to go. Did you know her when you were alive? Anything you want to say before I send you away?"

"I didn't know her at all," he said, still grinning. "But *she* called *me* on her Ouija board. I was *invited* to be here."

"No, you weren't," I said simply. He tried to defend himself by explaining exactly how he had been invited by Liza and her friend, who had been playing with a Ouija board at a sleepover, and while Liza did confirm his story, it didn't make it any better.

Now it was the woman's turn. She hadn't said a word since I'd arrived and I wanted to know what her deal was. She didn't look mean, and when I told Liza there was also a woman in the house, Liza's face paled.

When I got to her house, she actually had two ghosts attached to her, a woman and a man.

"It's Nana, isn't it?" she wondered.

"Your grandmother?" I asked, assuming Liza had called her grandmother "Nana," but both Liza and the ghost were shaking their heads no.

"Ghost Nana," Liza said quietly. "I've been talking to her on the Ouija board."

"Oh, for goodness' sake!" I exclaimed.

"She's the reason I called you!" Liza said in her defense. "She kept saying 'the man' and 'Watch out for the man,' and it was freaking me out!"

"Well, I think we know what she meant by that," I agreed.

"She also kept saying 'shortbread cookies' or something about shortbread pie with cookies or something."

I looked at Nana, who was nodding happily. She knew that Liza's husband loved lemon pies, and Nana had a recipe she wanted to give to Liza for a lemon meringue pie made with shortbread cookies.

Needless to say, when I left Liza's house after clearing it for her, she handed me her Ouija board.

"Can you get rid of this for me?"

"I'd be happy to," I agreed.

NANA'S LEMON SHORTBREAD PIE

CRUST

Butter

1 package Nabisco shortbread cookies, finely crushed

FILLING

3 eggs, separated

Juice and grated rind of 1½ lemons

1 can Eagle Brand milk (sweetened)

1 tablespoon granulated sugar

▶ Preheat oven to 350º. To make crust, grease pie plate generously with butter. Line bottom of pie plate with crushed cookies, pressing into butter.

To make filling, combine egg yolks, lemon juice, and grated rind in a large bowl. Add Eagle Brand milk and mix well. Transfer filling to prepared pie plate. Beat sugar and egg whites together until stiff peaks form. Spread meringue mixture on top of pie. Bake for 20 minutes, watching closely. Remove from oven and put in a cool place until time to serve.

ORANGE ROCK COOKIES

Earthbound spirits are exactly like they were when they were alive. That's something that amazes people, but it's true. There is nothing about dying that changes your personality. You don't get that sense of peace with the world until you actually cross over. One of the quirks you do gain upon dying is a curiosity to see who remembered and cared about you. This is why I think I run into so many spirits who seem reluctant to talk. It's not that they are too shy or too private, it's that they want to test the people they're attached to and see if they are remembered and missed. They figure if they just talk to me, then they're giving the answer away and they're really curious to see if so-and-so remembers them or still thinks of them.

Opal ran into such a spirit from her childhood. When she called me, she assumed the ghost in her house was her daughter, who had died from cancer at a young age. She'd only been 28 and had left behind a beautiful little girl, Caitlin. Opal was now raising her granddaughter, and they spoke openly and often about Caitlin's mother. In fact, they both dreamed of her frequently, of talking to her and getting advice. That was my first clue that the young woman who was in the home with them was not Opal's daughter. If you've dreamed of a loved one and communicated with them in dreams after they've died, then they have already crossed over.

The problem was, the earthbound spirit was very unwilling to talk to me. She was tall with dark hair and looked to be in her late 20s. To be absolutely certain, Opal showed me a picture of her daughter, which allowed me to confirm that it was not her.

"You know, it's funny," Opal said. "I've always felt like there was someone here, ever since I was a little girl about Caitlin's age, about 8 years old." She knew it wasn't her parents or grandparents—they'd all been alive when she first had the feeling like someone else was there—and she didn't have any siblings, so it couldn't have been them.

"The only other person I was close to as a girl was Anna," she said. "She was a Ukrainian girl who came and stayed with us. My parents sponsored her or something. Anyway, she barely spoke any English, and we used to read my storybooks so she could learn English. We always had a special bond because of that, even though she was much older than me."

I was watching the ghost the whole time Opal was talking, and sure enough, the earthbound spirit started grinning ear to ear.

"She got sick and died when I was about 6," Opal continued. "Nobody talked about her after that—it was sort of strange. But I never forgot her. She was my best friend back then. We used to make these cookies together that Anna called Orange Rock Cookies. I really missed her after she died."

The problem was, the earthbound spirit was very unwilling to talk to me. She was tall and looked to be in her late 20s. To be absolutely certain, Opal showed me a picture of her daughter, which allowed me to confirm that it was not her.

Opal was getting bleary-eyed and stopped herself, mumbling an apology. When I looked over at the ghost again, she also appeared to have tears on her cheeks. "Are you Anna?" I asked, and the ghost nodded. When I told Opal, she cried out in joy. They reminisced for a few minutes, and Anna asked if I would pass on the cookie recipe so Opal could make them with Caitlin.

That made Opal even happier, and when Opal asked Anna to take a message to her daughter in the White Light, Anna agreed. She hadn't wanted to leave, I could tell, but with a sense of purpose and of doing something Opal so badly wanted her to do, it was enough to get her to cross over.

ORANGE ROCK COOKIES

½ cup butter
⅔ cup granulated sugar
2 eggs
3 cups sifted all-purpose flour
⅓ teaspoon salt
3 teaspoon baking powder
Grated rind of 2 oranges
Strained juice of 1 orange
Milk (optional)

▶ Preheat oven to 375º. Cream butter and sugar in a large bowl; beat in eggs, 1 at a time. In a separate bowl, combine flour, salt, and baking powder. Stir flour mixture into butter mixture; stir in orange rind and juice until a stiff dough forms. (If dough is too stiff, add orange juice or milk, if desired.) Grease a baking sheet with butter. Drop dough from tip of tablespoon onto baking sheet; bake for 10 minutes.

SNAIL TAILS

POPPY SEED CAKE WITH BUTTERCREAM FROSTING

I learned very early on that earthbound spirits behave just as they did when they were alive. If a person was mean alive, they'll be mean dead. If they were quiet and kind, then they'll still be quiet and kind. That is what frustrates me about so many Hollywood movies that have ghosts: If Hollywood were to be believed, then I'd expect everyone who died to suddenly turn into a rampaging fiend bent on destruction. Nothing could be farther from the truth, of course.

My years of experience with passing messages from deceased loved ones to their living relatives have also taught me a lot about diplomacy. People are the same dead as they were alive, and a lot of people lack basic tact—both the living and the dead. I try very hard to not insert myself into some family squabble or other when I'm helping my clients, and to do that I often have to finesse the fine points. I don't change anything—the message still gets through—I just tone it down or play up the positive parts.

That was the case with Madeline and her sister, Annie. I was actually introduced to them as Grandma Madeline and Aunt Annie because it was Madeline's granddaughter, Maddie, who called me. She wanted me at the visitation of her grandmother, Madeline, so she could ask her a few last-minute things. Unfortunately, there's no better way to start a family squabble than to put me in a funeral home when half the family doesn't want me there, so I never agree to go unless an immediate relative invites me—and only if they agree not to tell everyone until I'm gone. Since Maddie was an immediate family member and she agreed to tell only her great-aunt Annie, I agreed to go to the funeral home.

After the visitation was over, I hung back with Maddie and Annie, and they got to ask Madeline everything they wanted. It was the usual mix of personal family things and some family business things—Madeline had left two homes behind, in Florida and Ohio—but there was nothing very salacious about any of it. They'd just wanted me there to tie up the "who gets what" sort of loose ends. Then, once everything was squared away and the goodbyes had been said, Maddie spoke up and said there was one last thing she wanted.

"Grandma Madeline?" she asked. "Whatever happened to your recipe for poppy seed cake?"

"It's with all my recipes," she replied, but Maddie frowned and shook her head.

"No. I looked all over your house here in Ohio. I found all of your recipe books, but none of them had the poppy seed cake. Did you take it to Florida?"

Now Grandma Madeline shook her head. "No, no—all my recipe books should be here."

While this conversation was being relayed, I noticed that Annie got awfully quiet and a bit nervous. She looked guilty, in other words. She was sitting behind Maddie, so her niece didn't see it, but I did—and so did Grandma Madeline. She caught my eye and nodded toward her sister.

"She has it," Madeline said to me. "I'd bet anything she took it from my house the day I died!"

Which is when my diplomatic skills kicked in. I couldn't exactly turn to Annie and accuse her of taking it, but I couldn't just let it go either.

"Annie?" I said, getting her attention. "Madeline wonders if you borrowed it that one time, and maybe you forgot to return it?"

Annie's face looked shocked, then her eyes lit up. "Yes! I bet that's what happened! I think maybe I did borrow it before she went down to Florida for the winter. Is it red, with a coffee cup on the cover?"

"Oh, you're good," Madeline said to me, giving me a wink. "But I don't think she's going to be able to find it, if you know what I mean. Can I just give you the recipe for the cake Maddie wants?"

So I wrote down the recipe and gave it to Maddie.

Quite by chance, several years later, I ran into Maddie and asked her about the red cookbook with the coffee cup on the cover, and if her Aunt Annie had ever found it and given it to her.

"No," Maddie replied. "She just can't find it anywhere!"

POPPY SEED CAKE

¾ cup poppy seeds
1½ cups milk, divided
¾ cup butter
1½ cups granulated sugar
2 cups sifted all-purpose flour
½ teaspoon salt
2 teaspoons baking powder
4 egg whites
Buttercream Frosting

▶ Soak poppy seeds in ¾ cup milk overnight. Preheat oven to 375º. Cream ¾ cup butter in a large bowl; gradually add granulated sugar. Stir in poppy seeds. Stir flour, salt, and baking powder together in a separate large bowl. Add flour mixture to butter mixture alternately with remaining ¾ cup milk. Fold in stiffly beaten egg whites. Grease (with butter) and flour 2 (8-inch) round cake pans. Transfer batter to prepared pans; bake for about 45 minutes; cool. Spread with Buttercream Frosting.

BUTTERCREAM FROSTING

4 tablespoons butter
2 cups powdered sugar, divided
1 teaspoon vanilla extract
½ teaspoon almond extract
3 tablespoons heavy whipping cream

▶ Cream 4 tablespoons butter. Mix in 1 cup powdered sugar. Beat in vanilla and almond extracts. Stir in cream with remaining 1 cup sugar, 1 tablespoon at a time, until frosting mixture reaches spreading consistency.

SIMPLE LOAF CAKE WITH STRAWBERRY SAUCE

It might seem morbid, but have you ever wondered what you'd want if you knew it was your time to pass away? Is there a song you'd want to hear? A favorite movie you'd want to watch again? Or a certain recipe you'd want to smell and taste one last time? If Ralph had thought of these things, he was unfortunately in no shape to tell anyone when I met him. He was confined to what can best be described as a "hospital recliner," and the room smelled of medicine. He was old—at least 90—and the pain medications he was on left him a shell of his former self. The only good part of his hospice care was that it was being conducted at home, with his daughter Lizzy at his side.

Lizzy had called me because she was sure her grandmother—Ralph's wife, Joyce—was in the house. Ralph called out to Joyce from time to time, and while Lizzy could have dismissed it as the ravings of a dying mind, she could also *tell* that, when he called out to Joyce, he really believed she was there.

"He has so little energy lately too," Lizzy explained. "He gets drained much more quickly than before."

Lizzy was right. When I got there, Joyce was in the house, but she wasn't the one sapping all of Ralph's energy. There was also a male ghost in the house, and he was like an energy vacuum. He just stood and scowled at me, apparently angry with anything and everything. What was strange is that he looked just like Ralph.

"Uncle Raymond?" Lizzy guessed in disbelief. The ghost nodded. "That's dad's twin brother. They didn't get along at all when they were alive."

"To be honest, he doesn't look like he wants to get along now either," I said. Lizzy didn't have anything to say to him, and I knew he wasn't doing anything but draining his brother's energy, so I made the White Light and talked him into it as quickly as I could. Then it was Joyce's turn.

"He doesn't have long now," she said to me, with a nod toward her husband. She'd only died a few years before, and she'd stayed behind so they could cross over together.

"Is there anything you want to tell him or Lizzy?" I asked.

"He wants some loaf cake," she replied. "Tell Lizzy he wants some of his loaf cake before he dies."

I passed the message on to Lizzy, and it made complete sense to her. Joyce's loaf cake with strawberry sauce had been a family favorite, but especially Ralph's. He wanted it all the time, and he never seemed to get sick of it.

"But I don't have the recipe," Lizzy admitted. "I wouldn't know where to begin."

"Tell her to get a pen and paper," Joyce said. "I can give it to her. She really must make it for her dad. He's going to die very soon now."

Lizzy called me a week later and asked me to come to her father's funeral. Ralph had died

There was also a male ghost in the house, and he was like an energy vacuum. He just stood and scowled at me, apparently angry with anything and everything.

within the week, just as Joyce had predicted, and since he'd been so out of it at the end, she didn't feel she'd ever got to properly say good-bye. At the funeral home, Joyce and Ralph were both there, holding hands and waiting to cross over.

"Thank you," Ralph said to me. "Just smelling that loaf cake cooking again and having that last, tiny bite of it—that meant so much to me and made the end so much easier."

SIMPLE LOAF CAKE WITH STRAWBERRY SAUCE

Butter
1½ cups all-purpose flour
2 teaspoons baking powder
¼ teaspoon salt
3 large eggs
1 cup granulated sugar
½ cup sour cream
2 teaspoons pure vanilla extract
½ cup flavorless oil (such as canola)
Strawberry Sauce (recipe below)

▶ Preheat oven to 350º. Generously butter a loaf pan. Whisk together flour, baking powder, and salt in a large bowl. In a separate bowl, whisk together eggs, 1 cup sugar, sour cream, and vanilla until well blended. Add flour mixture to egg mixture; stir until smooth. Whisk in oil thoroughly. Transfer batter to loaf pan and bake for 50–55 minutes or until a wooden pick inserted in center of cake comes out clean. Top with Strawberry Sauce.

STRAWBERRY SAUCE

1 pint fresh strawberries
1 cup granulated sugar
Juice of ½ lemon
½ cup white wine (optional)
1 cup heavy whipping cream
1 tablespoon potato flour

▶ Combine all ingredients in a saucepan. Bring to a boil, stirring constantly to prevent burning, until mixture starts to thicken; remove from heat.

TED'S COCONUT KISSES

When I'm visiting friends, they usually know better than to invite other people over at the same time. You'd be amazed at how many conversations come around to ghost stories, and from there it's only a matter of time before what I can do gets revealed. After that, there's no more relaxing for me! It's like I'm back on the clock, answering questions and telling stories. Not to say it's particularly hard for me to tell stories—I love to!—but when I'm expecting a night off, I like to have it.

That's why it took me by surprise when my friend Sharon said she had invited her neighbor Carly over to visit with us. I was dumbfounded when she also announced that Carly thought she had a ghost, which is why she wanted to stop by and visit. The only thing that saved the afternoon was the big plate of cookies Carly arrived with!

Ted, my husband, was with me, and his eyes lit up when he saw that some of the cookies were macaroons. Ted's a huge fan of coconut, especially coconut cookies, but since I am not, he really doesn't get them much at home. As Ted reached for his second, I noticed that the ghost who had come in with Carly—because yes, there was a man attached to her—was scowling a little.

"These are delicious!" Ted said.

"The macaroons?" Carly replied. "Thank you!" That made the ghost scowl even deeper.

"Those are *not* macaroons," he mumbled. "Why does she *always* call them macaroons?"

"Well, what do you call them?" I asked the ghost. He told me they were Coconut Kisses, not macaroons. I didn't want to bicker about what the difference could possibly be, so I asked him who he was instead.

Turns out his name was also Ted, to which Carly responded, "Grouchy Uncle Ted?"

"He didn't introduce himself that way," I said diplomatically. Carly had me ask him if he had a wife and what her name was, which confirmed that it was indeed Aunt Irene's husband, grouchy Uncle Ted.

"He was always so particular about everything," Carly explained. "He'd sit there and grouch about everything that wasn't exactly the way he liked it."

"Actually, he's complaining now," I admitted, then explained to Carly what he'd said about the cookies.

"Oh, I know what he called them," Carly said. "But everyone else on the planet calls them macaroons, so that's what I call them now too."

"No!" Uncle Ted disagreed. "They are *not* macaroons! Macaroons have flour in them and these cookies do not. Is she even making them right? They have to cool on a damp cloth before you try to take them out of the pan." Uncle Ted—perhaps in an effort to prove how

You'd be amazed at how many conversations come around to ghost stories, and from there it's only a matter of time before what I can do gets revealed. After that, there's no more relaxing for me! It's like I'm back on the clock.

particular he really was—then asked me to copy down his recipe to make sure Carly was at least making them right.

I passed along the recipe and Carly nodded as she looked it over. "Yes, that's how they're made. I don't need this," she said, handing the recipe back to me. So I made the White Light for Uncle Ted. Thankfully, he saw Irene in it and crossed right over without another thought.

TED'S COCONUT KISSES

1¼ cups shredded coconut
⅓ cup sweetened condensed milk
½ teaspoon vanilla extract
1 egg white
Vegetable cooking spray

▶ Preheat oven to 350º. Stir together coconut, condensed milk, and vanilla in a large bowl. Beat egg white until stiff, and fold into coconut mixture. Grease a baking sheet with cooking spray. Drop batter by teaspoonfuls onto baking sheet. Bake for 15–20 minutes. Cool pan on a folded damp cloth for several minutes before carefully lifting kisses from pan with a spatula. (This method helps to avoid breaking the kisses.)

One day, Roberta finally talked: The reason she always clammed up about her unwanted visitor is that she knew the lady who came in was a ghost, so there was nothing anyone could do.

—Cranberry Cordial

MISCELLANEOUS

CRANBERRY CORDIAL

Janice's mother, Roberta, was supposed to have a private room at the nursing home, but she always complained about an "old lady" who kept coming into her room and bothering her. The home was full of old ladies, of course, so narrowing it down to a specific person was nearly impossible, especially since Roberta clammed up at the mention of her. She'd bring it up, then seem to realize something and stop talking.

Roberta didn't have dementia or any of the so-called brain-wasting diseases. She was only 70 and still had all her mental capacities. What held her back was the damage to her body caused by a long life of battling alcoholism. She'd been sober for years before she'd gone to the nursing home, but time and alcohol had already taken their toll. Now she was so physically run-down that she required the level of care only a nursing home could provide.

One day, Roberta finally talked: The reason she always clammed up about her unwanted visitor is that she knew the lady who came in was a ghost, so there was nothing anyone could do.

"A ghost?" Janice checked, and her mother nodded.

"She comes in almost every night. She's trying to make me start drinking again."

"What do you mean?"

"She tells me I should drink, that I'll live longer if I do," Roberta said. That was enough for Janice, so she called me to see if I could help.

I don't usually see clients at nursing homes for two reasons. One, nursing homes are always full of earthbound spirits—mostly deceased spouses waiting for loved ones to pass away—and it can quickly turn into a madhouse for me. And two, most rooms are not private, so I can't protect the room against any further ghosts, making it almost pointless for me to go out, just to get rid of one pesky spirit. But Janice was a good talker, and with her mother being in a private room, she convinced me to visit her.

The facility was very nice—very clean and without that typical nursing-home smell. Roberta told me that there was only the one ghost she ever saw. Sometimes she just heard her, but she always visited, every night, with the same message: "You should drink more." I asked a few questions, and we figured out that the times Roberta saw her were usually around the full moon, which makes sense because earthbound spirits always have more energy around a full moon. I had a feeling this ghost that was visiting Roberta most likely visited more often than once a day, but she'd save her energy to get that one message across every night: "Drink more." Sure enough, as we were talking, a curious ghost wandered into the room.

"Have you been bothering this lady?" I asked her. The ghost shook her head, "No," so I asked if she'd been telling Roberta to drink. She kind of paused, then slowly nodded her head, "Yes."

"She should drink," the ghost explained. "I drank a little glass of cordial every day, and that's how I made it to 103."

I had to agree, she did look really, really old and quite frail. I could see why Roberta had been bothered by her but not scared. She said her name was Lilibeth and she had died in the nursing home. When she was alive, she not only drank a small glass of cranberry cordial every day, she also made it herself and kept it squirreled away in her room once she was moved to the home. Later, Janice confirmed all of that with the nurses.

"But I don't just tell *her* to drink," Lilibeth said, pointing at Roberta. "I go into every room and tell them all to drink—it's what kept me alive so long!"

I told her I didn't necessarily agree with that and also explained how she didn't know who she was saying that to or what other medical conditions they might have that would make alcohol very dangerous. I told her that there was really nothing she could do here—most of the people couldn't even see or hear her—and that she should go into the White Light and be with her husband again. She agreed, but before she left, I just had to know . . . I'd never heard of a recipe for cranberry cordial, so I asked her if she'd give it to me.

"Of course," she agreed with a smile, probably thinking I was going to have a glass every day!

CRANBERRY CORDIAL

1 pound fresh cranberries, coarsely crushed

2 cups granulated sugar

4 cinnamon sticks

4 cloves

1 fifth vodka

▶ Mix all ingredients in a holding vessel. Stir once a day for 7 days. Let stand for 1 month. Strain off the muck and allow to age for 2 more months. Strain again and place in sterilized jars for storage.

DEVILED EGGS

One recipe I am proud of is my deviled eggs. Whenever we have a party to go to and we're asked to bring something, I always take my deviled eggs, and they're always a hit. I don't say this to brag; I say it because I guess you could say I have a thing for deviled eggs. As my own recipe is my favorite, I'm always curious to try other people's to see how they stack up. Such was the case when I cleared the home of Eugene and Vera, a first-generation immigrant couple from Poland.

After I was done, they insisted on taking Ted and me out to eat at a "very special place." It was a little Polish restaurant offering an authentic taste of the old country. The menu was very Polish, very heavy and yeasty food. Things like duck-blood soup, potato dumplings, pork and sauerkraut, herrings and beets—and deviled eggs. Ted, thanks to his Polish roots, was all over the duck-blood soup, and I was curious about the deviled eggs. Ted loved the soup, but I thought the eggs were just okay. The ghost who showed up with the food didn't think much of either of them.

"That soup's not thick enough!" she yelled out. She was a heavy woman wearing a hairnet under her babushka—very Polish and, I had no doubt, once a chef at the restaurant. I tried to ignore her so we could finish our meal.

"How are the eggs?" Vera wondered, since I'd told her how I liked to try every deviled egg I came across.

"They're okay," I said. "But I think I still like mine better."

Well, the ghost in the babushka exploded! "If you had *my* deviled eggs, you'd like them!" she hollered. "Those aren't good deviled eggs! I tried to tell them!"

"I'm sorry, Vera and Eugene," I said, leaning in to them. "But there's actually an earthbound spirit here with us now, and she's kind of upset."

"Oh!" Vera gasped. "What about?"

"Deviled eggs!"

I turned back to the ghost and suggested she give me her recipe so I could have real deviled eggs later, when I got home—it would be the only way to make a fair comparison. But she wasn't having it. She crossed her arms, shook her head, and refused to give up her personal recipe.

"You know, my husband, Ted—his mother came from Poland," I said. "Can't you give me the recipe for him, so he can see what real Polish deviled eggs taste like?"

She mumbled a bit more and pretended to be cutting a hard bargain, but she finally gave in and gave me the recipe. Thing is, the recipe is so odd, I had her repeat it three times. I can't say I like them better than my own deviled eggs, but I can say this is the most unusual recipe for deviled eggs I've ever seen. And besides the recipe itself, she was also insistent that you only use goose or duck eggs to make them!

I turned back to the ghost and suggested she give me her recipe so I could have real deviled eggs later, when I got home—it would be the only way to make a fair comparison. She crossed her arms, shook her head, and refused.

DEVILED EGGS

6 hard-cooked duck or goose eggs, peeled
1 tablespoon chopped fresh chives
3 tablespoons butter, divided
2–3 tablespoons sour cream
Salt and black pepper to taste
Breadcrumbs

▶ Using a very sharp knife, cut eggs lengthwise. Scoop out egg yolks into a large bowl; chop yolks fine, and mix in chives, 1 tablespoon butter, sour cream, salt, and pepper. Return yolk mixture to egg whites and cover with breadcrumbs. Melt remaining 2 tablespoons butter in a large skillet, and fry prepared eggs quickly, open sides down. Serve immediately.

Note: The egg-yolk mixture may also be spooned into clean scallop shells. Brown the breadcrumbs in butter, then pour over top of stuffed shells. Place in a hot oven for a few minutes to heat through.

DILL PICKLES

I am often asked, "What's in the White Light that you make for earthbound spirits to cross over?" The answer is: "I don't know." I can't see into the White Light, and I can't see any spirits that have crossed over. Any ideas I have about what's on the other side are purely my conjecture, based on inferences from what spirits have said to me as they're crossing over. I'm certain there is always someone there, waiting for you on the other side, to guide you across. I'm also sure that once you cross over, the problems of our plane of existence no longer weigh on you. Maybe people want to be sure they can come back once they cross over, but from my experience, I'm not sure many people want to come back. Not because they suddenly stop caring for their loved ones, but because they achieve a level of peace that allows them to let go. To be honest, I also think a lot of earthbound spirits end up wishing they hadn't stayed behind, and once they have that chance to finally cross over, there's very little that could stop them. But the pull of loved ones is strong, as is the fear of missing something once you're gone.

Martha was like that. I met her at a roadside fruit-and-veggie stand in Pennsylvania. When my husband, Ted, and I got out of the car, I commented on how strong the scent of dill was in the air—there must have been a bush nearby—and that I wished I had a good recipe for dill pickles. That was when Martha first tried to get my attention—waving her arms, shouting, jumping up and down—but I ignored her. I can't stop for every single ghost I see; otherwise, I'd never get anything done!

Ted and I did some shopping. When I saw a bag of baby cucumbers, I commented again that they'd be perfect for pickles, if I only had a recipe. Martha went nuts. She yelled, she waved her arms, she jumped up and down, she flapped her skirt, and when I finally said, "*What?*" she froze and gaped at me.

"You can see me?" she wondered.

"Did I scare you?" I replied. She nodded and let go of her dress, straightening it out and looking at me. "So what did you want?" I asked.

"I have a great recipe for dill pickles!"

"Oh!" I said, quite surprised at her answer. "Well, that would be fantastic! How long have you been dead?"

"Years and years and years," she said. "I had a heart attack about 15 years ago."

"Why didn't you cross over?"

"My husband is still here," she said sadly. "And my kids—they're grown up now, but now there are my grandkids."

"You know, you can still visit them after you cross over," I told her.

"I don't know," she considered. "My grandkids can see and talk to me now, just like my own kids could, once upon a time."

"But they outgrew it?" I assumed. She nodded. "And you know your grandkids will outgrow it, too, right?" She thought for a second, then nodded again. "But if you cross over, you can still visit them—all of them, including your husband—in their dreams. Besides, don't you want to see any of your deceased relatives?"

"My mother," she replied without hesitation.

I got the recipe for dill pickles from her, then made the White Light and told her that her mother would undoubtedly be in it. She stood and looked and looked and looked, but she didn't move.

"Don't you see anyone in there?" I asked her. She stepped forward and looked again, then turned back toward me with a beaming smile.

"My daughter Angie is there!" she said. "My dear Angie—she died when she was only 7!"

Martha didn't wait for me to reply. Instead, she quite literally ran into the White Light.

It makes me feel good to see loved ones reunite after so long apart. Which is why it doesn't make sense to me that so many people choose to stay behind. It's also why I simply can't do a talk or put together a collection of my stories without once again imparting my two most valuable lessons: One, there really is no reason to stay behind, no matter how much you want to try and help; and two, if you do become earthbound after you've died, all you have to do is find a funeral home and walk into someone else's White Light—it's a doorway to the other side, not the entrance to someone's personal room.

DILL PICKLES

Small cucumbers
Fresh dill sprigs
Garlic cloves (optional)
1 quart white vinegar
3 quarts water
1 tablespoon alum
¾ cup noniodized salt

▶ Slice cucumbers and pack into hot pint jars. Place several dill sprigs in each jar. (Add a clove of garlic to each jar, if desired.) Bring vinegar, 3 quarts water, alum, and salt to a boil in a saucepan. Pour over pickles, and seal jars.

FIG PUFFS WITH WINE SAUCE

I try not to make a big production when I go to someone's home to help an earthbound spirit cross over. People ask me to stay for dinner from time to time, mostly to be polite, and I usually decline. If the spirit was a relative, especially, it starts to feel like I'm overstaying my welcome. Maybe it's just me, but to look at it another way, if I did stay to dinner with everyone who offered, I'd rarely eat at home! When I'm out of town, it's easier to talk me into it. Such was the case after I had helped a spirit cross over at the home of a judge in Atlanta.

"Please, stay and have dinner with us," Judge Wilkens requested.

"I simply couldn't," I replied, but he just grinned pleasantly.

"We had actually counted on it. We'd like to take you out for dessert, which means we have to eat dinner first."

So I stayed, and when we went out for dessert, I saw why he was insistent. People like to show off their hometowns, and he had a favorite spot he wanted to share that boasted three floors of desserts. It was like a dessert buffet, and they also brought more desserts around to your table, wheeled over on serving carts. That was when the evening soured, at least for me. Not because of the desserts or the company, but because of the ghost who arrived at our table with the cart.

As the waiter was describing all of the desserts, I couldn't help but watch this ghost. He

was scowling so intensely, I got the feeling he really believed looks could kill. It was too much. I had to know what his problem was, and if his problem was the waiter, I'd hate to hear what kind of odd things had been going on in his life with a ghost like that following him around.

"What's wrong?" I asked the ghost directly, without any pretense. I wasn't in the mood to play the "you can see me" game. Apparently, the ghost wasn't either because he didn't miss a beat.

"That dessert does not belong on this cart!" he cried. "No, no, *no!*"

"The dessert?" I asked. Fortunately for the waiter, he was apparently not the problem.

"They have just ruined the fig puff!" the ghost declared.

"What's your name?" I asked. "Maybe I can help."

He stopped for a second, huffed once, then replied, "Albert. We developed that fig puff here, and they've ruined it! It was my partner's grandmother's recipe—thank goodness she isn't here to see what they've done!"

"What did they do to it?"

"They flambé it!" Albert declared, as if it was the most obvious thing in the world.

"Judge Wilkens," I said, turning my attention back to my host. "Have you ever had the fig puff?"

"Yes," he replied. "But I didn't care for it."

*He was scowling so intensely,
I got the feeling he really
believed looks could kill.
It was too much. I had to know
what his problem was, and if
his problem was the waiter,
I'd hate to hear what kind of
odd things had been going on
in his life.*

"See? See?" Albert cried. "They ruined it!"

"If I order it and ask them not to flambé it, will it be the way you made it?" I asked him. Albert waggled his head in a sort of yes-and-no way, so I finally managed to get it out of him how the fig puff should be made. When I ordered it—passing on directions from Albert as a request for how I'd like it prepared—the waiter seemed to be hiding his shock, and Judge Wilkens seemed confused. After the waiter had left, I let the judge in on what was going on.

"And this chef is here now?" he checked. I nodded. Then I made sure to get the complete recipe for Albert's fig puff.

"Are you ready to cross over now?" I asked him once I had the recipe down.

"Absolutely not!" he declared, and then he stormed off!

FIG PUFFS WITH WINE SAUCE

1½ cups sifted all-purpose flour
1½ teaspoons baking powder
½ teaspoon salt
3 tablespoons shortening
¾ cup chopped figs
1 egg, beaten
¾ cup milk
Wine Sauce (recipe below)

▶ Preheat oven to 375º. Stir together flour, baking powder, and salt in a large bowl. Cut in shortening and add figs, mixing well. Stir in egg and milk. Grease cups of muffin pan with shortening; transfer batter into prepared pan, and bake for about 20 minutes. Serve hot with Wine Sauce.

WINE SAUCE

½ cup butter
½ cup granulated sugar
½ cup heavy whipping cream
¼ cup sherry

▶ Cream butter and sugar in a bowl. Pour in whipping cream, then set bowl over a pan of hot water. Beat with a rotary mixer until butter mixture is light and fluffy. Add sherry slowly and serve at once.

FRANK'S MEAD

Jenny was worried about her father, Ed. At 80, he was old and arthritic, but, until recently, she hadn't feared for dementia. He'd always been sharp, and he still enjoyed reading and doing crosswords, so it didn't seem like anything was going to slow him down. Recently, though, he'd seemed to take a turn for the worse. He had a runny nose that just wouldn't go away, and he seemed more tired than normal—both pretty average conditions for a man his age, but Jenny just felt like there was something more to it.

"The cat is acting funny too," she admitted to me. "Its litter box is in the basement, but she just refuses to go down there anymore, and she'll sit and bat at the air like she's playing with an invisible toy."

"Is there anything else?" I wondered. I could tell by her tone that there was, and I've learned that, quite often, a person's gut is telling them the right thing. Whether we realize it or not, we all pick up on the energy of earthbound spirits, so oftentimes those hunches are actually true.

"Well, we've been having a lot of electrical problems recently."

"And . . .?"

Jenny sighed and finally came out with it. "Dad's neighbor died recently. He and Dad weren't best friends, but they were civil and they borrowed tools and things from each other. I think it's him, but I can't imagine what he'd want."

Jenny's hunch was absolutely correct. Ed's neighbor, Frank, was in the house, and he really didn't want anything. He was there simply because Ed's energy reminded him of days gone by and made him feel good.

"He loved my mead," Frank said wistfully, which was about the last thing I expected to ever hear from a ghost.

"Mead?" I checked, then asked Ed about it. He nodded and smiled.

"That's true. Frank made really good mead. He'd always bring me some, and we'd sit and drink it and chat for a while."

"Mead," I stated. "Okay. Would you like me to get the recipe from Frank, if he can remember it?" Ed's eyes lit up.

"That would be great! Can you do that?"

Frank was beaming a wide smile, too, and he remembered every word of his recipe. After reciting it to me, he crossed over quite happily.

"Is there anything else?" I wondered. I could tell by her tone that there was. I've learned that, quite often, a person's gut is telling them the right thing. Whether we realize it or not, we all pick up on the energy of earthbound spirits, so oftentimes those hunches are actually true.

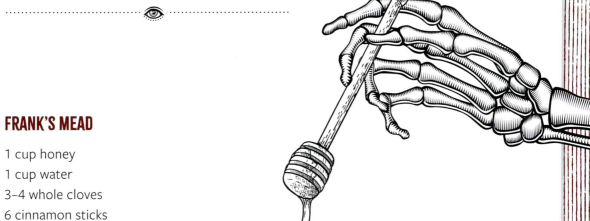

FRANK'S MEAD

1 cup honey
1 cup water
3–4 whole cloves
6 cinnamon sticks
1 small piece nutmeg
1 (3-inch) piece vanilla bean
1 (½-inch) strip orange rind
2 cups grain alcohol

▶ Bring honey and 1 cup water to a boil in a saucepan, and carefully remove all scum. Add cloves, cinnamon, nutmeg, vanilla bean, and orange rind. Return to a boil; remove from heat, let stand for a minute or two, and again bring to a boil. Cover and set aside for at least 30 minutes to steep; strain. Bring to a boil again, and then pour in alcohol. Stir well. Remove and discard bean pod, and serve piping hot.

HOMEMADE NOODLES

Clara had invited me to her home to do a "ghost chat," where someone calls me to come to a private event and speak to them and their invited guests about what I can do and some of the things I've seen. I don't do any mass ghost clearings at ghost chats because if I started doing that—for all 30-plus guests invited to these things—I'd be there all night! People do always ask if there are any ghosts in the host's house, and I'm fine with doing that much. In Clara's case, she and her husband, Rich, were absolutely certain they did not have any ghosts in their home—but they were just as certainly wrong!

I went over to the house early for a light lunch with Clara and Rich. I don't often do that, but in this case the house was far off the beaten path and more than two hours from my house, so I knew I'd need some food before the ghost chat started. Clara was planning finger foods and desserts for the chat, but I knew I'd need more than that to get me through and back home after, so I asked her if there were any good restaurants close to her house. To cut a long story short, that's when she suggested I just join her and Rich for lunch, and since she really couldn't think of anywhere nearby to eat, I accepted.

Lunch was quite delicious and featured a homemade chicken-noodle soup, for which Clara had even made the noodles. It was tasty, but I did notice that it was very thick, much thicker than I'm used to seeing with chicken-noodle soup. The earthbound spirit in Clara's house also noticed the same thing.

The ghost was an older, elegant-looking woman. She had perfectly manicured nails and pretty, well-kept hair, and she had an air of refinement about her—something in the way she held herself and moved around the room. Usually when someone hosting a ghost chat has an earthbound spirit attached to her, the ghost immediately makes itself known to me the moment I arrive. But not this lady. She made absolutely no effort to catch my eye, and to be fair, I didn't make any effort to catch hers. After all, I wasn't there to do a clearing, and Clara and Rich had already told me there was no way they had a ghost, so I assumed she wasn't bothering them in any way. Judging by her demeanor, I figured this ghost knew all about me and what I could do and had decided I was a scam artist, so she couldn't be bothered to try to speak to me.

After lunch, Clara asked if I enjoyed the soup. I said that I did, and I asked if it was a family recipe.

"It was my Grandma Gigi's noodle recipe," Clara explained.

At that point, I heard the ghost mumble, "Oh, she *makes* the noodles correctly, but she doesn't *cook* them correctly."

That piqued my curiosity, so I caught her eye and said, "What do you mean, she doesn't cook them correctly?"

Usually when someone hosting a ghost chat has an earthbound spirit attached to her, the ghost immediately makes itself known to me the moment I arrive. But not this lady. She made absolutely no effort to catch my eye.

⟡

The spirit gaped at me for a few seconds, then breathed, "You really *can* see me!"

"Yes I can," I replied, talking to her in my head as I always do with earthbound spirits. "And I'm curious about what you meant."

"Oh, it's the noodles," this woman said. "She cooks the raw noodles right in with the soup."

"You mean she doesn't boil them separately and drain them?"

"Exactly!" she declared. "That's how you're supposed to do it! But no, she cooks them right in with the soup, and it just ruins it. It makes it far too thick."

I couldn't argue with her, and since I'd gotten her stirred up, she took the chance to vent about another thing that bothered her: the hand towels. Apparently, Clara had

inherited some towels that this woman—whom I soon discovered was Grandma Gigi—had made. On each of the four towels a different scene was embroidered, depicting one of the four seasons. Grandma Gigi was adamant that they should be displayed in the order she had made them: spring, summer, fall, and winter. She had even moved them into the correct order several times, but Clara just blamed Rich and moved them back!

Later, at the ghost chat, someone asked the usual question: "Is there a ghost in this house?" I asked Grandma Gigi if she wanted her presence known, and she said she did. Clara and Rich were both stunned, but based on my description alone they knew exactly who it was.

Later, at the ghost chat, someone asked the usual question: "Is there a ghost in this house?" I asked Grandma Gigi if she wanted her presence known.

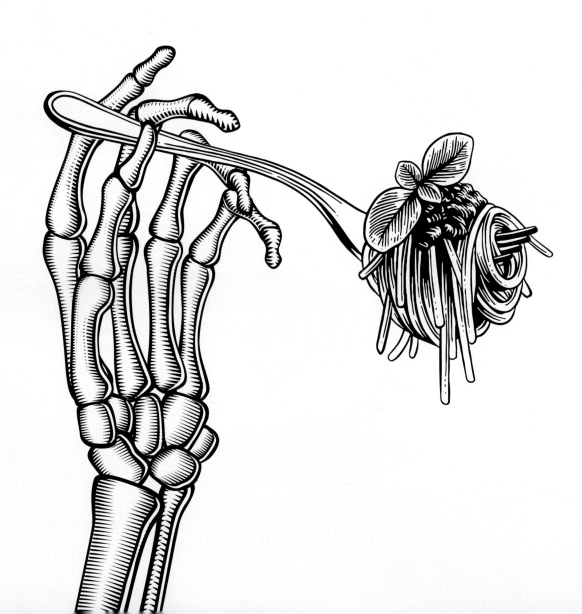

"Tell her she's making me nuts with those noodles!" Grandma Gigi practically begged me. I didn't want to call Clara out in her own home and in front of her guests, so I softened it and asked if she did anything different with the noodles when she cooked her soup. Clara glanced at Rich, who ducked his head shyly.

"I cook them *in* the soup," she admitted.

"Okay—that's what Grandma Gigi wants to ask you about. She wants to know why you do that."

"It was Rich's idea!" Clara said. "He wanted thicker soup, and he said that's how his mother used to make it! I knew I wasn't following the recipe!"

Grandma Gigi was happy to see that her point had been made, then moved on to the issue of the hand towels. Clara defended how she hung them, because they looked better in the order she used (which was true), but she acquiesced and told her grandma she'd put them in the "right" order—and then she apologized to Rich for blaming him.

"There's one thing she can do for me now," Clara said then. "I'm sure my recipe is correct for her homemade noodles, but I've always wanted to double-check it because I didn't copy it down myself. Does she remember it?"

"I'll give it to her if she promises to make the soup correctly!" Grandma Gigi declared without hesitation.

HOMEMADE NOODLES

2 eggs, lightly beaten
½ teaspoon salt
2¼ cups sifted all-purpose flour
2–3 tablespoons lukewarm water

▶ Stir eggs, salt, and flour together on a pastry board, adding 2–3 tablespoons water to form an elastic dough. Add more flour, if necessary. Work until little bubbles begin to form in the dough. Divide dough in two, roll out very thin on lightly floured board, and sprinkle with a little flour to help the dough dry. Let stand for a few minutes, then roll up, jelly-roll fashion, and cut into strips. Cook in salted boiling water for 5–10 minutes according to thickness. Drain well. Noodles may be stored in the refrigerator until needed. (Simply run hot water over chilled noodles to warm before eating.)

PARSLEY SANDWICH SAUCE

The hardest earthbound spirits to deal with are the ones I come across when I'm not supposed to be working. I learned pretty early on that I had to ignore them, just as you might a random person in the grocery store who looks down on their luck. If you tried to help every person you came across who looked like they needed help, you'd never get anything done. Of course, there are always exceptions. Just like sometimes we do reach out to help a complete stranger, sometimes I do reach out to see if I can help a spirit, whether anyone has asked me to or not.

Such was the case one day when I was in New York City. I wasn't there to help any spirits cross over, but when we got to the restaurant for lunch, I couldn't stop myself. We ate at this beautiful deli—all hardwood decor and sturdy old-fashioned chairs. One of the friends I was with knew the owner of the place, an older gentleman named Ben. He joined us shortly after we'd sat down, and he looked quite dejected, to be honest with you. My friend asked him what was wrong.

"I don't know," he said slowly. "It's just not fun anymore. We have troubles in the kitchen all the time these days—trouble with the waiters, trouble with everything. I think it's time to retire."

Ben looked to be around 75, but my friend tried to talk him out of it. To hear her talk, it was the only deli worth anything in New York,

and Ben leaving it would be like a mother abandoning her child. (You have to love New Yorkers for their dramatic flair!) As they were talking, though, I looked around and took in my surroundings, which is when I noticed another older gentlemen across the room who looked just as dejected as Ben. Thing is, the other gentleman was a ghost.

I managed to catch the ghost's eye and asked him to come closer. He looked shocked, then relieved, and he came over to the table. Ben was going on about some parsley butter or parsley spread or something they used to make, the lost recipe for which he pegged as the beginning of the end.

"When Cliff died, that was it," he was saying. "Nobody knew how to make that secret sauce, and now the sandwiches just aren't any good."

"I'm Cliff!" the ghost said to me jubilantly. "Me and Ben go way back. I worked here for 40 years, and he's right—they don't have a clue how to make my sauce. Can you give him the recipe for me?"

Now I was about to break my other cardinal rule—the first being not to get involved with random ghosts. The other rule is not to tell people who haven't asked me to help them that there's a ghost. So I tried to be diplomatic.

"You know, maybe I know that recipe," I tried.

"How could you?" Ben almost wailed. He wasn't angry, just upset. My friend looked at me, and I gave her a subtle nod. She knew exactly what was going on.

"No, I think she does," she said slowly and filled Ben in on what I can do. Ben just gaped; then his expression slowly lifted, and he smiled widely.

"Is Cliff here? Now?"

"Yes, he is," I said. "And he wants to give you the recipe."

Ben was only too happy to take it down. Then he called one of the waiters over and asked him to get one of the cooks. A cook came out, and Ben handed him the recipe.

"Richard, this is the recipe for Cliff's sauce," he said. "Go and make it and bring it out to me."

Richard glanced over the recipe and sort of turned up his nose. "I don't think this is it, Ben," he admitted. "This doesn't look right at all."

"Just make it. Please? And make sure you follow it *exactly*."

Richard went off as ordered, and while he was gone, Ben and Cliff wrapped up a few things they'd left undone—the usual list of apologies and regrets and memories. When Richard came back, Ben grabbed a breadstick, dunked a healthy dollop of the sauce onto it, and took a big bite. His face lit up.

"This is it!" he declared. "This *is* it!"

PARSLEY SANDWICH SAUCE

½ cup flat-leaf parsley
1 medium-size onion, finely chopped
2 tablespoons olive oil
2 tablespoons sour cream
1 tablespoon granulated sugar
Salt and black pepper to taste

▶ Mix all ingredients together; spread parsley mixture evenly on sandwiches. Refrigerate leftovers.

POTATO REFRIGERATOR ROLLS

Brianna often woke up in the middle of the night and smelled the good, strong smell of baking bread, but she knew there was no one cooking anything, at least not at 2 o'clock in the morning! The first few times it happened, she assumed her mother had been up late baking, but there was never anything baked the next day when she went downstairs. When she asked her parents about it, her dad, Ross, admitted that he had also smelled something a few times, but her mom, Mary, had not.

It's not unusual for ghosts to make their presence known using the sense of smell. Smell is a strange sense in that it can trigger our memories in ways the other senses can't. We've all had that experience of smelling a certain scent and being flooded with memories and the emotions attached to them—perhaps the cologne a favorite uncle wore or the pipe tobacco Grandpa used to smoke. Earthbound spirits seem to be able to tap into this and can actually create the scents that will remind people of them.

In this case, I have to assume that is exactly what was going on, but the spirit in the home was very shy and barely shared anything with me. When I went out to the house, there was no ghost I could see, but I knew she was there. Usually, they come into the room where I am, out of curiosity if nothing else, but this time the ghost stayed put, in a room on the second floor.

"Does the smell remind you of anyone?" I asked Brianna.

"Not really," she admitted, then looked over at her dad. He was nodding.

"It smells just like your aunt's rolls, Mary," he said to his wife. "Remember when we had to stay at your parents' house while our first house was being built? Your aunt made those rolls for dinner all the time. She'd make them on Saturday and they'd last all week."

"Right . . ." Mary said thoughtfully. "Aunt Charlotte . . ."

"That's it!" Brianna suddenly declared. "It *does* smell like Aunt Charlotte's rolls!"

"Hold on a second," I said. "How can you make rolls on Saturday and have them last all week? That doesn't make sense!"

Mary chuckled and shrugged. "I don't know. But that's what Aunt Charlotte did. She only baked on Saturday, but we always had rolls."

I knew the ghost upstairs was hearing all of this, but she still wasn't coming down. I asked Mary to go to the bottom of the stairs and call up to her, to call out for Aunt Charlotte and ask her to come down. Eventually, the ghost did come downstairs. She peeked in to the room where we were, and when I told them that she was about 60 and acting painfully shy, they all smiled.

"That's Aunt Charlotte!" they agreed.

I looked over at her—she'd finally come all the way into the room—and she was nodding.

It's not unusual for ghosts to make their presence known using the sense of smell. Smell is a strange sense in that it can trigger our memories in ways the other senses can't.

"Are you cooking at night?" I asked her, to which she blushed—a ghost actually blushed! She was clearly afraid to speak, but I had to know how these magical rolls that lasted all week were made, so I asked her if she knew what they were talking about.

She nodded again, then took in a deep breath and said, "They have mashed potatoes in them, that's why."

Apparently, she made them with mashed potatoes—perfect for leftovers from the night before—and yeast. They still had to rise before cooking, but the potatoes meant you could store the dough in the refrigerator and cut off enough to make however many rolls you needed on a certain night.

"Can you get the recipe from her?" Mary asked. "I'd *love* to taste those rolls again!"

"Me too!" Brianna and her dad excitedly agreed in unison.

POTATO REFRIGERATOR ROLLS

1 cup freshly cooked mashed potatoes
⅔ cup shortening, softened
½ cup granulated sugar
1 teaspoon salt
2 eggs, well beaten
1 cup milk
1 cake (packet) yeast
½ cup lukewarm water
6–8 cups sifted all-purpose flour

▶ Stir mashed potatoes in a large bowl until smooth; mix in shortening, sugar, salt, and eggs. Pour milk into a saucepan; scald and cool to lukewarm. Dissolve yeast in ½ cup water and stir into milk. Stir milk mixture into potato mixture. Stir in flour until a firm dough forms. Turn dough out onto a floured surface; knead thoroughly. Grease a large bowl with shortening; transfer dough to bowl. Cover and let rise in a warm place (85º), free from drafts, until doubled in bulk. Knead again slightly, brush with melted shortening, and return to bowl. Cover tightly and store in refrigerator until needed.

About 1 hour before baking time, cut off as much dough as needed, shape as desired, then cover and let rise until very light.

Preheat oven to 400º. Bake for 15–20 minutes, according to size. Dough may be stored in the refrigerator for up to 1 week. Makes 2½–3 dozen rolls.

QUINCE HONEY JAM

I was helping a woman named Donna. She'd called me for all the usual reasons, including electronics on the fritz, constant colds and runny noses, and the sound of footsteps in empty rooms. There was a female ghost in her house, but she was entirely unhelpful. She wouldn't tell me her name, she wouldn't say how she'd died or how long she'd been there, and she wouldn't tell me how she'd become attached to Donna. She didn't seem like a relative or anyone Donna knew—I described her in great detail, but she didn't sound familiar to Donna—so I'd given up and was getting ready to have her leave.

"How will I keep other ghosts away?" Donna asked. "If I can pick up this stranger from goodness-knows-where, how will I stop other . . . strangers from coming home with me?"

"Oh, I have some quince seeds," I said. Donna's brow furrowed and she looked at me like she hadn't heard me correctly.

"Quince seeds?" she asked. "What good will that do?"

"They aren't ordinary quince seeds," I admitted. "I have relatives in Italy who do something to them—they won't tell me what—and it creates some kind of barrier that earthbound spirits cannot cross. If you keep one in your purse or in a locket, they won't be able to attach to you. And before I leave, I'll put them over all the entrances to the house, which will stop them from being able to come in."

"Quince seeds," she repeated, taking in what I'd said. I know my explanation of what they can do isn't the best, but since I really don't understand how they work myself, there isn't much more information I can offer. I do know they work, and I do know that just any old quince seeds don't help at all—they have to have done to them whatever it is my relatives in Italy do.

"The only other thing I know is that a quince is a cross between an apple and a pear," I offered. "And that they're not much good for cooking."

"Nonsense!" the ghost suddenly chimed in. "There's plenty you can do with quince. They're just hard to work with, so nobody can be bothered. I have a recipe for a quince jam that will change *anyone's* mind."

"Oh, okay," I said. "I'd like to have that—I've always wondered what people do with quince. Will you give it to me?"

She did, and as I finished writing she waved her hand in Donna's direction and said, "She had a beautiful big quince bush when she moved in here, but she ripped it out!"

"When was that?" I asked.

"Oh, 25 years ago," the ghost replied.

I confirmed with Donna that it was true. When she'd first moved into the house, she had removed a huge bush at the end of the property.

"So was this your house?" I asked the ghost.

"It doesn't matter!" she declared as she marched into the White Light. "Never mind!"

There was a female ghost in her house, but she was entirely unhelpful. She wouldn't tell me her name, she wouldn't say how she'd died or how long she'd been there, and she wouldn't tell me how she'd become attached to Donna.

PICKLED HONEY BEES

QUINCE HONEY JAM

5 pounds granulated sugar
2 cups boiling water
5 quinces, grated
Grated lemon (optional)

▶ Heat sugar and 2 cups boiling water in a large saucepan, stirring until sugar dissolves. Add quince; bring to a boil, and cook for 18 minutes. Add grated lemon, if desired. Pour quince mixture into jars. Cool before sealing with paraffin.

RICE-AND-NUT LOAF

Sometimes I wonder why people even call me. Sarah rubbed me the wrong way immediately, and it didn't get better.

"It's about time you called back," she said when I told her who I was.

"Well, I'm very busy," I sighed. For someone calling for my help, she didn't sound very appreciative to talk to me.

"I know about you," she said with an odd tone in her voice. "I've seen you on TV, and I've heard you on the radio, and I've read your books."

"Okay," I agreed. "And?" By this point, I could already tell there was a ghost in her house, but I wasn't about to tell her that. Not until she asked. She was one of the strangest kinds of skeptic: She believed, but without actual proof, she still wouldn't let herself admit that. She knew all about me because she'd been looking for that elusive proof all this time, and now that something odd was happening in her home, she almost blamed me for it.

Her problems were with her cat. Or rather, she was only concerned for the well-being of her cat, Cha Cha. The cat was 4 years old, but within the last few months it had suddenly stopped using its litter box in the basement and was going potty all over the house. That was about the same time Sarah had noticed doors that were open one minute, then closed the next, especially the basement door.

"Cha Cha's been locked down there several times," Sarah said with a sigh.

"Well, you do have a ghost in the house," I finally admitted, and we set up a time for me to visit.

When I got there, I saw a ghost standing near the basement door, watching us. She had flaming red hair and looked much more adventurous than Sarah, who had mousy brown hair pulled back in a bun and was dressed as if she thought looking like an old maid was good fashion sense. I was sure the ghost wasn't a friend, but she didn't look like a relative either. I assumed the ghost had hitched a ride and had come into the house some other way, attached to an old piece of furniture or a used dress, but Sarah assured me she didn't shop at secondhand stores and couldn't think of anything she'd brought into the house new in the last few months.

"Well, there's a ghost here," I said "She has really bright-red hair."

"Oh my God!" Sarah gasped. "Carol died six months ago!"

"Who was Carol?"

"My neighbor . . ." she trailed off and her face soured again, back to her old-maid demeanor. "She always wanted to visit and gossip, but she had horrible allergies and made me lock Cha Cha upstairs."

By this time, Carol had wandered into the room. At first, I thought she'd realized we were talking about her, but as I watched, I saw that she was chasing the poor cat.

"Carol!" I called out. "Leave that cat alone!"

She stood up straight and glowered at me.

"You've been locking that cat in the basement, haven't you?" I asked the spirit. She didn't agree outright, but her posture and "you got me" look said it all. No wonder the poor cat wasn't using its litter box anymore.

Carol had obviously just had enough of Cha Cha, for whatever petty reason a nosy neighbor would have, but I got the impression she'd actually figured out that messing with the cat was a great way to get back at Sarah. Then I inadvertently gave her an even better way.

"What's that cooking?" I asked as Sarah and I moved into the sitting room. "It smells delicious."

"It's a rice-and-nut loaf," she said shortly. "It's my specialty. It's cooling."

"Liar!" Carol bellowed at her. "That's *my* specialty! That was *my* recipe! She's been passing it off as her own!"

"It smells really good," I said to Sarah. "I've never heard of a rice-and-nut loaf. Can I have the recipe?"

"No," Sarah replied. "It's my specialty."

"Oh, for goodness' sake!" Carol cut in. "She doesn't even make it right. I left out something on purpose when I gave her the recipe."

"Would *you* give it to me, then?" I asked the ghost.

"Of course I will," she said with a mischievous grin. "And I'll give it to you the right way."

RICE-AND-NUT LOAF

2 cups cooked rice

2 eggs, well beaten

2 cups tomatoes, chopped, seeded, and skinned

1 teaspoon salt

¼ teaspoon black pepper

½ cup chopped walnuts

1 tablespoon butter

½ cup breadcrumbs

GARNISH: minced fresh parsley

▶ Preheat oven to 350º. Stir together rice, eggs, tomato, salt, pepper, and walnuts in a large bowl. Grease a baking dish with butter, and transfer rice mixture to prepared dish. Melt 1 tablespoon butter in a small saucepan and stir in breadcrumbs; spread over rice mixture. Bake for 25 minutes. Turn out onto a warm serving platter and garnish, if desired. Slice to serve, like you would a meatloaf.

SWEET QUINCE PRESERVES

Chad could hear someone in the attic moving things around. He thought it was squirrels or raccoons at first, but when he went to investigate, he saw evidence that boxes had been moved—boxes that were far too heavy for a small animal to drag. The trails through the dust and grime were unmistakable, though: The boxes had moved. When the activity spread downstairs and pictures in the house started to be rearranged, Chad knew for sure there was something in the house, even though his wife, Antonia, said it was nothing.

"I'm the one who's home all the time," he said to her. He'd just undergone back surgery and was spending his days at home recovering. "I hear the noises and I feel like I'm being watched. I *know* there's someone here."

Antonia gave in, and they called me. There was a woman named Bea in the house. Chad didn't recognize the name.

"I knew his Uncle Glen," Bea told me. "And I knew his cousins when they lived here."

"That's right," Chad said, when I passed along what the ghost had told me. "Uncle Glen did live here, but he died a long time ago. That was back when the family was . . . well, I guess the word is *estranged*. We've worked it out now, but I wouldn't know anyone from back then."

Bea told me she'd lived next door. There were several fruit trees between the houses, and they shared the fruit and often the recipes they made using them.

"There's also a quince bush out there," Bea told me. "That's a cross between an apple and a pear, so we had apples, pears, and quince to choose from."

"I've heard quince is hard to cook with," I told her, and she nodded sagely.

"Ask the young lady to show you her finger."

I looked over at Antonia and told her what Bea had said. Antonia blushed slightly, then held up her left hand. The tip of her ring finger was missing.

"I was trying to cut up a quince to make quince preserves," she explained. "It's a very hard fruit and the knife slipped. . . ."

"Oh, I'm sorry," I said, hoping it wasn't too painful a memory.

"It's okay," she replied with a smile. "I'm just clumsy."

"I've heard quince preserves are delicious," I said. "Where did you get your recipe?"

"Well, that's what's strange," Antonia admitted. "I don't know. I found it on the floor in the den one day, but Chad and I didn't put it there, and we don't keep any cookbooks up there."

I looked over at Bea and asked, "Did you put it there?"

"Nope," she said. "But I do have a recipe for quince preserves."

I was suspicious, so I played along. "Can you remember it?" I wondered. "I'd love to have it."

Bea did remember it, so I jotted it down. Later, I had Antonia go and get the recipe she'd

The boxes had moved. When the activity spread downstairs and pictures in the house started to be rearranged, Chad knew for sure there was something in the house, even though his wife, Antonia, said it was nothing.

found in the den and we compared them. They were identical, almost word for word. The only differences were so minor, they were no doubt the result of me trying to write as fast as Bea was talking.

"That's so strange," Antonia said. "Why wouldn't she tell us it was hers?"

"Who knows?' I replied. "Maybe it really wasn't. Maybe one of Chad's relatives copied it from her."

Chad shook his head. "Maybe, but then how did it get up in the den? That room was empty when we moved in. There aren't other ghosts here, are there?" he suddenly added, looking around as if he could spot them.

"No," I said reassuringly. "Your house is clear now."

Some days, I end up with more questions than answers!

SWEET QUINCE PRESERVES

3½ pounds quinces, peeled and seeded
Juice of 1 lemon
1¾ pounds granulated sugar

▶ To prepare quinces, remove peel and trim centers, the way you would an apple, then cut into thin chunks and put into a bowl of water to cover. Add lemon juice to prevent quince from turning dark. Place in a strainer and rinse under running water.

Place quince chunks in a large pot, and add enough water to reach the top of the fruit. Add sugar, cover, and bring just to a boil. Lower heat to medium-high. Remove cover and cook, stirring occasionally, until syrup coats a spoon. Do not overcook. (The color of a raw quince is similar to a pear's; when it cooks, it turns a reddish color, from light pink to dark red.) Cool for 30 minutes. Spoon into jars with airtight seals, and seal. Makes 6–7 cups.

TROPICAL DELIGHT SALAD

You wouldn't think a fruit salad would be that hard to mess up, which might explain why Annie was so upset. My husband, Ted, and I were staying at a condo in Hawaii on the island of Kauai, and we were trying to enjoy what was billed as the best brunch on the island, except that every few minutes there was a crash and scuffle as another patron dropped a plate of food. After the fourth or fifth time, I started to pay close attention to where the noise was coming from.

We were seated near the center table that had all of the different salads on it. As I watched, I saw a small, athletic woman, maybe 20 years old, standing near the table in a chef's smock with a scarf holding back her hair. She was an earthbound spirit; as I watched her, I quickly pieced together what was happening. Whenever someone would take some of a certain salad, this woman would lean over and tip their plate or nudge them or in some other way cause them to drop it. Mind you, the cleanup from these messes was a big production, especially if someone's food tipped into the dishes on the serving table. The staff would trundle out, break down the table, clean up the mess, then put everything back the way it was.

And this woman was clearly enjoying it. But I'd had enough. It was disruptive and, quite frankly, mean. So I got up and walked over to the table, looking over the salads as if I was trying to find one to eat.

In front of me were a mother and her boy. The boy was all of 7, and as he reached for a particular salad, I saw the ghost waltz over and start to reach out for his plate.

"Don't you *dare*," I warned her. Thankfully, I speak with these earthbound spirits mentally, or that little boy would have thought he'd done something wrong. The ghost heard me, though, and she *knew* she'd been caught.

"You can see me?" she gasped, backing off a step.

"Yes. And I want to know what you think you're doing."

She huffed and her expression darkened as she pointed at the fruit salad the little boy was helping himself to. "That was *my* family's recipe and they're not making it right!"

By now, the boy and his mother had moved on, and I stepped up to the salad in question. "Looks fine to me," I said.

"Well it's *not* right," she insisted. "And I won't let them serve it until they make it right!"

"What's wrong with it?" I asked.

"The dressing is all wrong. They didn't use mayonnaise like they should. And there should be pineapple in it."

"Look," I said, "you're disrupting everyone's meals, and we've paid good money for this brunch. So you come back with me to my table and we'll talk."

She huffed again, but she agreed and followed me back. Ted knew by the look on my

I saw the ghost waltz over and start to reach out for his plate.

face that there was a ghost somewhere nearby that I was talking to, and he sort of rolled his eyes and smirked.

Her name was something very long and Hawaiian, but she said everyone called her Annie. She claimed she'd been a chef at the restaurant who had died in a surfing accident. Her mom, whom they called Queenie, used to make the fruit salad out at her guava plantation and had given the recipe to Annie, who made it for the restaurant.

"But now they've messed it up!" she summed up. "And I won't let them!"

In an effort to have a peaceful brunch with my husband, I brokered a deal with her: If she gave me the exact recipe and crossed over, I'd see that it got back to the kitchen. I couldn't guarantee they'd use it, but I could promise I'd at least put it in their hands.

"You tell them it was Annie's recipe from Queenie and they'll use it," she stated, but I got the feeling she was trying to convince herself more than me. Still, she agreed that her current situation of knocking plates out of strangers' hands wasn't all that satisfying and decided maybe it would be best if she just moved on.

So I got the recipe, and we managed to finish our brunch in peace.

TROPICAL DELIGHT SALAD

2 oranges
2 bananas
1 cup French dressing
Lettuce leaves
1 cup mayonnaise
½ cup whipped cream
⅔ cup grated pineapple, well drained

▶ Peel oranges, removing white membrane. Separate into sections, removing skin and keeping sections whole. Peel bananas and cut into quarters to same length as orange sections. Put orange and banana pieces into a bowl and cover with French dressing; let stand for 1 hour. Drain.

Divide lettuce leaves evenly among 4 salad plates. Alternately arrange 3 orange sections and 3 banana pieces to form the shape of a flower on top of lettuce leaves on each plate.

Combine mayonnaise, whipped cream, and pineapple in a bowl. Dollop a generous tablespoon of pineapple mixture in center of flower on each plate.

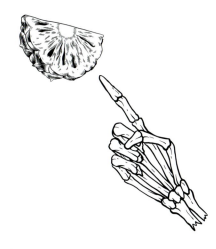

WARD'S COFFEE LIQUEUR

College dorms are a lot like nursing homes when it comes to ghosts, and I'm just as unsure about visiting them as I am about visiting nursing homes. They're always full of ghosts and the rooms aren't private, so there's generally very little I can do. Making it slightly worse is the fact that most of the ghosts are college-age kids, and they're pretty angry and upset about being dead.

Helen convinced me to visit her son, Brian, though. He had a private room, so at least I'd be able to protect it from further intrusions, but the ghosts were affecting his grades (Mom said) and freaking him out (Brian said). He could hear people arguing in his room. It sounded like a young couple fighting, though he couldn't make out exactly what they were saying—it was like hearing raised voices through a wall. Besides that, he always felt *watched*, like he was never truly alone in his own room.

The problem, I discovered, was Ward and Colleen, a couple of students who had dated—and died—in the 1980s. They were arguing, too, about how they had died. According to Colleen, Ward was driving drunk and had caused the car accident that killed them. Ward thought it had been Colleen's fault because she was drunk, too, and had been goofing around.

"But *you* got *me* drunk!" she yelled at him. "With that stupid Kahlúa you made!"

"You *loved* it!" he shouted back. "I didn't *force* you to drink it!"

"Okay, okay!" I broke in. "Let's not start this again." I turned to Helen and told her everything I'd gotten out of the ghosts so far and asked her to go and check with the resident assistant on the floor to see if it was true. I knew it was, of course, but I wanted to speak with Brian alone.

After she'd gone, I asked Brian if he drank. He waggled his head and admitted that he did.

"What's weird is, I've been looking for a good recipe for coffee liqueur," he said. That might have been a coincidence, but I kind of doubted it. Sometimes a common bond like that can make earthbound spirits latch on. Now, I was also curious about this recipe because I had one myself that was pretty good, but I wanted to compare notes, especially since Ward said his version was made with bourbon, not vodka. I wasn't going to give the recipe to Brian, though—I'm sure he found his own in his own way, but I wasn't going to help. I just told him that this was a good lesson to not drink and drive.

When his mom came back, she told us that it was all true, that a young man named Ward had lived in the dorm. He'd been dating a high-school senior in town, and they had died in a drunk-driving accident. While she was telling us what the RA had said, I jotted down Ward's recipe, so it looked like I was taking notes on the story. Then the kids crossed over without any more fuss.

He could hear people arguing in his room. It sounded like a young couple fighting, though he couldn't make out exactly what they were saying—it was like hearing raised voices through a wall. Besides that, he always felt watched, like he was never truly alone in his own room.

WARD'S COFFEE LIQUEUR

1 cup water
2 cups granulated sugar
2 cups double-strength coffee
1 fifth bourbon
1 cinnamon stick
1 vanilla bean

▶ Bring 1 cup water and sugar to a boil in a saucepan; simmer for 5 minutes. Cool. In a separate pan, boil 2 cups coffee until reduced to 1 cup. Cool. Combine sugar mixture, coffee, bourbon, cinnamon stick, and vanilla bean. Pour into holding vessel. Age for at least 3 months. Discard bean pod.

FINAL THOUGHTS

A BETTER WAY TO PRESENT A FISH

There is one last story I'd like to share. It's one of my favorite food-related stories, but it doesn't involve a recipe. Ted and I were at a restaurant in Maine. I was there doing some work for a client who lived in Ohio but had a beach house near Kennebunkport that needed clearing out. Because I had some other work to do in the area, he let me stay at the house after I had cleared it. It was a nice spot—we could even see the Bush compound from the beach—and we went out to eat a couple of nights, once at a fancier restaurant.

We were seated next to a table of six, and they had all ordered fish. When their plates were brought out, they certainly contained fish—the whole fish, fins, head, eyes, and all. I was just telling Ted how I'd heard fish should be cooked and served whole, but that you'd never catch me doing it, when I suddenly noticed a ghost come shooting out of somewhere, dressed in a full chef's uniform—hat, smock, and everything. I didn't see where he came from, but he dashed right over to the table and stood glaring at the waiter.

"What?" Ted asked when he saw my face. "Is there someone here?"

"Yeah . . ." I agreed slowly. The ghost chef was standing there cussing up a storm and shaking his finger at the waiter.

"This is *horrible!*" he was complaining. "Why didn't they listen to me? This is all wrong! No one wants to look at the eyes!"

As if on cue, a teenage girl who was seated at the table emitted a dramatic "Ew!" and then scrunched up her nose in disgust.

"See? See?" he said. He started moving, then pacing around the table and looking at the presentation of all the fish on the plates. When he got close to us, I managed to get his attention and asked him what was wrong.

"When you cook fish, you cover the eyes," he said simply. "There are ways to cook and present it correctly, with the eyes covered, and when the waiter prepares the plate, he should remove the head." Then he stopped and stood up straight and tall, a mild look of surprise on his face. "And how am I talking to you?"

It's pretty easy to convince ghosts that I can see and talk to them, so it didn't take me long to explain. Then it was my turn to ask some questions. Apparently, he'd worked at the restaurant under the former owner, and he was very big into the correct presentation of food.

"It's how you set yourself apart from all the other restaurants," he explained. "It adds to the ambience—or detracts from it," he added with a glance at the next table.

"So what would you suggest for the fish?" I wondered.

"No one wants to see dead eyes," he said. "You use lemon to garnish the plate and cover the eyes, or you remove them and replace them with peppermints. Or you design a nice flourish from tartar sauce, like you would with icing on a cake. What you don't do is leave the eyes staring at the guests like that!"

"Did you get another recipe?" Ted wondered, unable to hear the conversation I was having in my head with the chef.

"No," I said to him. "But at least now I know how to present a whole fish, if I ever cook one."

It may seem odd that a chef would stay behind and get upset about the correct presentation of fish, but I'd be willing to bet he'd been just as fixated on correct presentation in life. What I've seen time and time again while collecting recipes is that, above all else, people are people, whether they're dead or alive, and when it comes to what they pride themselves on, they want to make sure it gets done correctly. Whether that's the correct way to present a fish, the right ingredients to use in a casserole, or the type of chocolate you use in a torte, people who used to take care of family and guests with the fruits of their kitchen don't like to see those recipes changed.

I have realized that recipes have come to signify something more to some people than just good food. In many ways, they have become tiny heirlooms to be treated with reverence. In many cases, they are the one thing a person wants to be remembered for. To them, recipes signify the love they felt for their families or the pride they derived from their professions. These dishes nourished loved ones for decades or made countless patrons happy, and even after death many earthbound spirits want to continue sharing them with their guests or those they care about.

Even more than that, the recipes from private kitchens all across America are testaments to the power of family: that warmth and care an aunt or mother or grandfather always wants to be able to offer. There is so much more to food than simply eating. Food is memories, food is celebrations, food is remembrances—food is *family*. And when you think of it like that, I can conceive of no better tribute to someone than passing on their best or favorite recipe.

INDEX

PHOTO CREDITS

All photos copyright of their respective photographers.
Mary Ann Winkowski photograph by **Stephan Hastings**
David Powers photograph by **Ken Powers**

ADK branding background by **chyworks/shutterstock.com**

All images used under license from Shutterstock.com:
AKaiser: ix (containers), 23 (fly), 73 (knife), 173 (fly, stove); **aksol:** 177; **Babich Alexander:** 121 (cake); **Alexander_P:** 179 (pickle jar); **Kovalov Anatolii:** title pages (spider); **Art and Roam:** title page (planchette); **Arthur Balitskii:** 171 (old man, coconuts); **AVA Bitter:** 45 (meat cleaver), 53 (beef ribs), 77 (campfire), 97 (picnic basket), 101 (meat fork), 103 (baker's hat), 109 (chickens and chicken leg), 123 (soup ladle), 127 (boiling pot), 149 (campfire); **chempina:** 65 (prayer beads/rosary); **Croisy:** 41 (eyeball); **Evgenii Doljenkov:** 43 (corn); **Epine:** 33 (wok), 41 (raisins), 145 (elderberries); **Extezy:** title pages (design mustache), vii (design element); **fahmisans:** 121 (front skull), 123 (skulls); **Foxys Graphic:** 49 (cow); **kacanx:** 199 (skeleton hand); **Kseniakrop:** 45 (turkey dinner), 91 (recipe book); **mamita:** 27 (mushroom); **Mehaniq:** old paper backgrounds; **mikesj11:** page edge design element (vinage lines); **Moloko88:** 9 (eye); **MoreVector:** 87 (beer), 175 (cordial glass); **nadiia_oborska:** 129 (spoons); **Nata_Alhontess:** 9 (hourglass), 19 (pea pod), 21 (green onions, white onion, ½ tomato), 23 (¼ tomato), 29 (beet), 33 (pea pods),47 (½ apple), 55 (potatoes, egg), 67 (potatoes), 73 (asparagus and knife), 89 (celery), 91 (dill), 97 (candleabra), 99 (cabbage), 103 (lemon slice), 157 (lemon), 159 (candles), 163 (lemon), 189 (parsley, bread slices); **NATALIA-P:** title page (floral corners); **Maisei Raman:** 15 (feather in hand), 23 (fork in hand), 33 (hand), 41 (hand), 79 (skeleton hand), 145 (female hand); **roughedges_stock:** 79 (bananas), 169 (strawberry), 186 (fork), 199 (pineapple slice), 201 (coffee cup); **Sketch Master:** 85 (ginger), 109 (garlic), 115 (tamales), 131 (potion bottle); **SpicyTruffel:** title pages and main/cookbook section headers (vector font), 99 (letter "C"); **Bodor Tivadar:** 7 (broom, cauldron), 13 (web), 21 (spider), 29 (gravestone), 43 (spider), 47 (bee), 49 (gravestone cross), 53 (stethoscope), 57 (gravestone circle cross), 85 (bat), 91 (spider), 105 (salt and pepper), 109 (raven), 115 (apron), 117 (pearl necklace), 119 (coffin), 147 (doll), 161 (pumpkin), 169 (web), 175 (cranberries), 183 (honey stick), 193 (bee, jar), 195, 197 (jar); **vector_ann:** 137 (teacups); **Vectorgoods studio:** 49 (milk pail)

The Story of AdventureKEEN

We are an independent nature and outdoor activity publisher. Our founding dates back more than 40 years, guided then and now by our love of being in the woods and on the water, by our passion for reading and books, and by the sense of wonder and discovery made possible by spending time recreating outdoors in beautiful places.

It is our mission to share that wonder and fun with our readers, especially with those who haven't yet experienced all the physical and mental health benefits that nature and outdoor activity can bring.

In addition, we strive to teach about responsible recreation so that the natural resources and habitats we cherish and rely upon will be available for future generations.

We are a small team deeply rooted in the places where we live and work. We have been shaped by our communities of origin—primarily Birmingham, Alabama; Cincinnati, Ohio; and the northern suburbs of Minneapolis, Minnesota. Drawing on the decades of experience of our staff and our awareness of the industry, the marketplace, and the world at large, we have shaped a unique vision and mission for a company that serves our readers and authors.

We hope to meet you out on the trail someday.

#bewellbeoutdoors

ABOUT *The* AUTHORS

MARY ANN WINKOWSKI was born in Cleveland, Ohio. Her earliest memories include talking to earthbound spirits and helping them cross over into the White Light. Mary Ann's reputation has spread worldwide. She has been a consultant to the CBS hit television show *Ghost Whisperer,* has appeared on numerous TV and radio programs, and has spoken at countless lectures, all while raising two daughters and foster parenting. Her abilities have offered solace to countless people, either by reuniting them with loved ones who have died or by removing unwanted spirits and negative energy. In early 2024, Mary Ann semi-retired. She no longer conducts personal visits for clearings or does phone consultations. She is limiting her time to select appearances and personal Zoom consultations, which can be booked on her website: **maryannwinkowski.com.**

DAVID POWERS earned a degree in creative writing from Ohio University. He has since worked as a freelance music critic; a section editor at an alternative newsweekly; and a technical writer, creating help files for a leading software developer. His fiction has appeared under the name David Christopher. He launched *OH Hellmouth,* a fictional accounting of "weird" Ohio presented in a blog format, at **graveworm.com.**